International Political Economy Series

Series Editor: **Timothy M. Shaw**, Visiting Professor, University of Massachusetts Boston, USA and Emeritus Professor, University of London, UK

The global political economy is in flux as a series of cumulative crises impacts its organization and governance. The IPE series has tracked its development in both analysis and structure over the last three decades. It has always had a concentration on the global South. Now the South increasingly challenges the North as the centre of development, also reflected in a growing number of submissions and publications on indebted Eurozone economies in Southern Europe.

An indispensable resource for scholars and researchers, the series examines a variety of capitalisms and connections by focusing on emerging economies, companies and sectors, debates and policies. It informs diverse policy communities as the established trans-Atlantic North declines and 'the rest', especially the BRICS, rise.

Bringing together some of the very best titles in the International Political Economy series' history, the IPE Classics showcase these titles and their continued relevance, all now available in paperback, updated with new material by the authors and a foreword by series editor Timothy M. Shaw.

Titles include:

Shaun Breslin
CHINA AND THE GLOBAL POLITICAL ECONOMY

Kevin C. Dunn and Timothy M. Shaw
AFRICA'S CHALLENGE TO INTERNATIONAL RELATIONS THEORY

Randall Germain
GLOBALIZATION AND ITS CRITICS
Perspectives from Political Economy

Stephen Gill
GLOBALIZATION, DEMOCRATIZATION AND MULTILATERALISM

John Harriss, Kristian Stokke and Olle Törnquist
POLITICISING DEMOCRACY
The New Local Politics of Democratisation

David Hulme and Michael Edwards
NGOs, STATES AND DONORS
Too Close for Comfort?

Sharon Stichter and Jane L. Parpart
WOMEN, EMPLOYMENT AND THE FAMILY IN THE INTERNATIONAL DIVISION OF LABOUR

Peter Utting and José Carlos Marques
CORPORATE SOCIAL RESPONSIBILITY AND REGULATORY GOVERNANCE
Towards Inclusive Development?

International Political Economy Series
Series Standing Order ISBN 978–0–333–71708–0 hardcover
Series Standing Order ISBN 978–0–333–71110–1 paperback

You can receive future titles in this series as they are published by placing a standing order. Please contact your bookseller or, in case of difficulty, write to us at the address below with your name and address, the title of the series and one of the ISBNs quoted above.

Customer Services Department, Macmillan Distribution Ltd, Houndmills, Basingstoke, Hampshire RG21 6XS, England

Politicising Democracy
The New Local Politics of Democratisation

Edited by

John Harriss
Professor of International Studies, Simon Fraser University, Canada

Kristian Stokke
Professor of Human Geography, University of Oslo, Norway

and

Olle Törnquist
Professor of Political Science, University of Oslo, Norway

First published in 2004
This edition published in paperback 2013 by
PALGRAVE MACMILLAN

Palgrave Macmillan in the UK is an imprint of Macmillan Publishers Limited, registered in England, company number 785998, of Houndmills, Basingstoke, Hampshire RG21 6XS.

Palgrave Macmillan in the US is a division of St Martin's Press LLC, 175 Fifth Avenue, New York, NY 10010.

Palgrave Macmillan is the global academic imprint of the above companies and has companies and representatives throughout the world.

Palgrave® and Macmillan® are registered trademarks in the United States, the United Kingdom, Europe and other countries

ISBN: 978–1–403–93481–9 hardback
ISBN: 978–1–137–35519–5 paperback

This book is printed on paper suitable for recycling and made from fully managed and sustained forest sources. Logging, pulping and manufacturing processes are expected to conform to the environmental regulations of the country of origin.

A catalogue record for this book is available from the British Library.

A catalog record for this book is available from the Library of Congress.

Library of Congress

2013   431252

Contents

List of Tables

Foreword: Learning from the IPE Series Classics Over Three Decades

Timothy M. Shaw

> UNDP 2013 Human Development Report – 'The Rise of the South: Human Progress in a Diverse World' – ...will examine the profound shift in global dynamics that is being driven by the fast-rising powers in the developing world – and the implications of this phenomenon for human development...Looking ahead at the critical long-term challenges facing the international community, from inequality to sustainability to global governance...
>
> (www.hdr.org/en/mediacentre/ humandevelopmentreportpresskits/ 2013report/)

I am delighted, honoured and humbled to craft this Foreword for the initial set of Classics to be reissued in paperback from the IPE Series, accompanied by new Prefaces. Both I and my students/colleagues/networks have been greatly informed over a trio of decades as both analytic and existential 'worlds' have changed in myriad ways as indicated in the opening citation from the 2013 UNDP HDR on the rise of the South.

Symbolic of this exponential transformation is this very Series, which has always concentrated on the 'global South'. Thirty years ago, colleagues and editors alike were quite sceptical about the viability of such a limited focus; and indeed initially we only managed to publish a half-dozen titles per annum. By contrast, since the start of the second decade of the 21st century, the IPE Series has been proud to produce over 20 titles a year. As Jan Nederveen Pieterse (2011: 22) has asserted, the established N–S axis is indeed being superseded by an E–S one:

> ...the rise of emerging societies is a major turn in globalization...North-South relations have been dominant for 200 years and now an East-South turn is taking shape. The 2008 economic crisis is part of a global rebalancing process.

This overview juxtaposes a set of parallel/overlapping perspectives to consider whether the several 'worlds' – from North Atlantic/Pacific and onto Eurozone PIIGS versus 'second world' (Khanna 2009) of Brazil, Russia, India, China, South Africa (BRICS) / Columbia, Indonesia, Vietnam, Egypt, Turkey, South Africa (CIVETS) / Mexico, Indonesia, South Korea, Turkey (MIST) / Vietnam, Indonesia, South Africa, Turkey, Argentina (VISTA) – have grown together or apart as global crises and reordering have proceeded (see myriad heterogeneous analyses such as Cooper and Antkiewicz 2008, Cooper and Flemes 2013, Cooper and Subacchi 2010, *Economist* 2012, Gray and Murphy 2013, Lee et al. 2012, Pieterse 2011, USNIC 2012, WEF 2012 and World Bank 2012 as well as O'Neill 2011). In turn, 'contemporary' 'global' issues – wide varieties of ecology, gender, governance, health, norms, technology etc (see part (v) below) – have confronted established analytic assumptions/traditions and actors/policies leading to myriad 'transnational' coalitions and heterogeneous initiatives/processes/regulation schemes as overviewed in Bernstein and Cashore (2008), Dingwerth (2008), Hale and Held (2011) et al. (see part (vii) below). Such extra or semi-state hybrid governance increasingly challenges and supersedes exclusively interstate international organization/law. Clark and Hoque (2012) have assembled a stellar, heterogeneous team to consider any such 'post-American world' (Zakaria 2011): what salient, sustainable features of 'the rest' (Shaw 2012b)?

My overall impression or assumption is that IPE with such a focus on the global South increasingly overshadows – trumps?! – IDS, IR (but cf Bremmer 2012 and Bremmer and Rediker 2012 on resilience/revival of Political Science (PS) as analysis of Emerging Markets (EMs) (www.eurasiagroup.net)), area/business/gender/security studies, and established orthodox social science 'disciplines' such as economics, political science, sociology etc. In turn, IPE may yet increasingly face challenges from analysis broadly construed as 'global studies', especially in the US whose universities never really did 'development'. So I seek to identify areas where such a version of IPE generates similarities to or differences from such approaches, along with 'silences' in each plus divergent ranking of factors among them.

Every title in this set of Classic editions includes a contemporary update on both existential and theoretical developments: from 'Asian' to 'global' crises, from newly industrializing countries (NICs) to BRICs and onto PIIGS and BRICS/CIVETS/MIST/VISTA, Price Waterhouse Cooper's (PWC) E7 (PWC 2013). These sets of Emerging Markets embody slightly different sets of assumptions/directions/implications; PWC expanded the 'Next-11' of Goldman Sachs (i.e. 15 without RSA) to 17 significant EMs by 2050 (Hawksworth and Cookson 2008). Symptomatically, the initial iconic acronym was proposed at the start of the new century by a leading economist working for a global financial corporation – Jim O'Neill (2011) of Goldman Sachs (www2.goldmansachs.com) – who marked and reinforced his initial coup with celebration of its first decade. As he notes, global restructuring has been accelerated by the simultaneous decline not only of the US and UK but also the southern members of the eurozone. Many now predict China to become the largest economy by 2025 and India to catch-up with the US by 2050 (Hawksworth and Cookson 2008: 3). PWC (2013: 6 and 8) suggests that:

> The E7 countries could overtake the G7 as early as 2017 in PPP terms ... the E7 countries could potentially be around 75% larger than the G7 countries by the end of 2050 in PPP terms ...
>
> By 2050, China, the US and India are likely to be the three largest economies in the world ...

But Stuart Brown (2013: 168–170) notes that there are competing prophecies about the cross-over date when China trumps the US, starting with the International Monetary Fund (IMF) advancing it to 2016.

Meanwhile, global architecture is very fluid: the inter-governmental Financial Stability Board (www.financialstabilityboard.org) is matched by think tank networks like the World Economic Forum's (WEF) Risk Response Network (RRN) (www.weforum.org/global-risks-2012) and the Global Risk Institute (www.globalriskinstitute.com); all creations in response to the global crisis towards the end of the first decade. As the G8 morphed into G20 (Cooper and Antkiwicz 2008, Cooper and Subbachi 2010) a variety of analysts attempted to map the emerging world, including Parag Khanna's (2009) second world and Fareed Zakaria's rest: for example: the WEF's Global Redesign Initiative (GRI), which included a small state caucus centred on Qatar, Singapore and Switzerland (Cooper and Momani 2011) (for a readers' guide to GRI see www.umb.edu/cgs/research/global_redesign_initiative), to the Constructive Powers Initiative advanced by Mexico (www.consejomexicano.org/en/constructive-powers), which brought older and newer middle powers together (Jordaan 2003) such as the old Anglo Commonwealth with *inter alia* Indonesia, Japan and South Korea.

And at the end of 2012, from both sides of the pond, the US National Intelligence Council produced 'Global Trends 2030: Alternative Worlds' (GT 2030) (www.gt2030.com), which identified four 'megatrends' like 'diffusion of power' and 'food, water, energy nexus'; a half-dozen 'game-changers'; and four 'potential worlds' from more to less conflict/ inequality, including the possibilities of either China-US collaboration or of a 'nonstate world'. And Chatham House in London reported on 'Resources Futures' (Lee et al. 2012: 2) with a focus on 'the new political economy of resources' and the possibility of natural resource (NR) governance by 'Resource 30' (R30) of major producers/consumers, importers/exporters (www.chathamhouse.org/resourcesfutures): G20 including the BRICs, but not BRICS (i.e. no RSA), plus Chile, Iran, Malaysia, Netherlands, Nigeria, Norway, Singapore, Switzerland, Thailand, UAE and Venezuela.

And in the case of the most marginal continent, Africa, its possible renaissance was anticipated at the turn of the decade by Boston Consulting Group (BCG), Centre for Global Development (CGD), McKinsey et al. (Shaw 2012a), with the *Economist* admitting in January 2011 that it might have to treat Africa as the 'hopeful' rather than 'hopeless' continent. In December 2012, James Francis in the African MSN Report cited Africa's 15 biggest companies: from Sonatrach (Algeria) and Sonangol (Angola) and Sasol (RSA) through MTN, Shoprite, Vodacom and Massmart/Walmart to SAPPI (www.african.howzit.msn.com/ africa's-15-biggest-companies/).

The demand or need for 'development' is shifting away from the poorest countries, including 'fragile states' (Brock et al. 2012, www.foreignpolicy.com/failedstates), to poor communities in the second (and first?!) worlds: the other side of the rise of the middle classes in the global South (Sumner and Mallett 2012). Moreover, the supply of development resources is also moving away from the old North towards the BRICS (Chin and Quadir 2012) and other new official donors like South Korea and Turkey plus private foundations like Gates, faith-based organisations (FBOs), remittances from diasporas, Sovereign Wealth Funds (SWFs) and novel sources of finance such as taxes on carbon, climate change, emissions, financial transactions etc (Besada and Kindornay 2013).

(i) Varieties of development

'Development' was a notion related to post-war decolonisation and bipolarity. It was popularised in the 'Third World' in the 1960s, often in relation to 'state socialism', one-party even one-man rule, but superseded by neo-liberalism and the Washington Consensus. Yet the NICs then BRICs pointed to another way by contrast to those in decline like fragile states (Brock et al. 2012); such 'developmentalism' (Kyung-Sup et al. 2012) has now even reached Africa (UNECA

2011 and 2012). But, as indicated in the previous paragraph, while the 'global' middle class grows in the South, so do inequalities along with non-communicable diseases (NCDs) like cancer, heart diseases and diabetes. Given the elusiveness as well as limitations of the Millennium Development Goals (MDGs) (Wilkinson and Hulme 2012), the UN is already debating post-2015 development desiderata (www.un.org/millenniumgoals/beyond2015) including appropriate, innovative forms of governance as encouraged by networks around international non-governmental organizations (INGOs) (www.beyond2015.org) and think tanks (www.post2015.org). As already indicated, Andy Summer and Richard Mallett (2012) suggest that 'development' in the present decade is very different from earlier periods as the number of fragile states declines: given the rise of the global middle class, the poor are now concentrated in the second world. Aid is now about cooperation not finance as a range of flows is attracted to the global south including private capital, foreign direct investment (FDI), philanthropy/FBOs, remittances, let alone money-laundering (Shaxson 2012); Official Development Assistance (ODA) is a shrinking proportion of transnational transfers (Brown 2011 and 2013: 24–28).

(ii) Varieties of capitalisms

The world of capitalisms has never been more diverse: from old trans-Atlantic and -Pacific to new – the global South with its own diversities such as Brazilian, Chinese, Indian and South African 'varieties of capitalisms'. Andrea Goldstein (2007) introduced emerging market MNCs (multinational corporations) in this Series, including a distinctive second index: five pages of company names of emerging market multinational corporations (EMNCs) (see next paragraph). And in the post-neo-liberal era, state-owned enterprises (SOEs), especially national oil companies (NOCs) (Xu 2012), are burgeoning. Both US/UK neo-liberal, continental/Scandinavian corporatist and Japanese/East Asian developmentalist 'paradigms' are having to rethink and reflect changing state-economy/society relations beyond ubiquitous 'partnerships' (Overbeek and van Apeldoorn 2012). Furthermore, if we go beyond the formal and legal, then myriad informal sectors and transnational organized crime (TOC) / money-laundering are ubiquitous (see (vi) below).

For the first time, in the *'Fortune* Global 500' of (July) 2012, MNC head quarters (HQs) were more numerous in Asia than in either Europe or North America. There were 73 Chinese MNCs so ranked (up from 11 a decade ago in 2002) along with 13 in South Korea and eight each in Brazil and India. Each of the BRICS hosted some global brands: Geely, Huawei and Lenovo (China), Hyundai, Kia and Samsung (Korea); Embraer and Vale (Brazil); Infosys, Reliance and Tata (India); Anglo American, De Beers and SABMiller (RSA) etc.

The pair of dominant economies in Sub-Saharan Africa (SSA) is unquestionably Nigeria and South Africa; yet, despite being increasingly connected, they display strikingly different forms of 'African' capitalisms. They both have venerable economic histories, most recently within heterogeneous British imperial networks; and both have gone through profound political as well as economic changes in the new century: from military and minority rule, respectively, both with diasporic and global engagements, including being out of the Commonwealth family for considerable periods each. Whilst distinctive in per capita incomes, they are both highly unequal; for example, Nigeria boasts over 150 private jets owned by its entrepreneurs, pastors, stars, etc.

Nigeria, including its mega-cities like Lagos and Ibadan, is a highly informal political economy with a small formal sector (beer, consumer goods such as soft drinks and soaps, finance, telecommunications etc); by contrast, despite its ubiquitous shanty-towns, South Africa is based on a well-established formal economy centred on mining, manufacturing, farming, finance, services etc. Both have significant diasporas in the global North, especially the UK and US, including Nigeria's in RSA, especially Jo'burg, remitting funds back home. Since majority democratic rule, South African companies and supply-chains, brands and franchises have penetrated the continent, initially into Eastern from Southern Africa, but now increasingly into West Africa and Angola. So MTN's largest market for cell-phone connectivity is now Nigeria; DStv, Shoprite, Stanbic, Woolworth etc. are also present, especially in two of the very few formal shopping malls in Lagos.

South African banks compete in Nigeria with national (established like First and Union and new generation) and regional banks: Access, Eco (in over 30 African countries), Enterprise, Diamond, FCMB, Fidelity, GT (Guaranty Trust), Keystone, Marketplace, UBA (now partially owned by China), Unity, Wema, Zenith etc. And one or two global banks, like Citi and Standard Chartered, are now present in Nigerian cities.

Nigeria's press remains remarkably free and lively despite competition from mobile-phones, social media, TV and websites: *Guardian, Nation, Punch, This Day* etc. Its choice of cell providers includes Airtel, Glo and Etisalat as well as MTN. Its entrepreneurs are developing their own fast food franchises to compete with KFC, Spur etc: Chicken Republic, Mama Cass, Mr Biggs, Rocket Express, Royal Table, Tastee Chicken, Sweet Sensation etc. And it has a huge range of private gas stations in addition to Mobil and Total: Acorn, Bunker, World etc...

Nigeria's variety of African capitalism includes a burgeoning market for second hand EU and US cars and trucks, and a burgeoning born-again religious sector with myriad churches and pastors, some now very large, with endless colourful names such as several Winners' chapels and the (15th in December 2012) Holy Ghost Congress of the Redeemed Christian Church of God at Redemption Camp. Nigerian Pentecostalism has been exported to the diaspora and elsewhere, including the born-again Christian channel on DStv. And characteristic of personal energy, style and networks, Nigeria's Nollywood is now the largest movie industry in the world (*Forbes*, 19 April 2011) in terms of volume – African Magic on DStv. By contrast, South Africa's TV and film production is more limited, formal and international, however stylish. Both countries are sports mad, Nigeria for (men's) soccer: British and EU brands dominate – Arsenal, Barcelona, Chelsea, Manchester United, Real Madrid etc – with Nigerian amongst other players in European clubs.

(iii) Emerging economies/states/societies

The salience of 'emerging markets', especially the BRICs and other political economies in the second world, has led to debates about the similarities and differences among emerging economies/middle classes/multinational companies/states/societies etc, informed by different disciplinary canons; for example, by contrast to Goldstein on EMNCs, Pieterse (2011) privileges sociologically informed emerging societies. In turn, especially in IR, there are burgeoning analyses of emerging powers/regional and otherwise (Flemes 2010, Jordaan 2003, Nel and Nolte 2010, Nel et al. 2012), some of which might inform new regionalist perspectives, especially as these are increasingly impacted by the divergence between BRICS and PIIGS.

(iv) New regionalisms

The proliferation of states post-bipolarity has led to a parallel proliferation of regions, especially if diversities of non-state, informal even illegal regions are so considered. And the eurozone crisis concentrated in the PIIGS has eroded the salience of the EU as model, leading to a recognition of a variety of 'new' regionalisms (Flemes 2010, Shaw et al. 2011).These include instances of 'African agency' (Lorenz and Rempe 2013) like South African franchises and supply chains reaching to West Africa and the Trilateral FTA (Free Trade Agreement) among Common Market of Eastern and Southern Africa (COMESA), East African Community (EAC) and Southern African Development Community (SADC) (T-FTA) (Hartzenberg et al. 2012) along with older/newer regional conflicts like South China Sea (SCS) and Great Lakes Region (GLR) plus the regional as well as global dimensions of, say, piracy off the coast of Somalia.

(v) Emerging 'global' issues
Over the past quarter-century, the IPE Series has treated a growing number of global issues arising in the global South, as well as those resulting from excessive consumption/pollution in the North such as NCDs like diabetes. In the immediate future, these issues will include environmental and other consequences of climate change and health viruses/zoonoses. They will also extend to myriad computer viruses and cyber-crime (Kshetri 2013). Some suggest that we may be running out of basic commodities like energy (Klare 2012) and water, let alone rare-earth elements (REEs). Finally, after recent global and regional crises, the governance of the global economy is at stake: the financialisation syndrome of Debt Bond Rating Agencies (DBRAs), derivatives, Exchange-Traded Funds (ETFs) / Exchange-Traded Note (ETNs), hedge and pension funds, SWFs etc (Overbeek and Apeldoorn 2012).

(vi) Informal and illegal economies: from fragile to developmental states?
Developing out of the internet, new mobile technologies increasingly facilitate the informal/illegal, as well as otherwise. The 'informal sector' is increasingly recognised in the discipline of anthropology etc. as the illegal in the field of IPE (Friman 2009, Naylor 2005 etc.); these are increasingly informed by telling Small Arms Survey (SAS) annual reports after more than decade with a focus on fragile states (www.smallarmssurvey.org).

Similarly, TOC is increasingly transnational with the proliferation of (young/male) gangs from myriad states (see Knight and Keating (2010), chapter 12). In response, the field of IPE needs to develop analyses and prescriptions from the established informed annual Small Arms Survey and Latin American then Global Commission on Drugs and Drug Policy/Health (www.globalcommission

ondrugs.org); and now at start of new decade onto Ideas Google re the illicit (www.google.com/ideas/focus.html).

Such pressures lead to communities going beyond national and human security towards 'citizen security' as a notion developed in communities of fear in today's Central America and the Caribbean; see UNDP (2012b).

(vii) Varieties of transnational governance

Just as 'governance' is being redefined/rearticulated (Bevir 2011), so the 'transnational' is being rediscovered/rehabilitated (Dingwerth 2008, Hale and Held 2012) following marginalization after its initial articulation at the start of the 1970s by Keohane and Nye (1972): they identified major varieties of transnational relations such as communications, conflict, education, environment, labour, MNCs, religions etc. And Stuart Brown (2011) updated such perspectives with a more economics-centred framework which included civil society, remittances etc.

In turn, I would add contemporary transnational issues such as brands and franchises; conspicuous consumption by emerging middle classes; world sports, such as Federation Internationale de Football Association (FIFA) and International Olympic Committee (IOC); global events from World Fairs to Olympics and world soccer; logistics and supply-chains (legal and formal and otherwise); mobile digital technologies; newly recognized film centres such as Bollywood and Nollywood including diasporas, film festivals, tie-ins etc; new media such as Facebook and Twitter; but such heterogeneous relations/perspectives deserve much more further attention: real IPE in current decade of the 21st century.

(viii) IPE of global development/studies by mid-century?

In conclusion I juxtapose a trio of changes which will probably impact the IPE of the global South in policy and practice and may lead towards the greater privileging as well as theorizing of 'global studies' (O'Bryne and Hensby 2011):

(a) exponential global restructuring in myriad areas, from economics and ecology to diplomacy and security (Besada and Kindornay 2013, Overbeek and Apeldoorn 2012);

(b) changes in the IPE and technologies of publishing including competition from digital and mobile devices; and

(c) shifts in global higher education towards a variety of international interdisciplinary perspectives/methodologies/technologies – from 'ivy' and 'open' universities to Executive Masters in

Business Administration (EMBAs) and Massive Open Online Courses (MOOCs) – so my privileged personal experience of university education on three continents will become the norm, whether virtually or in real time.

In short, to bring my own academic and editorial roles together, I'm delighted to be ending my formal career animating a new interdisciplinary PhD at a public university in the US – University of Massachusetts – (my first time teaching there) on 'Global Governance and Human Security': reinforcing my continuing education, enhanced by the present burgeoning IPE Series, especially its Classics.

Bibliography

Berstein, Steven and Benjamin Cashore (2008) 'The Two-Level Logic of Non-State Market Driven Global Governance' in Volker Rittberger and Martin Nettesheim (eds) *Authority in the Global Political Economy* (London: Palgrave Macmillan), 276–313.

Besada, Hany and Shannon Kindornay (eds) (2013) *The Future of Multilateral Development Cooperation in a Changing Global Order* (London: Palgrave Macmillan for NSI, forthcoming).

Bevir, Mark (2011) *Sage Handbook of Governance* (London: Sage).

Bremmer, Ian (2012) *Every Nation for Itself: Winners and Losers in a G-Zero World* (New York: Penguin)

Bremmer, Ian and Douglas Rediker (eds) (2012) *What's Next: Essays on Geopolitics That Matter* (New York: Portfolio/Penguin).

Brock, Lothar, Hans-Henrik Holm, Georg Sorensen and Michael Stohl (2012) *Fragile States* (Cambridge: Polity).

Brown, Stuart (2013) *The Future of US Global Power: Delusions of Decline* (London: Palgrave Macmillan).

—— (ed.) (2011) *Transnational Transfers and Global Development* (London: Palgrave Macmillan).

Chin, Gregory and Fahim Quadir (eds) (2012) 'Rising States, Rising Donors and the Global Aid Regime' *Cambridge Review of International Affairs* 25(4): 493–649.

Cooper, Andrew F and Agata Antkiewicz (eds) (2008) *Emerging Powers in Global Governance: Lessons from the Heiligendamm Process* (Waterloo: WLU Press for CIGI).

Cooper, Andrew F and Bessma Momani (2011) 'Qatar and Expanded Contours of South-South Diplomacy' *International Spectator* 46(3), September: 113–128.

Cooper, Andrew F and Daniel Flemes (eds) (2013) 'Special Issue: Emerging Powers in Global Governance' *Third World Quarterly* (forthcoming).

Cooper, Andrew F and Timothy M Shaw (eds) (2013) *Diplomacies of Small States: Resilience versus Vulnerability?* second edn (London: Palgrave Macmillan).

Cooper, Andrew F and Paola Subacchi (eds) (2010) 'Global Economic Governance in Transition' *International Affairs* 86(3), May: 607–757.

Cornelissen, Scarlett, Fantu Cheru and Timothy M Shaw (eds) (2012) *Africa and International Relations in the Twenty-first Century: Still Challenging Theory?* (London: Palgrave Macmillan).

Dingwerth, Klaus (2008) 'Private Transnational Governance and the Developing World' *International Studies Quarterly* 52(3): 607–634.

Dunn, Kevin C and Timothy M Shaw (eds) (2001) *Africa's Challenge to International Relations Theory* (London: Palgrave Macmillan).

Economist (2012) *The World in 2013* (London) (www.economist.org/theworldin/2013)

Fanta, Emmanuel, Timothy M Shaw and Vanessa Tang (eds) (2013) *Comparative Regionalism for Development in the Twenty-first Century: Insights from the Global South* (Farnham: Ashgate for NETRIS).

Fioramonti, Lorenzo (eds) (2012) *Regions and Crises: New Challenges for Contemporary Regionalisms* (London: Palgrave Macmillan).

Flemes, Daniel (ed) (2010) *Regional Leadership in the Global System* (Farnham: Ashgate).

Friman, H Richard (ed) (2009) *Crime and the Global Political Economy* (Boulder: LRP. IPE Yearbook #16).

Goldstein, Andrea (2007) *Multinational Companies from Emerging Economies* (London: Palgrave Macmillan).

Gray, Kevin and Craig Murphy (eds) (2013) 'Special Issue: Rising Powers and the Future of Global Governance' *Third World Quarterly* (forthcoming).

Hale, Thomas and David Held (eds) (2012) *Handbook of Transnational Governance* (Cambridge: Polity).

Hanson, Kobena, George Kararach and Timothy M Shaw (eds) (2012) *Rethinking Development Challenges for Public Policy: Insights from Contemporary Africa* (London: Palgrave Macmillan for ACBF).

Hartzenberg, Trudi et al. (2012) *The Trilateral Free Trade Area: Towards a New African Integration Paradigm?* (Stellenbosch: Tralac).

Hawksworth, John and Gordon Cookson (2008) 'The World in 2050: Beyond the BRICs: A Broader Look at Emerging Market Growth' (London: PWC).

Jordaan, Eduard (2003) 'The Concept of Middle Power in IR: Distinguishing between Emerging and Traditional Middle Powers' *Politikon* 30(2), November: 165–181.

—— (2012) 'South Africa, Multilateralism and the Global Politics of Development' *European Journal of Development Research* 24(2), April: 283–299.

Keohane, Robert O and Joseph S Nye (eds) (1972) *Transnational Relations and World Politics* (Cambridge: Harvard University Press).

Khanna, Parag (2009) *The Second World: How Emerging Powers Are Redefining Global Competition in the Twenty-First Century* (New York: Random House).

Klare, Michael T (2012) *The Race for What's Left: The Global Scramble for the World's Last Resources* (New York: Metropolitan).

Kliman, Daniel M and Richard Fontaine (2012) 'Global Swing States: Brazil, India, Indonesia, Turkey and the Future of International Order' (Washington, DC: GMF).

Knight, W. Andy and Tom Keating (2010) *Global Politics* (Toronto: Oxford University Press), chapter 12.

Kshetri, Nir (2013) *Cybercrime and Cybersecurity in the Global South* (London: Palgrave Macmillan, forthcoming).

Kugelman, Michael (2009) *Land Grab? Race for the World's Farmland* (Washington, DC: Brookings).

Kyung-Sup, Chang, Ben Fine and Linda Weiss (eds) (2012) *Developmental Politics in Transition: The Neoliberal Era and beyond* (London: Palgrave Macmillan).

Lee, Bernice et al (2012) 'Resources Futures' (London: Chatham House, December) (www.chathamhouse.org/resourcesfutures).

Lorenz, Ulrike and Martin Rempe (eds) (2013) *Comparing Regionalisms in Africa: Mapping Agency* (Farnham: Ashgate, forthcoming).

Margulis, Matias E et al. (eds) (2013) 'Special Issue: Land Grabbing and Global Governance' *Globalizations* 10(1).

Naylor, R T (2005) *Wages of Crime: Black Markets, Illegal Finance and the Underworld Economy*, second edn (Ithaca: Cornell University Press).

Nel, Philip et al. (eds) (2012) 'Special Issue: Regional Powers and Global Redistribution' *Global Society* 26(3): 279–405.

Nel, Philip and Detlef Nolte (eds) (2010) 'Regional Powers in a Changing Global Order' *Review of International Studies* 36(4), October: 877–974.

O'Bryne, Darren J and Alexander Hensby (2011) *Theorising Global Studies* (London: Palgrave Macmillan).

OECD (2012) 'Economic Outlook, Analysis and Forecasts: Looking to 2060. Long-Term Growth Prospects for the World' (Paris).

O'Neill, Jim (2011) *The Growth Map: Economic Opportunity In the BRICs and Beyond* (New York: Portfolio/Penguin).

Overbeek, Henk and Bastiaan van Apeldoorn (eds) (2012) *Neoliberalism in Crisis* (London: Palgrave Macmillan)

Pieterse, Jan Nederveen (2011) 'Global Rebalancing: Crisis and the East-South Turn' *Development and Change* 42(1): 22–48.

Power, Marcus, Giles Mohan and May Tan-Mullins (2012) *China's Resource Diplomacy in Africa: Powering Development* (London: Palgrave Macmillan).

PWC (2013) 'World in 2050: The BRICs and Beyond: Prospects, Challenges and Opportunities' (London, January).

Ratha, Dilip et al. (2011) *Leveraging Remittances for Africa: Remittances, Skills and Investments* (Washington, DC: World Bank and AfDB).

Reuter, Peter (ed) *Draining Development: Controlling Flows of Illicit Funds from Developing Countries* (Washington, DC: World Bank) (www.openknowledge.worldbank.org).

Shaw, Timothy M (2012a) 'Africa's Quest for Developmental States: "Renaissance" for Whom?' *Third World Quarterly* 33(5): 837–851.

Shaw, Timothy M (2012b) 'The "Rest" and the Global South: Varieties of Actors, Issues and Coalitions.' In Sean Clark and Sabrina Hoque (eds) *Debating a "Post-American World': What Lies Ahead?* (Abingdon: Routledge), chapter 18.

Shaw, Timothy M, Andrew F Cooper and Gregory T Chin (2009) 'Emerging Powers and Africa: Implications for/from Global Governance?' *Politikon* 36(1), April: 27–44.

Shaw, Timothy M, J Andrew Grant and Scarlett Cornelissen (eds) (2011) *Ashgate Research Companion to Regionalisms* (Farnham: Ashgate).

Shaxson, Nicholas (2012) *Treasure Islands: Uncovering the Damage of Offshore Banking and Tax Havens* (New York: Palgrave Macmillan).

SID (2012) 'State of East Africa 2012: Deepening Integration, Intensifying Challenges' (Nairobi for TMEA).

Sinclair, Timothy (2012) *Global Governance* (Cambridge: Polity).

Singh, Priti and Raymond Izaralli (eds) (2012) *The Contemporary Caribbean: Issues and Challenges* (New Delhi: Shipra).

Sumner, Andy and Richard Mallett (2012)*The Future of Foreign Aid* (London: Palgrave Macmillan).

UNDP (2012a)*African Human Development Report: Towards a Food Secure Future* (New York, May)

UNDP (2012b) *Caribbean Human Development Report 2012: Human Development and the Shift to Better Citizen Security* (Port of Spain).

UNDP (2013) *Human Development Report 2013: The Rise of the South: Human Progress in a Diverse World* (New York, March).

UNDP (2014) *Human Development Report 2014: Beyond 2015: Accelerating Human Progress and Defining Goals* (New York, forthcoming).

UNECA (2011) *Economic Report on Africa 2011: Governing Development in Africa: The Role of the State in Economic Transformation* (Addis Ababa).

UNECA (2012) *Economic Report on Africa 2012: Unleashing Africa's Potential as a Pole of Global Growth* (Addis Ababa).

USNIC (2012) 'Global Trends 2030: Alternative Worlds' (Washington, DC: National Intelligence Council, December) (www.dni.gov/nic/globaltrends) (www.gt.com).

Vom Hau, Matthias, James Scott and David Hulme (2012) 'Beyond the BRICs: Alternative Strategies of Influence in the Global Politics of Development' *European Journal of Development Research* 24(2), April: 187–204.

Weiss, Thomas G (2013) *Global Governance* (Cambridge: Polity, forthcoming).

Wilkinson, Rorden and David Hulme (eds) (2012) *The Millennium Development Goals and Beyond: Global Development After 2015* (Abingdon: Routledge).

Wilkinson, Rorden and Thomas G Weiss (eds) (2013) *Global Governance* (Abingdon: Routledge, forthcoming).

World Bank (2012) *Global Economic Prospects June 2012: Managing Growth in a Volatile World* (Washington, DC, June).

World Economic Forum (WEF) (2012) *Global Risks 2012: An Initiative of The RRN* (Davos. Seventh edition)

Xing, Li with Abdulkadir Osman Farah (eds) (2013) *China-Africa Relations in an Era of Great Transformation* (Farnham: Ashgate, forthcoming).

Xu, Yi-chong (ed) (2012) *The Political Economy of State-Owned Enterprises in China and India* (London: Palgrave Macmillan).

Xu, Yi-chong and Gawdat Baghat (eds) (2011) *The Political Economy of Sovereign Wealth Funds* (London: Palgrave Macmillan).

Zakaria, Fareed (2011) *The Post-American World: Release 2.0* (New York: Norton. Updated and expanded edition).

www.africaminingvision.org
www.bcg.com
www.beyond2015.org
www.cgdev.org
www.chathamhouse.org
www.consejomexicano.org/en/constructive-powers
www.dni.gov/nic/globaltrends
www.economist.org/theworldin/2013

www.eiti.org
www.enoughproject.org
www.eurasiagroup.net
www.fareedzakaria.com
www.fatf/gafi.org
www.foreignpolicy.com
www.globalcommissionondrugs,org
www.globalpolicy.org
www.globalreporting.org
www.globalriskinstitute.com
www.globalwitness.org
www.google.com/ideas/focus/html
www.gt2030.com
www.hdr.org
www.isealalliance,org
www.jannederveenpieterse.com
www.kimberleyprocess.com
www.leadinggroup.org
www.mahbubani.net
www.mckinsey.com
www.normangirvan.info
www.openknowledge.worldbank.org
www.paragkhanna.com
www.post2015.org
www.pwc.com
www.reourcesfutures.org
www.smallarmssurvey.org
www.umb.edu/cgs/research/global_redesign_initiative
www.un.org/millenniumgoals/beyond2015
www.unodc.org
www.weforum.org
www.worldbank.org/globaloutlook
www2.goldmansachs.com

Lagos, December 2012 and
Boston, January 2013

Preface to the Second Edition

The work of the various scholars who have contributed to this book was completed in the very early years of the new century, and brought together by us in 2003. It was the first publication of an ever-growing network of scholars from around the world, organised by Kristian Stokke and Olle Törnquist from the University of Oslo, and animated by shared concerns about the reality of 'democracy' and of processes of democratisation, in the context of globalisation and of what was dubbed by Samuel Huntington as 'the third wave of democratisation'.[1] Since the first publication of *Politicising Democracy* in 2004 the three of us, and other members of the network, have continued our research and writing on these themes.[2] Törnquist and Stokke, with Neil Webster, edited a second book, *Rethinking Popular Representation*, published in 2009, and more recently the two of them have published a further collection, *Democratisation in the Global South: The Importance of Transformative Politics* (2013). Harriss is a contributor to both volumes. Here the three of us reflect upon the arguments developed through the three volumes.

The world has, of course, moved on and changed a good deal since we worked on the editing of *Politicising Democracy* on the small Swedish island of Hallö in the spring of 2003. Perhaps most significantly, the global economic crisis of 2008–09 – which has still not been fully resolved – has shaken both the philosophy on which the economic globalisation that took place in the later 20th century was based, and the ways in which it was sought to be realised. A good many scholars have noted, as we have done – we discuss the point in *Transformative Politics* – the parallels between these recent events and those of the later 19th and early 20th centuries, as they were analysed by Karl Polanyi in his classic, *The Great Transformation*.[3] He showed that the attempt to establish the self-regulating market economy, championed by economic liberals, brought a movement of reaction and resistance to it – he talks of the 'double movement' of contemporary history – as people resisted the commodification of their labour, and of the environment, and states intervened to save business from the effects of the attempt to treat money, too, as a commodity. History does not repeat itself, but recent events across the world may be interpreted in the same sort of way. Polanyi understood the rise both of fascism and of communism, and the emergence of Roosevelt's New Deal, as responses to the crisis brought about by the failure of the attempt to realise the self-regulating market economy. Across Europe democracy was either crushed or under threat. In the present, too, it is said by the Economist Intelligence Unit, in a report on the *2011 Index of Democracy*, that 'Global backsliding in democracy has been evident for some time and strengthened in the wake of the 2008–09 economic crisis'. The report notes that between 2006 and 2008 there was stagnation in the process of democratisation, between 2008 and 2010 regression across the world and that in 2011 there was a decline in democracy concentrated in Europe.[4] We believe, therefore, that the changes that have taken place since this book was first published, have gone to make the concerns that were its driver even more relevant.

Our title, *Politicising Democracy*, reflects what we thought was the practical need of the time, and the task for intellectuals like the authors whose work we brought together. The historical moment was that of 'democracy building' by the Western powers that still dominated the world (how remarkably the world has changed over the course of the past decade ...) – the hubris of which was already being exposed in the tragedy of Iraq. But in 2003 the idea that 'democracy' could be crafted through the introduction of forms of the liberal democratic institutions that had emerged in the West, was still widely accepted. Even beyond this there was an idea, influentially propounded by some in the World Bank, of crafting democracy as participation – an idea of introducing various participatory mechanisms, such as associations in civil society that would both build on and enhance 'social capital', and that would extend the limits of representative democracy. These propositions were closely bound up with the accent that was being placed at the time on decentralisation, including both the deconcentration of adminis-tration and the devolution of power to local government bodies, as a key means of improving the responsiveness and efficiency of govern-ment. Decentralisation would bring government closer to the people and make it both more transparent and more accountable. These were amongst the key principles of the arguments about 'good government', or 'good governance', that were articulated by the international finance institutions – and that reflected a technocratic view of government in which politics had no place.[5]

The position that we took, and that is elaborated through the chap-ters of the book, sought to counter these arguments, which we saw as *depoliticising* democracy. Hence our title.[6] The argument about 'crafting democracy as participation', in particular, though it held out the pros-pect of substantive democracy – of improved popular control, that is, of widely defined public affairs on the basis of political equality – seemed to us to deny the necessary reality of political competition and conflict. Arguments about the virtues of decentralisation seemed to assume common interests among people at local levels, whereas the reality – as research already showed, and as was brought out in chapters in the book – is that decentralised institutions are very often taken over and used to extend their powers by local elites. The introduction of the institutions of liberal democracy at national levels, too, had frequently been brought about through pacts between powerful elites in such a way as effectively to exclude ordinary people. The trends of increasing privatisation of matters of public interest, or the delegation of responsibility for them to elitist associations in civil society, effectively took them out of the public space. In all these ways, as well as through the nostrums of technocratic 'good governance', depoliticisation was taking place. The significance of politics, and especially of local politics, was being downplayed, and this was what we aimed to counter in the book.

On the positive side we were inspired, as we explained in our Introduction, by the arguments of Eric Olin Wright and Archon Fong about the potentials and the possibilities of 'empowered participatory governance', and by the empirical materials from experiments in different parts of the world on which they drew, and also by the parallel arguments of Leonardo Avritzer on the opening up of what he calls 'public space' in Latin America.[7] Yet these studies also raised the critical question of what determines the balance of power that makes these sorts of developments possible – and this underlined again the importance of analysing the politics of local political spheres. Each one of the chapters of the book has this focus – and our enquiry into what determines the establishment of a favourable balance of power has been pursued further through the work that appears in the two later books.

Politicising Democracy reaches some tentative conclusions, perhaps notably about the vital links between civic and political activism. *Contra* then fashionable arguments, deriving especially from the work on social capital by Robert Putnam[8] positing the causal primacy of the former, the studies of the book showed it is the inter-relationships of civic and political activism that matter, and that they actually may be driven by the latter. Further, the studies show, as Törnquist argues in the second of his chapters, that three sets of factors influence the capacities of actors to pursue democratic objectives. These are: (i) the locations of political actors in political and other fields – 'where are different groups active in the political terrain of state, business, self-managed units, and in-between them, the public sphere (where people can meet, communicate, organise and do things together)?'; (ii) the scope and the character of the politicisation of issues; (iii) modes of political inclusion. Nicos Mouzelis once distinguished between '*integration* of people into politics on the basis of relatively autonomous broad popular movements', as opposed to the elitist *incorporation* of people, lacking substantial organisations of their own, by means of *clientelism* and *populism*.[9] These are all factors that we have found significant in the later studies, brought together in *Rethinking Popular Representation* and *Transformative Politics*, our further enquiries into the conditions for building substantial democracy.

The depoliticisation of democracy is both partly produced by, and is a cause, of the flawed representation of the *demos* (the people), in many regimes. Flawed representation, in turn, we argue in *Rethinking Popular Representation*, is the consequence of both institution building that is the outcome of elite pacts and exclusive of the mass of the people, so that the institutions that are built remain embedded in an unfavourable distribution of resources and relations of power, and also of fragmented citizen participation. A democracy that provides a meaningful framework for ordinary people to improve their lives cannot be built only by 'getting the institutions right' – which has been such a popular mantra – based on the assumption that basic freedoms and liberal elections will yield popular inclusion in democratic politics. What is rather required are institutions that can counter the structural impediments that hamper popular democratic control over public affairs. The findings of the research brought together in *Rethinking* show the importance of building various forms of mediation between the demos and public affairs, broadly defined, through civil society and informal leaders and groups, as well as through political society. Representation by way of political parties and interest groups in political society remains important and deserves continued attention, but popular representation is also mediated by way of social movements, trade unions, non-governmental and community-based organization in civil society, as well as through informal leaders such as patrons, religious leaders and 'traditional' authorities, some but not all of which may be transformative. Several of the studies also showed the potential in the provision by governments of new nodes for ordinary citizens' representation beyond elections, through the setting up of institutional channels by means of which democratic organisations can interact directly with the state, as in arrangements for their participation in planning (in Kerala, India) and in budgeting (in Brazil). Understanding actual popular control over public affairs thus requires critical attention to the diversity of actual and potentially transformative channels of representation, as mediating links between the multitude of identities and interests at the level of demos and polycentric institutional arrangements at the level of public affairs.

Our conclusions in *Rethinking Popular Representation*, cited here from the introduction to *Transformative Politics* (2013: 6), are that popular representation

> ...calls for empowered citizens and stronger popular organisations with a voice and with the capacity to reform the system. It also calls for improved institutional nodes and clear democratic principles of representation that ensure strong linkages between popular organisations and institutions of public governance. Substantive popular representation rests, moreover, with the distribution of resources and relations of power as well as with resistance and organised struggle for change. Yet the pressure from below is not in itself sufficient for the generation of political change towards more substantial democratisation. *The design of public institutions for participation and representation (is) also crucial as they affect the ways in which people organise and mobilise. The successful introduction of institutions that are favourable for democratic popular organisation and mobilisation rests with a combination of leadership and demands from below* (emphasis added here).

These conclusions led then to the enquiry into the conditions for the emergence of such institutions through transformative democratic politics, the subject of the third book. *Democratization in the Global South: The Importance of Transformative Politics* argues that it is possible to make political advances on the basis of formal democratic institutions, even in deeply flawed democracies. While acknowledging the structural constraints for substantial democratization, we highlight the centrality of political agendas, strategies and alliances that use formal and minimalist democracy to introduce politics and policies that may enhance people's chances of achieving their aims while also improving democracy. This most recent book in our series on problems and dynamics of democratization in the Global South thus rests on an argument about a 'primacy of politics', but also insists that the prospects and dynamics for transformative democratic politics can only be properly understood with reference to contextual political economies of development. Both arguments are exemplified by the historical making of the 'Scandinavian model', rooted in social democratic ideology, politics and policies.[10] A key question in *Transformative Politics* is thus about the comparative relevance of these experiences for the contemporary Global South. Our general answer, despite critical nuances and qualifications, is on the affirmative side. If transformative democratic politics refers to fruitful links between popular organizations, political parties and the state in the context of formal democracy, there are also interesting contemporary cases in the global South, especially in the recent 'pink tide' revolutions throughout Latin America and in experiments towards local participatory governance.

Historical and contemporary experiences from Scandinavia and Latin America point to the importance of productive relations between popular movements, political parties and the state, both at the local and the national scale. They also point to the importance of the local scale of politics, as especially seen in Brazilian cities and municipalities. But the book also shows the possibilities for transformative dynamics from above, locally as well as on the central level, as seen in nascent tendencies towards post-clientelist politics and social security programmes emerging from middle class politics and reformist political elites. These are important tendencies that require critical attention, bearing in mind the problems of depoliticisation and flawed popular representation that we identified in *Politicising Democracy* and *Rethinking Popular Representation*. Our continued intellectual engagement with the problems and dynamics of substantial democratization, which started with the problems of depoliticised democracy, leads to the conclusion that substantiating democracy requires democratic transformative politics, as also indicated in the title and content of *Politicising Democracy*.

Notes

1. Huntington, Samuel P. (1991) *The Third Wave: Democratisation in the Late Twentieth Century*, University of Oklahoma Press, Norman.
2. In addition to the contributors to the present volume, we wish to acknowledge our debt and gratitude to Berit Aasen, Gunilla Andræ, Sofian Asgart, Gianpaolo Baiocchi, Sheri Berman, David Beetham, Einar Braathen, Inga Brandell, Paul R. Brass, Benedicte Bull, Nils Butenschön, Lars Buur, Harald Bøckman, Neera Chandhoke, Jos Chathukulam, Daniel Chavez, Premakumara de Silva, Nirmal Ranjith Dewasiri, Lars Engberg-Pedersen, Arild Engelsen Ruud, Fredrik Engelstad, Adam Habib, Eva-Lotta Hedman, Patrick Heller, Eric Hiariej, Sam Hickey, Peter P. Houtzager, Janaki Jayawardena, David Christoffer Jordhus-Lier, Preben Kaarsholm, Knut Kjeldstadli, Adrian Gurza Lavalle, Cornelis Lay, Ilda Lourenco-Lindell, Bertil Lintner, James Manor, Desmond McNeill, Joel S. Migdal, Marianne Millstein, Giles Mohan, Aris Arif Mundayat, Kristen Nordhaug, Nathan Quimpo, Pratikno, A.E. Priyono, Lars Rudebeck, Purwo Santoso, Willy P. Samadhi, James C. Scott, Elin Selboe, Nadarajah Shanmugaratnam, Gyda

Marås Sindre, Nur Iman Subono, Gerry van Klinken, Nicolaas Warouw, Neil Webster, Glyn Williams, and Øyvind Østerud.
3. See Polanyi, K. (1944/1957/2001) *The Great Transformation: The Political and Economic Origins of Our Time,* Beacon Press, Boston; and for recent discussions Harvey, D. (2005) *A Brief History of Neoliberalism,* Oxford University Press, Oxford, and Burawoy, M. (2010) 'From Polanyi to Pollyanna: the false optimism of global labor studies', *Global Labour Journal* 1(2), 301-313.
4. Economist Intelligence Unit (2011) *The Democracy Index 2011: Democracy Under Stress,* EIU, London.
5. The foundational statement is found in World Bank (1992) *Governance and Development,* World Bank, Washington, DC.
6. It was actually suggested to us by Peter Houtzager of the Institute of Development Studies, University of Sussex.
7. Fung, A. and Wright, E. O. (eds) (2003) *Deepening Democracy: Institutional Innovations in Empowered Participatory Governance,* Verso, London; Avritzer, L. (2002) *Democracy and the Public Space in Latin America,* Princeton University Press, Princeton.
8. Putnam, R. (1993) *Making Democracy Work: Civic Traditions in Modern Italy,* Princeton University Press, Princeton; Putnam, R. (2000) *Bowling Alone: The Collapse and Revival of American Community,* Simon & Schuster, New York.
9. Mouzelis, N. P. (1986) *Politics in the Semi-Periphery,* Macmillan, Basingstoke, italics in original.
10. Berman, S. (2006) *The Primacy of Politics. Social Democracy and the Making of Europe's Twentieth Century,* Cambridge University Press, Cambridge.

Notes on Contributors

Björn Beckman is Professor Emeritus of Political Science at the University of Stockholm. He is a scholar of politics of development, state and class formation, labour studies and civil society and democratisation in Africa, with a primary empirical focus on Nigeria and South Africa in comparative perspective. His recent publications include *Union Power in the Nigerian Textile Industry* (with Gunilla Andrae, 1999), *Labour Regimes and Liberalization: The Restructuring of State-Society Relations in Africa* (edited with Lloyd Sachikonye, 2001), and *Trade Unions and Party Politics: Labour Movements in Africa* (edited with Sakhela Buhlungu and Lloyd Sachikonye, 2009).

John Harriss is Professor of International Studies and the founding Director of the School for International Studies at Simon Fraser University in Vancouver, Canada. He taught previously at the University of East Anglia, and at the London School of Economics. He has researched and written on the economy and society of Tamil Nadu, in particular, for more years than he readily admits to. His publications include *Reinventing India* (with Stuart Corbridge, 2000), *India Today: Economy, Politics and Society* (with Stuart Corbridge and Craig Jeffrey, 2013), *Power Matters: Essays on Institutions, Politics and Society in India* (2006), and *Depoliticizing Development: The World Bank and Social Capital* (2001). He is a fan of English cricket, and an enthusiastic though not very skilful sailor.

Henk Schulte Nordholt is Professor of Asian History at Erasmus University Rotterdam, focusing on the experience of decentralisation, regional autonomy, and violence in Indonesia. He was the director of the research programmes based at KITLV (Royal Netherlands Institute of Southeast Asian and Caribbean Studies) on *Renegotiating Boundaries: Access, Agency and Identity in Post-Soeharto Indonesia* and *In Search of Middle Indonesia*. His publications include *Indonesia in Search of Transition* (with Irwan Abdullah, 2002) and *Renegotiating Boundaries: Local Politics in Post-Suharto Indonesia* (edited with Gerry van Klinken, 2007).

Sophie Oldfield is Associate Professor of Human Geography at the University of Cape Town. Her research focuses on urban social and political change, community and social movement politics, and state restructuring. Recent publications include *Reconfiguring Identities and Building Territory in India and South Africa* (with Philippe Gervais-Lambony and Frederic Landy, 2005), 'The Parallel Claims of Gated Communities and Land Invasions in a Southern City: Polarised State Responses', *Environment and Planning A* 41(3) (with C. Lemanski, 2009) and 'Moving beyond Polemics: Civil Society Politics in South Africa', *Critical Dialogue* 2(1) (2005).

Joel Rocamora is a Fellow and former Co-director of the Transnational Institute (Amsterdam) and of the Philippines Institute for Popular Democracy as well as the former President of *Akbayan* (Citizens Action Party). He is an expert on Philippines and Southeast Asian politics and development with a special focus on civil society, popular organisation, and constitutional reform. He is the author of the standard work on the PNI, the Indonesian Nationalist Party, and his publications include *Breaking Through: The Struggle within the Communist Party of the Philippines* (1994) and *Low Intensity Democracy: Political Power in the New World Order* (edited with Barry K. Gills and Richard Wilson, 1993).

Günther Schönleitner was Lord Dahrendorf scholar at the London School of Economics and Political Science (LSE), where he took his PhD in 2004. He holds a degree in Law from the University of Salzburg (Austria) and a Master's in Development Studies from the LSE. Prior to his doctoral studies he worked for eight years with an Austrian NGO, including four years in Brazil. His research interests include state–society relations, civil society participation, good governance, democratic consolidation, and social inclusion. He is now with the World Bank.

John T. Sidel is Professor of International and Comparative Politics at the LSE. His research interests and expertise lie within local politics in the Philippines and Indonesia, religious violence in Indonesia, and transnational movements in Southeast Asia. His books include *Capital, Coercion, and Crime: Bossism in the Philippines* (1999) and *Riots, Pogroms, Jihad: Religious Violence in Indonesia* (2006).

Kristian Stokke is Professor of Human Geography at the University of Oslo, specialising in movement politics, democratisation, and conflict transformation. His recent books include *Democratising Development: The Politics of Socio-economic Rights in South Africa* (edited with Peris Jones, 2005), *Rethinking Popular Representation* (edited with Olle Törnquist and Neil Webster, 2009), *Liberal Peace in Question: The Politics of State and Market Reforms in Sri Lanka* (edited with Jayadeva Uyangoda, 2011), and

Democratization in the Global South: The Importance of Transformative Politics (edited with Olle Törnquist, 2013).

P. K. Michael Tharakan writes on Kerala's history and problems of education and development, as well as on the People's Planning Campaign, about which he has a chapter in *Rethinking Popular Representation* (Olle Törnquist, Neil Webster, and Kristian Stokke (eds), 2009). He has recently retired as Vice Chancellor of Kannur University (India) and has been Sri Ramakrishna Hegde Chair Professor in Decentralisation and Governance at the Institute for Social and Economic Change (ISEC), Bangalore, Director of the Kerala Institute of Local Administration (KILA), and Associate Fellow at the Centre for Development Studies (CDS), Thiruvananthapuram.

Olle Törnquist is Professor of Political Science and Development Research at the University of Oslo. His fields of expertise include theories of politics and development, radical politics and problems of democratisation, all in a comparative and theoretical perspective with an empirical focus on South and East Asia. His recent books include *Making Democracy Meaningful: Problems and Options in Indonesia* (with A.E. Priyono and Willy P. Samadhi, 2007), *Rethinking Popular Representation* (with Neil Webster and Kristian Stokke, 2009), *Aceh: The Role of Democracy for Peace and Reconstruction* (with Stanley A. Prasetyo and Teresa Birks, 2011), and *Assessing the Dynamics of Democratisation* (forthcoming).

List of Abbreviations

Akbayan	Citizens Action Group (The Philippines)
ANC	African National Congress (South Africa)
BATMAN	Civil society coalition on participatory local governance (The Philippines)
CBOs	Community-based organisations
CMS	Municipal health councils (Brazil)
COSATU	Congress of South African Trade Unions (South Africa)
CPI-M	Communist Party of India (Marxist)
CUT	Leftist union federation (Brazil)
DPRD	Dewan Perwakilan Rakyat Daerah, Regional parliaments (Indonesia)
GEAR	Growth, Employment and Redistribution Programme (South Africa)
ICFTU	International Confederation of Free Trade Unions
ILO	International Labour Organization
INC	Indian National Congress (India)
IPG	Institute for Politics and Governance (The Philippines)
KSPB	Kerala State Planning Board (Kerala, India)
KSSP	Kerala Sasthra Sahithya Parishat, People's Science Movement (Kerala, India)
LDF	Left and Democratic Front (Kerala, India)
LSGIs	Local Self-Governing Institutions (Kerala, India)
MPAEC	Mandela Park Anti-Eviction Campaign (South Africa)
NGOs	Non-governmental organisations
NHGs	Neighbourhood Groups, Ayalkoottams (Kerala, India)
NLC	Nigeria Labour Congress (Nigeria)
PB	Participatory Budgeting
PR	Proportional representation electoral system
PT	Partido dos Trabalhadores, Workers' Party (Brazil)
PPC	People's Planning Campaign (Kerala, India)
RDP	Reconstruction and Development Programme (South Africa)
SAMWU	South African Municipal Workers Union (South Africa)
SRRMs	Socio-religious reform movements (Kerala, India)
UDF	United Democratic Front (India)

1

Introduction: The New Local Politics of Democratisation

John Harriss, Kristian Stokke and Olle Törnquist

Contemporary discourses about the politics of developing countries have brought together an unlikely set of bedfellows. Intellectuals and policy actors whose ideas are rooted in very different values and theoretical assumptions nonetheless converge around the view that there is a 'new politics' grounded in *local* political spaces and practices. The circumstances are those of globalisation, a diverse set of phenomena which include – or so it is argued – a hollowing out of nation states, in the sense that certain regulatory capacities have been reduced and transferred to institutions operating primarily at global or local scales (Jessop 2002). Simultaneously, local identities and identity politics are constructed anew in a context of global transformations (Appadurai 1996). Thus what some have labelled 'glocalisation' – simultaneous globalisation and localisation processes – is reconfiguring politics (Cox 1997). These transformations are also reflected in development theories and practices, which have increasingly turned to the 'local' as a prime site of development in the context of globalisation.

The dominantly liberal discourse emanating from the World Bank is one powerful voice expressing this idea, but there are remarkably comparable views being articulated by intellectuals who may be described as 'post-structuralists'. Meanwhile there are significant thinkers and activists from the left who advocate what appear to be similar ideas. All these groups of actors share a conception of the vitalisation of democracy (or the establishment of more meaningful alternatives to it) through popular participation in local public spheres.[1] Part of our purpose here is to tease out the significant differences between the ideas of these different groups of thinkers and policy actors; and then through the various chapters of this book to subject them to *political* analysis, taking account of the ways in which local politics work in different contexts in developing countries. These politics are characterised by 'changing continuities' (a phrase that we take from the chapter by Henk Schulte Nordholt). In other words previously existing structures of thought and action exercise a persisting influence upon the politics of the present and constrain (though they do not exclude) possibilities of change.

Localisation of politics in the context of globalisation

The contemporary world is characterised by both globalisation and *localisation of politics*.[2] Local politics have usually been given little attention within development studies; and local authorities, identities and associations used to be seen as traditional features or colonial constructions that would dissolve with modernisation and post-colonial state building. This reasoning reappeared in the 1990s through analyses that portray globalisation as a homogenising force that subordinates people and states everywhere to the global market and thereby eradicates local distinctiveness. Contrary to these expectations, however, localisation of politics has proved to be a product of modernity and an integral part of globalisation and the associated restructuring of nation-states.

Globalisation[3] processes are important, complex and contradictory features of the contemporary world that integrate some states, economies and societies into global networks and flows while marginalising others. Contrary to one popular belief globalisation does not mean the end of sovereign states and of politics, but rather open-ended transformations of state power and politics. Under pressure from global market forces and neo-liberal discourses, many states are undergoing transformations towards *de-statisation* (i.e. reduced state authority in favour of market liberalisation) and towards *de-nationalisation* (i.e. scalar reconfiguration of state power in favour of regionalisation and localisation). This means that political authority is becoming increasingly diffused among state, market and civil society actors at local, national, regional and global scales (Jessop 2002).

In terms of the scale of politics, a dual movement can be observed. On the one hand, the role of supranational institutions is increasing. Formal institutions at global and regional levels – such as the International Monetary Fund, the World Trade Organisation, United Nations, the World Bank and Regional Development Banks – exercise considerable power over the institutions and peoples of the South. They do this largely through economic and legal instruments but also through discursive power. These institutions create and sustain political and discursive frames for thinking and acting, frames which are strongly influenced by a technocratic and apolitical approach that is itself rooted in the most powerful global institution of all – the market (McNeill and Bøås 2003).

On the other hand, the local level of politics is also becoming more prominent. Localisation of politics is mediated through *institutional reforms* towards decentralisation, local democratisation and good governance, *development discourses* on local participation and civil society, and localised *political mobilisation* around local, national and global issues. The last two decades have seen a renewed interest among national governments and international development agencies in administrative decentralisation, i.e. a deliberate transfer of responsibilities from central state institutions to local state institutions (deconcentration) and to non-state actors (privatisation). There has also been an added emphasis in recent years on political decentralisation (devolution) of authority to local governments (Crook and Manor 1998, Olowu 2001). Such reforms are coupled with development discourses that emphasise local partnerships between actors in state, market and society. The common assumption is that mutually enabling relations between decentralised state institutions, local businesses and civil associations will generate economic growth, poverty alleviation and good governance.

There are few critical analyses of whether this localisation actually generates the expected outcomes, especially in terms of democratisation. Existing studies commonly emphasise the crafting of local institutions of governance and downplay local politics. This collection aims at filling this gap. Our purpose is to examine the conjunction of discourses and institutions that define local political spaces and the political practices of actors operating within these spaces, with a special emphasis on the implications of local politics for democratisation.

Democratic transitions in the context of globalisation

These processes of globalisation and localisation of politics coincide and relate to contemporary democratic transitions, what Samuel Huntington famously described as 'the third wave of democratisation' (Huntington 1991).[4] One set of calculations shows that 69 per cent of the countries of the world had authoritarian regimes in 1975, while only 24 per cent could be described as liberal democracies. By 1995 these proportions stood at 26 per cent and 48 per cent respectively. The proportion of countries that could be described as being liberal democracies had doubled over

20 years (Potter 1997). Another calculation is that 'In the 1980s and 1990s...some 81 countries took significant steps towards democracy' (UNDP 2002: 1). In some ways the occurrence of this wave of democratisation (meaning, simply, 'political changes moving in a democratic direction': Potter 1997: 3)[5] is surprising, since those social conditions that have been most important historically in bringing about democracy seem to have been *reduced* by globalisation, and they have certainly not very commonly been present in the countries that have undergone some degree of democratisation.[6] One recent account of the major theoretical approaches to the explanation of patterns of democratisation distinguishes the 'modernisation' approach, the 'structural' approach and the 'transition' approach (Potter 1997; Törnquist 1999). The first of these, exemplified in the work of Seymour Lipset (1959), focuses on socio-economic development and suggests that economic development and widespread higher education are conducive to democratisation, partly because they strengthen the 'moderate' middle class. Yet a good many of the countries that have experienced democratisation in the 'third wave' had not previously been doing at all well in terms of economic development, and their middle classes were not always expanding. At least one country, Indonesia, actually saw movement away from democracy during the period (of the New Order regime of President Soeharto) in which economic development accelerated and the middle class grew in significance. There the members of the middle classes mostly supported an authoritarian regime (Törnquist 2000). In the worlds' largest democracy India, moreover, while people from lower castes and classes are increasingly active in elections the middle classes are not. Rather they seem to bank on a combination of market driven politics and the reinvention of reactionary forms of democracy, including manipulation of religious and ethnic loyalties. (Hansen 1999; Corbridge and Harriss 2000).

The second, 'structural' approach, exemplified in the work of Barrington Moore (1966), and following him in that of Rueschemeyer *et al.* (1992), emphasises changing structures of class, state and transnational power. While Moore's dictum 'no bourgeoisie, no democracy' has been almost as problematic in Third World contexts as the modernisation and middle class thesis, Rueschemeyer *et al.* argue that a shift in the balance of class power in a society towards the working classes creates structural conditions that have, historically, been favourable to the development of democracy. Yet this has not been true of most of the countries that have recently experienced democratisation, and indeed it is very widely held that the circumstances of globalisation towards the end of the 20th century have quite seriously weakened the organised working class.

These circumstances have also hollowed out the state and reduced the significance of programmatic political parties, which historically have been further conditions of democratisation on the basis of popular interests (Castells 1996; Therborn 2001; Held and McGrew 2002; Scholte 2000). In his chapter, Beckman actually questions this pessimistic view with regard to labour. From a poor country perspective, he argues, capitalist relations of production are spreading; expansion of wage labour is taking place, and not just the marginalisation of many people but also the growth of huge new workplaces This is not necessarily taking place in all areas but it is in strategic sectors. And workers are indeed interested in basic civil and political rights, if for no other reason than in order to fight for their own so-called special interests. For some analysts, promising tendencies are found in on-going transformations of organised labour struggles towards *social movement unionism* (Munck 2002). This refers to attempts to link old and new movements in global and local labour and community struggles. These are based on broad conceptions of who the working people are and seek to break down binary oppositions between workplace and community, between economic and political struggles and between formal-sector workers and the working poor. Chapter 6 by Stokke and Oldfield discusses some opportunities and constraints in such local community-centred struggles for livelihood and against global neo-liberalism.

The apparent weaknesses, however, of both the modernisation and the structural approaches for the explanation of the third wave of democratisation have certainly contributed to the ascendancy in the contemporary literature of the 'transition' approach, exemplified in the work of O'Donnell and Schmitter (1986), Linz and Stepan (1996) and others, which focuses on the agency of political elites.[7] Democracy is here conceptualised as a set of government institutions and procedures (rather than 'rule by the people') that are negotiated between political leaders, especially between reformers within an authoritarian regime and moderate dissidents. This theory lends support to the notion that democracy can be 'crafted' because the political alliances that are conducive to democratisation can be encouraged by internationally promoted policy interventions in support of 'good governance', including privatisation and decentralisation, and the strengthening of civil society.[8]

As is often the case, the strength of one approach is the weakness of the other. Whereas the structure-oriented approaches provide limited insight into context-specific actors and processes (as illustrated by the failure to account for recent democratic transitions) the actor-oriented approach does not pay sufficient attention to structural contexts and constraints (as illustrated by their difficulties in explaining different experiences with democratic consolidation). Both remain largely within the confines of the self-contained territorial nation-state and pay scant attention to the role of processes at other scales (Whitehead 2002).[9] Following from such shortcomings, it can be argued that studies of democratisation should broaden the understanding of both *democracy* and of the *dynamics of democratisation*. On the first issue, the minimalist definition of 'formal' democracy as the regular holding of relatively free and fair elections should be replaced with a broader 'substantial' definition that emphasises the introduction of democratic principles, institutions and citizenship rights (Beetham 1999; Grugel 2002; Törnquist 2002b). This means that the test for democracy is not about the existence of formal democratic rights and institutions, but whether they have real meaning for people. On the second issue, current theories of democratisation should be replaced with more holistic approaches, focusing on how collective and individual actors engage in struggles to transform authoritarian states and build democracy but also how they are enabled and constrained by structured environments. This yields an analytical focus on (1) *the state* as an arena, an actor and an outcome of democratic transitions; (2) *civil society* as the space where associations and individuals can hold the state accountable and join in struggles for citizenship rights, and; (3) *globalisation* as the contemporary structural context for democratic transitions (Grugel 2002). Regarding the aforementioned question about the link between economic development and democratisation, it can now be observed that the global political economy of the present period reduces the political and economic options available to developing states, as it facilitates and demands transitions to a hegemonic model of economic liberalisation coupled with formal liberal democracy. This has led some observers to describe the new liberal democratic regimes in many African countries as 'choiceless democracies' (Mkandawire 1999), i.e. formal liberal democracies but with limited capacity to deepen democratisation in the context of economic globalisation and structural adjustment.

Approaching local democratic participation

'Crafting' democracy as participation

The possibility of crafting of democracy is very clearly reflected in the pronouncements of the most influential voice in international development, that of the World Bank – which is, we have argued, the voice of liberalism (or what is often but unnecessarily qualified as 'neo-liberalism'). The high water mark of economic liberalism in development policies, and the 'rolling back' of the state that economic liberalism advocated, was reached in the 1980s. By the 1990s it was recognised that the policies of economic liberalism, implemented in stabilisation and structural adjustment programmes, were failing partly because of failures of government. In 1992 the World Bank published a paper on *Governance and Development* in which it began to lay out a new approach, summarised as follows by Lewis Preston, then the President of the Bank, in his Forword to the paper:

> Good governance is an essential complement to sound economic policies. Efficient and accountable management by the public sector and a predictable and transparent policy framework are critical to the efficiency of markets and governments, and hence to economic development. The World Bank's increasing attention to issues of governance is an important part of our efforts to promote equitable and sustainable development (World Bank 1992: v).

'Good governance' – understandably, in view of the World Bank's formally non-political role – was defined in technical, managerialist terms. It involved, as well as 'sound public sector management', establishing a strong legal framework for development, and mechanisms for securing transparency and accountability. Though it might have been expected that the role of democratisation would have entered into the consideration of 'good governance', it did not – and, on the face of it, still does not. A great deal of information about governance, which it identifies as a 'hot topic', is readily available on the World Bank's website, but there is very little there about democracy.[10] The major statement that appeared in the *World Development Report* of 1997, particularly in chapter 7 of that Report, entitled 'Bringing the State Closer to People', more or less assumed the existence of electoral democracy. But perhaps because of a recognition of the limitations of 'electoral democracy', the Bank's real focus turned out to be 'participatory mechanisms' that are represented as extending and going beyond the limits of representative, electoral democracy. It is argued, for instance, that 'In most societies, democratic or not, citizens seek representation of their interests beyond the ballot as taxpayers, as users of public services, and increasingly as clients or members of non-governmental organisations (NGOs) and voluntary associations. Against a backdrop of competing social demands, rising expectations and variable government performance, these expressions of voice and participation are on the rise' (World Bank 1997: 113).[11] The World Bank has thus come to identify as a key element in good governance citizen participation, seen as being articulated by and through NGOs and a variety of local associations, which are in turn held to constitute civil society. It is also argued that the differences that exist between societies in terms of 'the depth and intensity of popular collective action' may be explained in terms of 'differing endowments of *social capital*, the informal rules, norms and long-term relationships that facilitate coordinated action' (World Bank 1997: 114, see also World Bank 2000; UNDP 2002). Thus the Bank has come to emphasise in its rhetoric, and to a much more limited extent in its practices (Bebbington *et al.*, forthcoming), a set of closely connected and partly overlapping concepts – participation, civil society and social capital – that are frequently associated empirically with NGOs and local voluntary associations, within the framework of decentralised and to a large extent also privatised government and administration. These concepts are in the end represented as standing in the place of what may be described as 'conventional' democratic politics, in which different interests and values are aggregated and articulated by political parties. It is a society-centred perspective which, as we have argued before, represents a 'depoliticised' view of processes of social change (Törnquist 1999; Mohan and Stokke 2000; Harriss 2002). These ideas hold out the prospect of a democracy with substance and depth but without political competition or conflict between different social groups and classes. It is this very particular construction of an increasingly unconstitutional, de-institutionalised and de-politicised democracy, created through the crafting of local organisations and facilitated by NGOs, which is now seen as being a condition both for 'good governance' and for successful economic development.

'Radical polycentrism'

Another interpretation of the perspective presented by the Bank is that it sensibly reflects the 'new politics' of the present – the politics of new social movements, of civic activism and of NGOs – as opposed to the 'old politics' of the labour movement and of programmatic political parties. This 'new politics' has been described by Peter Houtzager in terms of 'radical polycentrism': 'a loosely bounded set of ideas and beliefs that the uncoordinated and highly decentralised actions of civil society entities, market actors and local government agents are engaged in a mutually reinforcing movement to produce all good things for all people' (compare the normative arguments of UNDP 2002). Houtzager continues: 'both neo-liberal [e.g. World Bank] and post-structuralist development discourse and practice are radically polycentric and share a strong belief in the ability of local-level associational activity...to solve an ever-expanding list of problems'.[12]

The 'post-structuralist' discourse highlights the multitude of collective struggles around culturally constructed identities. Such movements are commonly portrayed as forms of resistance against the state and the market and are said to operate outside major political alignments and the formal political sphere (Laclau and Mouffe 1985; Shiva 1989; Escobar and Alvares 1992; Alvarez, *et al.* 1998). Thus, local civil society is conceptualised as a relatively autonomous site of resistance, while broader material and political processes are analytically marginalised (Mohan and Stokke 2000). Arturo Escobar's (1995) well-known critique of state-sponsored development is a strong statement along these lines (for a discussion see Corbridge 1998). Focusing on the power of representations, he argues that the development discourse suppresses local cultures, identities and histories and thus functions as mechanisms of oppression. This produces various forms of cultural resistance (e.g. grassroots movements and local knowledge) that entail a search for radical *alternatives to development* rather than simply more appropriate *development alternatives*. Amongst the 'post-structuralists' are also those in the diverse group of Indian scholars whom Bardhan (1997) calls the 'anarcho-communitarians', including Ashis Nandy, Rajni Kothari, and Partha Chatterjee, who are critical of the centralising and elitist character of the modernising state – which is not changed, they hold, by the institutions of liberal democracy. They too defend aspects of 'tradition' and espouse the cause of decentralised, autonomous community-based development.

The literature on social movements and resistance in civil society brings forth the issues of scale that we have discussed with reference to localisation of politics in the context of globalisation. For many post-structuralist thinkers answers to the problems of creating meaningful democracy and development in the context of globalisation are sought in local communities and their resistance from below. This poses the problem of breaking out of localism and scaling up place-based struggles to challenge the state or the global market in significant ways. For others, like Mary Kaldor in her book *Global Civil Society: An Answer to War* (2003) the answers are sought in what she calls the 'activist' vision of global civil society, which is 'about the empowerment of individuals and the extension of democracy...about "civilizing" or democratising globalisation, about the process through which groups, movements and individuals can demand a global rule of law, global justice and global

empowerment' (2003: 12). The actual civic organisations, social movements and transnational networks that constitute her global civil society, however, should have roots and bases in local public spheres as well
as involving new actors who have 'found it possible and necessary to
make alliances across borders and to address not just the state but international institutions as well' (2003: 76). Kaldor quite fairly distinguishes
this vision of global civil society from the 'neo-liberal' version propounded by the World Bank. Yet it too is in some senses a depoliticising
discourse, as Neera Chandhoke has argued, certainly if international
NGOs and transnational movements come to represent the poor people
of the 'Third World'. These organisations may be quite effective but
does their activity 'substitute for the activity we call politics?', Chandhoke
asks, when 'to be politicised is to acquire consciousness that collective
endeavours offer possibilities of self-realisation' (2002: 47). She worries
that what the development of global civil society actually connotes is
'the collapse of the idea that ordinary men and women are capable of
appropriating the political initiative' (2002: 47) (and so of moving
towards the realisation of democratic values). Kaldor surely does not
envisage that global civil society, as she defines it, works in this way,
but Chandhoke's concerns are justified because of the concentration in
Kaldor's work on transnational actors.[13]

The worries of Houtzager, Chandhoke and others are further substan-
tiated in Törnquist's case studies of popular politics of democratisation
(2002b and Chapter 9 in this book). In Kerala, Indonesia and the
Philippines, alike, he finds those he describes as 'fragmented pro-
democrats'. Their efforts tend to suffer, on the one hand, from the lack
of linkage between civil and political society activism at both central
and local levels and, on the other hand, divisive politicisation of single
issues, special interests and identities.

Experiments in popular democracy

There are some continuities between Kaldor's arguments and those of
another distinct group of thinkers and political actors, coming (like her)
from the left, but who have responded to the crisis of confidence within
the political left – arising from recognition of the failures of statist projects
of social transformation – by proposing new 'transformative democratic
strategies'. This is the phrase of Archon Fung and Erik Olin Wright who
have advanced ideas about what they refer to as 'empowered participatory
governance' (Fung and Wright 2003a). Comparable ideas are found also
in the recent work of Leonardo Avritzer (2002), writing about Brazil, and
in that of Hilary Wainwright (2003) who brings together experience

both from Brazil and from the United Kingdom. Interestingly and significantly, all these writers – Fung and Wright, Avritzer and Wainwright – refer extensively to the experience of Participatory Budgeting in Brazil, especially in the southern Brazilian city of Porto Alegre.

The challenge for the left, Fung and Wright say, is 'to develop transformative democratic strategies that can advance our traditional values – egalitarian social justice, individual liberty combined with popular control over collective decisions, and the flourishing of individuals in ways which enable them to realise their potentials' (2003a: 5). With their co-workers, they have analysed several recent attempts to realise such strategies, including the People's Planning Campaign in Kerala (which is also the subject of Chapter 5 by Tharakan and, in part, of Chapters 1 and 9 by Törnquist in this book) and the experience of Participatory Budgeting in Porto Alegre (referred to here in Schönleitner's chapter), as well as initiatives in North America. All of them involve action in local political spheres. There are three principles, they find, that are common to the democratic experiments that they have studied: they have a practical orientation, focussing on specific, tangible problems; they involve ordinary people who are affected by these problems and the officials who are close to them; and they involve the *deliberative* development of solutions to these problems. They represent, indeed, attempts to realise the idea of deliberative democracy, in which, it is held, by coming together and discussing the ideas and interests which they bring to public decision-making, it is possible for people to arrive at those decisions through a consensual process rather than by majority voting. It involves an idea of bargaining as taking place through conversation, much of which necessarily takes place in local public fora, requiring 'civility' (or respect for others' positions and values), and the application of reason, rather than the conflict of interests alone. 'In deliberative decision-making, (say Fung and Wright) participants listen to each other's positions and generate group choices after due consideration . . . (and although) . . . (r)eal world deliberations are often characterised by heated conflict, winners and losers (the) important feature of genuine deliberation is that participants find reasons that they can accept in collective actions, not necessarily that they completely endorse the action or find it maximally advantageous' (2003a: 19). There is an important assumption here that it is possible for individuals, through reasoned deliberation, to transform their preferences. Attempts to realise deliberative democracy, however, in common with democracy in general, confront the problem of inequality. Fung and Wright clearly recognise the danger that 'some participants will use their power to manipulate and enhance positions motivated by particularistic interests' (2003a: 20) and they argue that the chances that institutions designed to establish deliberative democracy will actually have their desired effects 'depends significantly upon the balances of power between actors.... When individuals cannot dominate others to secure their first best preference they are often more willing to deliberate' (2003a: 26). A fundamental question in regard to the sort of 'deepening' of democracy that Fung and Wright envisage, therefore, is that of what really determines this balance of power.

Let us ground this discussion by referring further to the example of Participatory Budgeting in Porto Alegre and elsewhere in Brazil (Abers 2000; Baiocchi 2001). This is an important case, as we mentioned, for Fung and Wright, and also for Leonardo Avritzer – whose work is discussed in Schönleitner's chapter in this book. Avritzer's starting point is with the view that the 'transition' theory of democratisation that has been especially well developed in regard to Latin America, and which – as a version of the theory of democratic elitism[14] – privileges the role of political elites, does not account for nor recognise the significance of recent popular political movements. He refers to the emergence of democratic forms of collective action in Argentina, Brazil and Mexico, in the human rights movement, in urban social movements which have, he says 'challenged one of the region's most deeply ingrained traditions – the idea that material improvements for ordinary citizens represent favors to be delivered by elite political mediators' (2002: 5), and the *Alianza Civica* in Mexico, created in response to citizen concerns about electoral fraud. These show, Avritzer thinks, the potential that is there for establishing what he refers to as 'public space' and a form of popular democracy that goes well beyond competition between elites: it is 'a conception that links the emergence of political democracy to the formation of a *public space in which citizens can participate as equals*, and by arguing ['deliberating'] about collective projects for society, guide formal decision-making' (2002: 5, emphasis added). Elsewhere he says that he aims to develop 'a theory of democratisation based on the con-struction of what I call participatory publics' (2002: 35) – and the idea of 'participatory publics' clearly implies public deliberation over political matters in the local political sphere. Indeed Avritzer's 'public space' requires the existence of public fora where face-to-face deliberation can take place. A concrete case of the creation of what he means by public space is in the experience of Participatory Budgeting (PB). Here, building (according to Avritzer's account) on initiatives made in the first place by The Union of Neighbourhood Associations of Porto Alegre, the

Workers' Party (*Partido dos Trabhalhadores*, or PT), once it had secured office in the municipal government, has established a set of arrangements whereby it is possible for large numbers of people to join in deliberation and decision-making on public projects and investments, and to monitor their outcomes. The People's Planning Campaign in Kerala attempted very much the same thing. What is distinctive about PB in Porto Alegre for Avritzer – and what helps to make it such an important experiment – is that it involves deliberation and institutional mechanisms which connect that 'public reasoning' with the political system in a way that is stronger than just 'influence',[15] whilst not conflating deliberation with administration (which is the critical failing of many attempts at realising 'participation').

Avritzer's work combines positive analysis and normative reasoning in such a way that it is sometimes difficult to distinguish the one from the other. He aims to show that democratic collective action, within Latin American societies, has opened a space for political participation and challenged 'traditional (hierarchical and clientelist) understandings of politics' (2002: 3), and that there are institutional designs (as in PB) whereby the democratic practices that have emerged may be linked into the political system: there are ways, then, of transferring 'democratic potentials that emerge at the societal level to the political arena through participatory designs' (2002: 9) – and ultimately perhaps of changing the entire political culture. But he also recognises the potential or actual conflict between the kind of democratic action that he analyses – and this normative understanding of democratisation – and the old clientelist structures and hierarchical culture of Latin American politics. The demands that have arisen within Latin American societies come into conflict with 'political society', as for instance in Brazil and Mexico, where 'The autonomy of neighbourhood associations and the public presentation of demands were undermined by the reintroduction of clientelism, which became [once again] one of the principal ways of building political majorities' (2002: 7).

A realistic assessment, therefore, of the prospects for the sort of participatory deliberative democracy that Avritzer advocates, and that may have been realised in Porto Alegre and in some other cases (Fung and Wright 2001; Wainwright 2003), calls for analysis of the politics of the local political sphere. As a matter of fact, in several of the cases that seem to have worked (like Porto Alegre) or to have had some limited success (such as the People's Planning Campaign in Kerala) the role of political vehicles that have successfully mobilised people from the lower classes – and hence shifted the balance of social power – seems to have been one of the crucial factors. In Porto Alegre, which, like Brazil in general is marked by considerable inequality, it is hard to imagine that the condition that Avritzer identifies as being necessary – the creation of 'a public space in which citizens can participate as equals' – would have been satisfied without the securing of political power in the city by the PT and then the progressive top-down measures from the mayor's office, at the expense of the elected but often clientelistic councillors. Similarly, according to Tharakan and Törnquist, radical civil society activists in Kerala would never have been able to launch the massive People's Planning Campaign had it not been for successful simultaneous engagement and partial support from the Left Front government – particularly sections of the CPI-M – and access to the powerful state planning board. Unhappily, it was also other sections of the party and of the Left, in this case, that hijacked some parts of the Campaign, bringing them within the framework of conventional clientelistic politics and thus contributing to its undermining. But there is no question that the role of the PT in Porto Alegre, or of politically organised activists in Kerala contradicts Avritzer's idea that democratic forces arise from within society and have to be transmitted into the political system or into 'political society', when it seems quite clear that without the commitment of the political parties and activists in these cases public space would not have been opened up at all.[16] It surely remains a moot point as to whether it is ever possible to establish deliberative structures in a social context where a small number of relatively powerful people can exercise dominance and so 'secure their first best preferences' (Fung and Wright, quoted above); and a moot point, too, as to whether the kind of civility, or civic values that are an essential aspect of public deliberation are produced by the deliberative process or are instead a precondition for it.

'New politics' and the agenda of the book

The discourses that Houtzager labels as those of 'radical polycentrism' – whether of the liberals or the post-structuralists – evade the problem of power. They sideline, if they do not altogether ignore the role of political society, including political parties that negotiate between and aggregate together different interests and values, and contend for the authority to make decisions on matters of public importance. It is true that political activists, in turn, may be elitist and lack genuine bases on the ground, in civil society. But a major problem seems to be that of what Törnquist calls 'pro-democratic fragmentation', when there are insufficient links between civic and political activism, as well as divisive single issues, interests and identities. On the other hand, the thinkers and activists from the left to whose ideas on popular democracy we have referred, do recognise the need for links between civic and political activism and the generation of common agendas. Their main strategy is to facilitate and design the best possible public spaces for popular deliberation. But it is far from clear how it is possible to create those spaces in the first place, and then actually to practice 'deliberation', given the balance of power in most societies.

Public decision making through deliberation may sometimes be possible, but collective action in any society invariably involves contention – and that means what is generally understood as 'politics' (which begins whenever two or more people try to realise some objective together). This is brushed away in much of the society-centric discourse about participation and civil society, and in discourses about community. Of course there are new trends and features in contemporary politics. It probably is true that workplaces are less significant political arenas than they were, and communities more so; there are 'new' social movements; and there is a congeries of new types of associations, including the burgeoning numbers of NGOs in many countries. But there is still no substitute for a citizen based state and independent political vehicles. It is theoretically misleading to try to conceptualise 'civil society' except in relation to the state (Chandhoke 2002). As a matter of historical fact, significant developments in civil society in the best studied cases of the United States (Skocpol 1992; Fiorina and Skocpol 1999) and of Italy (Tarrow 1994) seem to have *followed from* rather than to have given rise to significant developments through state and politics. The reality and the possibilities of substantial democratisation – movement towards people's capacity actually to make use of democratic means to promote democratic ends (in Törnquist's terminology in Chapter 9 in this book) – necessarily involves citizens who are made politically equal by meaningful constitutional rights and institutions, and who as actors and agents of political society are in contention for the authority to make public decisions. Whereas much of the mainstream development discourse (including, ironically, that of the critics of 'development') is marked by a strong tendency to essentialise and romanticise local communities, and to downplay questions of citizenship and power (and inequality), the aim of this book is to develop critical examinations specifically of local power relations and politics. All the chapters of the book have an analytical focus, first, on the factors that may open up local political spaces so as to create what Avritzer describes as 'public space', and, secondly on the factors that influence the capacities of actors to make use of and further improve the rights and institutions within these spaces – thereby furthering a process of substantial democratisation.

Analysing local politics and democratisation

Our discussion points to a need to understand the local politics of democratisation in relational and contextual terms. Our approach to the analysis of local politics and democratisation combines analysis of the balance of power with that of the ways in which actors try to master and alter those conditions by employing and developing, or avoiding and undermining democratic instruments in local and non-local political spaces.

An illustrative way of conceptualising power relations is suggested by a reading of the work of Pierre Bourdieu (Stokke 2002).[17] Bourdieu – as a theoretician of power – seeks to conceptualise both the structural balance of power and the practices of actors. Three core concepts in Bourdieu's (1990, 1991) work are those, first, of 'habitus', second, his particular conception of 'capital', and thirdly the idea of a social 'field'. Bourdieu uses the term 'habitus' to refer to 'dispositions' – or internalised norms, understandings and patterns of behaviour – which clearly differ from one group of people to another. They are acquired, structured and durable and they establish classificatory principles and organising principles of action that in turn generate 'practice', in different social fields. A 'field', for Bourdieu, is a relational space of positions, occupied by actors, and the forces, or relations of power obtaining between those positions. Both 'positions' and 'forces', the key aspects of any social field, are defined – in turn – by the various forms of capital: *economic capital* (material wealth in the form of property, money, etc.),[18] *social capital* (social resources in the form of networks and contacts based on mutual recognition) and *cultural capital* (informational assets in the forms of knowledge and skills acquired through socialisation and education).These fundamental forms of capital are different forms of power, and they are convertible, the one to another. The most powerful conversion to be made is to a fourth form of capital: *symbolic capital* (meaning legitimate authority in the form of prestige, honour and reputation). This is of central importance in any political field for legitimate authority implies above all the power to create the 'official version of the social world'. People's actions, then, and their strategies, derive from their dispositions and their positions (implying access to different forms and combinations of capital) in the social field, and their perceptions of it. 'Practice', over time, may bring about change in both the constitution of the field and in habitus.

Bourdieu's idea of 'habitus' may be understood in terms of the more familiar concepts of 'institutions' and 'culture'. When Bourdieu talks of 'dispositions', as we have explained, he is referring to structured patterns of behaviour and the norms and understandings associated with them. He implies the existence of 'institutions', or the formal and informal rules that constrain and facilitate human action and social interaction, and 'culture', or the habits of thought and behaviour, and the meaning underlying them, that are characteristic of a particular group of people. Understood in this way the two terms have inter-linking or partly over-lapping meanings. Formal, particularly legal rules and contracts are always and necessarily 'embedded in deep, informal social strata, often involving such factors as trust, duty and obligation (so that) a formal contract always takes on the particular hue of the informal social culture in which it is embedded' (Hodgson 2001: 304) Mamdani's account (1996) of the construction of 'Indirect Rule' in Africa shows just this kind of complex relationship between legal institutions and an informal social culture in which they are embedded, and which they were both influenced by and also contributed to forming. In colonial and post-colonial Africa the distinction between customary law and 'modern' law has clearly been of fundamental significance in defining the political terrain. The power of the native chiefs in local politics arises from the establishment of customary law. While certain political and public spaces were generated among the usually urban white settlers-cum-citizens, and while these spaces were later on 'africanised' in the process of national independence, little changed with regard to the indirectly ruled majority of the population. They generally remained, as they had been in the colonial era, 'subjects' rather than citizens. Without major changes in these respects it may be counterproductive to craft decentralisation, civil society and electoral democracies. Nordholt (in this volume) develops a comparable argument in relation to the current process of decentralisation in Indonesia. With regard to Latin America, too, it has been argued that 'the development of Latin American societies always involved different combinations of traditions, in particular different combinations of universalism with the specific particularisms formed in the region prior to its encounter with the main Western tradition' (Avritzer 2002: 70).

The institutional and cultural context (habitus) and *the balance of social power* in a political field are intrinsically inter-related. Political fields are according to Bourdieu characterised by a competition for the legitimate right to speak on behalf of others. Positions as spokespersons may be based on personal symbolic capital (e.g. fame, honour and popularity), but more significantly reside within state institutions and political parties and are granted to individuals as representatives. This means that the balance of power in local political spheres will influence and be influenced by the resources (in terms of different forms of capital) of political institutions and actors and the relations among them.

This provides some critical guidelines for analyses of local politics. The possibilities for strategic practices within a political field are shaped, in the first place, by the institutional and cultural constitution of political spheres and by the balance of power within these. The fundamental question, then, is what social movement analysts call the 'political opportunity structure' – referring to opportunities and hindrances such as the degree of openness of the political field, the presence of allies and the risk of repression. Bourdieu's focus on institutionalised political capital highlights the critical role of political parties. Whether or not political parties have programmatic ideologies, whether they have symbolic power, and whether or not they are themselves institutionalised and embedded in local communities, are factors of wide significance. In Brazil the Workers' Party is now institutionalised in a way that the right wing parties are not. In India, similarly, the left parties have organisation and an institutionalised presence, certainly in the states of Kerala and West Bengal, that other parties generally do not have.[19] This is likely to make a considerable difference, in fact, to the nature and functioning of civil society organisations. Houtzager, Lavalle and Acharya, for example, report from recent research in Sao Paulo that 'the actors most likely to participate [in the institutional arrangements recently established for citizen participation] are those with institutionalised ties to two traditional political actors – political parties and the state. Ties to unions and the Catholic Church, however, do not affect civil society actors' propensity to participate' (Houtzager *et al.* 2003: 5–6). Similarly, as is shown in the chapters by Tharakan and Törnquist, while it is true that the development of the relatively vibrant associational life of Kerala is rooted in the socio-religious organisations of the 19th century that fought caste dominance and demanded equal rights, the development of more universalistic solidarities and wider mass movements came with the growth of class-based movements and organising amongst socialists and communists – since the mid-1960s mainly that of the CPI-M. The extent and nature of political competition is another vitally important factor. Heller has shown how political competition has influenced the extent and character of democratic decentralisation in Porto Alegre and Kerala on the one hand as compared with South Africa on the other. The compulsions of political competition drove the Workers' Party in Porto Alegre and a substantial number of members of the CPI-M in Kerala to try to reach out to new political constituencies through decentralisation, whereas, he argues, 'in the absence of countervailing forces, either in the form of viable opposition parties or autonomous social movements the African National Congress has succumbed to the centralising and autocratic tendencies of the iron law of oligarchy' (Heller 2001: 157).

Bourdieu's concrete studies focus mainly on the powers and practices of dominating forces. He rarely conceptualised and studied – although he actively supported – the efforts of dominated groups. This means that his work provides more insight into the mechanisms and continuities of domination than into processes and moments of transformation. A fundamental question then is how actors strategise to increase their capacity to pursue democratic objectives within a political field. Törnquist (1999, 2002a) argues that three sets of factors are especially important in studies of the strategies and capacities of different political actors.

The first set of factors addresses the location of political actors in political and other fields: where are different groups active in the political terrain of state, business, self-managed units and, in between them, the public sphere (where people can meet, communicate, organise and do things together)? And what of central as against local political levels and the linkages between them? Törnquist's comparative research indicates, for instance, that new pro-democrats are often weak within the state and at workplaces but comparatively strong within self-managed units (such as NGOs and cooperatives) and in the public sphere. It is also clear that fragmentation and the lack of links between different sectors and political levels have been a frequent and serious problem.

The second set of factors covers the politicisation of issues, interests, ideas and identities. Törnquist observes that, apart from what is prioritised, it is the *character* of politicisation that seems to be crucial. Pro-democrats tend to focus on single issues and specific group interests, and are rarely able to transform this into a synthesis of broader interests, perspectives and ideologies. This leaves them vulnerable to fragmentation and 'alternative' ethnic and religious unities. We may also think in terms of the differing combinations of individual/collective action and self-help/ claims-making. In tackling their problems, people may make claims upon the state, at some level, as individuals, probably through patrons. This is what generally happens in the slums of Delhi, where unelected local leaders, known as *pradhans*, who are themselves linked to political leaders in different parties, are key intermediaries for most people.[20] Or people may make claims on the basis of collective action. Again in Delhi, this is happening now under the leadership of a movement for homeless people initiated by the former prime minister V. P. Singh. Or people may seek to resolve their problems through collective action with the purpose of self-help, as for example when they combine together with others to obtain land for housing. A further aspect of politicisation is that of whether or not, and in what ways, claims and issues are aggregated together (Collier *et al.* 2002).

The third set of factors raises questions about how and at what level(s) actors mobilise support for their policies. In other terms: what is the mode of political inclusion? Nicos Mouzelis (1986) has suggested that we may distinguish historically 'between the *integration* of people into politics on the basis of relatively autonomous broad popular movements generated by comprehensive economic development (as in many parts of Western Europe), and the elitist *incorporation* of people with less solid organisations of their own' (Törnquist 1999: 155). Incorporation has two distinct forms: *clientelism* and *populism*. 'Clientelism' refers to the existence of bosses on different levels who have the capacity to deliver patronage in return for services and votes. The Congress Party in India for instance, in the 1950s and 1960s was organised by clientelism: 'That chain of important individuals stretching from village to state, and eventually to the national capital, welded by bonds of patronage, was one central feature of Congress's success into the 1960s' (Kohli 1990: 186). Populism provides another framework for bringing the lower classes into politics. In this case charismatic political leaders are able to mobilise people directly – in the way, for example, that Indira Gandhi was able to in India in the early 1970s when she was able to reach the people with a populist discourse, over the heads of the party bosses and faction leaders. The term 'populism' embraces a range of political ideologies and leaders. What is common to them is an appeal to an idea of an undifferentiated 'common people', who are either excluded from or only have limited access to privilege. Populist politics proposes to secure access to spheres of privilege, but without necessarily changing the system which generates differentiation in the first place. These concepts are ideal types and in practice it is possible to find differing combinations of populism and clientelism, or of integration and incorporation. The CPI-M in the state of West Bengal, for example, has integrated people into politics on the basis of a broad popular movement, but it also involves structures of clientelism. The two major Dravidian parties of the south Indian state of Tamil Nadu are both fairly described as 'populist' but one (the AIDMK) relies much more on the charisma of the leader than the other (the DMK), which does have a good deal of local organisation and structures of clientelism (Widlund 2000).

Integration of people into politics on the basis of relatively autonomous broad movements, on the other hand, is what pro-democrats usually strive for. Historically one may distinguish with Sidney Tarrow (1994) between two basic forms of 'mobilisation structures' that help movements to coordinate and persist over time by linking the 'centre' (of formally organised leadership), and the 'periphery' (of collective action in the field). One goes back to the anarchist and syndicalist tradition of trusting people's natural and spontaneous ability to resist oppression and exploitation through autonomous collective action – even though in reality organic leaders often function as spearheads. Today's networking and polycentric groups are quite firmly within this stream. The other tradition stresses political ideology, organisation and intervention through integrated structures of parties, unions and self-help organisations – which, however, in reality may hamper dynamic collective action. This tradition rests primarily with the European social democratic movements but also organisations of a similar kind in the developing world, such as the CPI-M in Kerala and to a certain degree the Workers' Party in Brazil.

The contributions

The aim of a systematic approach of this kind is not to prescribe how local politics and democratisation should be analysed but rather to initiate a discussion on the direction in which it may be fruitful to proceed. Whilst addressing the overall theme of local politics and democratisation, the individual contributions to this book address very different actors and contexts and do so by way of distinct approaches. In general terms, Chapters 2 and 3 (Henk Schulte Nordholt and John T. Sidel) examine the field of changing continuities in local elite politics; Chapters 4 and 5 (Günther Schönleitner and P. K. Michael Tharakan) analyse deliberative arrangements between local government and civil society, and; Chapters 6–9 (Kristian Stokke and Sophie Oldfield, Joel Rocamora, Björn Beckman and Olle Törnquist) address the local political spaces and strategies of popular movements.

Henk Schulte Nordholt critically examines the assumption that Indonesia is undergoing a transition from authoritarian centralist rule by a strong state towards a new democratic and decentralised system of governance in which civil society will play a prominent role. Nordholt challenges the simplistic notion of 'transition' as a fundamental and irreversible shift from one situation to another and especially the expectation that decentralisation reforms will automatically produce local democracy. Contrary to this model, Nordholt demonstrates the need for contextual analyses of the 'changing continuities' in political relations and practices. One such changing continuity is the persistence of patrimonial hierarchies from pre-colonial politics through the 'New Order' period to post-Soeharto politics. This yields a blurring of boundaries between state, society and market, between formal institutions and informal networks and between centre and periphery. In the context of entrenched patrimonial practices, decentralisation does not necessarily result in democratisation and good local governance. Instead Nordholt identifies tendencies towards decentralisation of corruption and political violence, which are likely to prevent the establishment of democratic transparency and accountability at the local level. Indeed decentralisation offers regional elites with access to strategic political positions new opportunities to expand and maintain patrimonial political networks.

John T. Sidel further investigates these links between decentralisation, local elites and democratisation through a comparative analysis of local bossism in the Philippines, Thailand and Indonesia. Contrary to the assumptions made by advocates of decentralisation, and in agreement with Nordholt's critique, Sidel argues that local elites may hamper rather than promote local democratisation. He provides a critique of the dominant view that local strongmen flourish in web-like societies and utilise their societal power to capture parts of the state. This capturing of state power is said to cause state weakness and impede policy implementation. Sidel argues on the contrary that local strongmen are shaped by the opportunities and constraints for accumulation and monopolisation of local economic and political power, which are provided by the macro- and micro-structures of the state. He especially emphasises the subordination of the state to elected officials at an early stage of capitalist development (described as 'primitive accumulation'), and asserts that democratisation and decentralisation have given local powerbrokers unprecedented political and economic opportunities. This conception of local bossism leads the author to the conclusion that democratisation through decentralisation requires societal challenges and constraints to the rules of bosses. This theme is further developed in subsequent chapters of this book.

Günther Schönleitner develops the theme of participatory governance through an analysis of local arrangements for political participation in Brazil. Focusing on deliberative sector-policy councils – joint decision-making bodies of local government and civil society – the author discusses the democratising effects of deliberation. The point of departure is Avritzer's (2002) normative assumption that institutionalised fora for face-to-face deliberations over contentious issues enable the transfer of democratic practices from civil society to a political society with ambiguous stances towards democracy. Schönleitner argues that this democratising effect of deliberative public spaces must be examined contextually rather than assumed *a priori*. Towards this end, he provides a comparative analysis of four local health councils, displaying different combinations of local government commitment to deliberation and associational vibrancy in civil society. This comparative analysis leads to the conclusion that democratisation through deliberative public spaces requires a positive interaction between an appropriate institutional design that ensures deliberative equality, government commitment to deliberation and civic participation in local deliberations. In reality, the different combinations of government commitment and civic organising that exist in Brazil produce diverse political outcomes, ranging from situations with highly unequal power relations and top-down political incorporation to situations with political equality and bottom-up political integration.

P. K. Michael Tharakan is also concerned with arrangements for deliberation between local government and civil society. Complementing Schönleitner's comparative analysis of deliberative public spaces in Brazil, Tharakan provides a contextual and historical account of the development of the campaign for decentralised participatory planning within the state of Kerala (India). He outlines the roots of the Communist Party in popular movements, emphasising the mobilisation of underprivileged groups and the use of state power to implement comprehensive land reforms in the 1970s and a campaign for democratic decentralisation from the mid-1990s. The latter was conceived and implemented as a 'top-to-bottom' programme with the expectation that it would take root within civil society and thereby be turned into a 'bottom up' programme for radical social change. Tharakan observes that this expectation of participatory planning driven by movements in civil society – facilitated and supported by a left party with a long history of social mobilisation – has not proven valid. Instead there has been a process of divisive politicisation of associational life according to clientelistic party affiliations. This exclusionary party-politicisation of civil society combined with the problems of mobilising marginalised social groups and providing significant socioeconomic benefits remain hurdles in the course of deliberative planning in Kerala.

The remaining four chapters share a common concern with the ways in which different collective actors – popular movements, trade unions and political parties – make use of local and non-local political spaces to pursue instrumental and democratic interests. *Kristian Stokke* and *Sophie*

Oldfield analyse the challenges of substantial democratisation in the context of the post-apartheid state and economic liberalisation in South Africa. The authors observe that material deprivation and state repression of popular protests have produced and radicalised new post-apartheid social movements, which politicise socio-economic rights. Contestation over the meaning of democratisation, and especially the relationship between economic liberalisation and social justice, are at the core of this new struggle. These movements display a diversity of strategies *vis-à-vis* state actors, combining various forms of political collaboration and adversarial struggle. On the one hand, political engagement may grant access to resources for community development, though it may also undermine the movements' legitimacy as autonomous representatives of marginalised groups. One the other hand, adversarial struggle may mobilise community support, but may also label a movement as a disruptive force that is targeted for state repression. Stokke and Oldfield conclude that the present period is characterised by growing mistrust between civil society movements and state actors. The post-apartheid state's way of handling this challenge from the new social movements will be decisive for the future of substantial democratisation in South Africa.

A persistent challenge for new popular movements in South Africa and elsewhere is the need to 'scale up' from local single issues to an ideological and co-ordinated political movement. *Joel Rocamora* addresses this challenge of building a social movement-based political party while engaging in local participatory governance in the Philippines. This is examined through an analytical focus on the strategies and experiences of *Akbayan* (Citizens Action Party) and *BATMAN*, the main civil society coalition working on participatory local governance. Akbayan has emerged from social movements of workers, peasants, urban poor, women and others, but also with close links to work within BATMAN to maximise the participatory and governance potential of decentralisation. While the main organisational challenge of BATMAN is to scale up from local governance issues, Akbayan's challenge is to accumulate political power within a political system characterised by a polarised conflict between right-wing populism and militant leftism, and a general political crisis of both. The new left-centre movement that is being built through Akbayan and BATMAN is consciously different from established parties, especially in its focus on pluralism and democracy within the movement, on the local political arena of the *barangay* and on goals of political and economic reforms.

Björn Beckman examines the capacity of trade unions to represent the interests of their own members and in support of wider popular and democratic interests. The author counters the view that unions are being marginalised by globalisation processes and constitute obsolete obstacles to institutional reforms. On the contrary, trade unions actively engage in reform processes and remain one of very few institutions that have the organisational capacity to represent popular interests and ensure their political inclusion. Most importantly, unions have the capacity of developing institutions that are vital for regulation of conflicts of interests and thereby sustain economic and political reforms (e.g. institutionalisation of union-based labour regimes protecting workers' rights to organise and bargain collectively). Since union rights are both a form and a basis for general political rights, unions also have a vested interest in these rights and play an important role in democratic movements. These arguments are grounded in analytical comparisons of unions and liberalisation in Nigeria, South Africa and Uganda. Whereas South Africa is a case with major union engagement in reform processes, Ugandan unions have largely been destroyed and marginalised. The Nigerian experiences fall somewhere between these two, displaying evidence of both union achievements and failures.

Olle Törnquist provides a conceptual and contextual analysis of the challenges of substantial democratisation. He defines the essence of democracy as popular control of public affairs based on political equality. Substantial democratisation means that people in general possess sufficient powers to make use of significant democratic rights and institutions. Following from this, Törnquist examines conceptual obstacles and political solutions for promoting substantial democratisation. One main obstacle is found in hegemonic conceptions of democratisation, focusing on negotiations and pacts between authoritarian and democratic elites rather than popular struggles for democratisation. This understanding of transitions has yielded a narrow and insufficient focus on institutional changes, while obscuring the role of both structural preconditions and popular mass action for substantial democratisation. Another major obstacle is found in the 'political deficit' of popular experiments for substantial democratisation. Just as in Porto Alegre, thinkers and activists affiliated with the popular democratic experiments in Kerala, the Philippines and Indonesia realise the need to link polycentric activities in civil society with politics and government, but it remains unclear how such public spaces emerge, endure and expand. Thus, there is a need for expanding the contextual and comparative knowledge, among academics and activists alike, of the *politics* of fighting for and implementing substantial democratisation.

Törnquist's conclusion brings us back to the starting point for this introductory chapter: Although the recent past has witnessed a wave of democratic transitions, many of these have yielded formal and minimalist liberal democracies rather than processes of substantial democratisation. Furthering these transitions towards substantial democratisation requires that democratic rights and institutions are re-appropriated by capable and committed actors. The argument that runs through this book – in sharp contrast to the common de-politicisation of development and democracy in mainstream academic and political discourse – is for the need to bring the political back into democratisation, in other words, for *politicising democracy*.

Notes

1. In accordance with what has become common practice, we shall use 'sphere' and 'space' synonymously. This may refer to institutional frameworks, forums and practices that are public and open (as opposed to private and closed), for people to come together and deliberate and negotiate. Sphere/space may also, for instance, refer to political institutions and practices – which may then be more or less public. The concept of 'arena', on the other hand, is used to indicate more structured and formalised parts of such (more or less public) spaces and has a metaphorical association with the idea of a game, which is particularly apposite in regard to politics. When we want to indicate the room for manoeuvre that may be available for an actor outside or inside the public or political sphere we will specify that in terms of 'space for action'. Likewise, when we only talk of politics in a territorial sense we will indicate that with formulations such as 'politics at the local level' or 'village politics'.
2. In general terms, localisation refers to the 'grounding' of human activities in specific places. We use 'localisation of politics' to refer to the location of state power and politics to sub-national spatial scales.
3. Globalisation refers to 'a process (or set of processes) which embodies a transformation in the spatial organization of social relations and transactions ... generating transcontinental or interregional flows and networks of activity, interaction, and the exercise of power' (Held *et al.*, 1999: 16). This suggests that globalisation should be understood as multiple processes (rather than just economic integration) and open-ended transformations (rather than an historical end-point or epoch).
4. The first ('long') wave, according to Huntington, developed in Europe, the United States, Argentina and some British colonies between the early 19th and early 20th centuries; the second ('short') wave after the Second World War up to the early 1960s, in the former colonies and in West Germany, Italy and Japan. Each was followed by a 'reverse wave', as for example when most Latin American countries reverted to authoritarian forms of rule in the later 1960s and early 1970s.
5. This definition of democratisation, of course, begs the question of 'what is democracy?'. This is not the place to enter into an extended discussion of a vast literature. At the core of the idea of democracy are the principles of *popular control* (the Greek words that make up the English 'democracy' mean 'rule by the people') and its concomitant, *political equality* (necessary if there is to be meaningful popular control). The variety of ways in which these core principles

have been sought to be realised is explained in terms of ten different 'models of democracy', by David Held (1996). Beyond this, as Laurence Whitehead (2002) has argued, persuasively, democracy should be seen as an ideal, to be defined and approached by social actors – or in his words as an open-ended process, subject to reflexive definition.

6. According to Larry Diamond *et al.* (1997), the number of liberal democracies has increased in the third wave, but not by nearly so much as that of narrowly electoral democracies. He suggests that the proportion of countries with liberal democracies increased from less than 30 per cent in 1974 to just over 40 per cent in 1991, and that this proportion then remained more or less the same through to 1996. Diamond describes 'electoral democracies' as those regimes in which multiple parties regularly compete for power through at least relatively free and fair elections, while the term 'liberal democracy' for him embraces protections for individual and group freedoms, inclusive pluralism in civil society and political parties, civilian control over the military, institutions to hold officeholders accountable, and a strong rule of law secured through an independent, impartial judiciary.

7. This is the approach that is reflected in a general work such as Laurence Whitehead's recent book *Democratization* (2002).

8. Whereas it had generally been held previously (in line with the modernisation approach) that economic development was a key condition for democratisation this understanding of causality began to be reversed in the 1990s, when it started to be argued that successful economic development actually requires the establishment of democracy. For example, Baroness Chalker, the then Minister for Overseas Development in the British government (the post that was renamed as Minister for International Development in 1997), argued in 1991 that 'a major new thrust in our policy is to promote pluralistic systems which work for and respond to individuals in society. In political terms this means democracy ... we firmly believe that democratic reforms are necessary in many countries for broad-based sustainable development' (quoted from notes made at the time by John Harriss). She and others had in mind a set-up with competitive party systems, regular and fair elections, an independent judiciary, a free press and protection of human rights – and these (certainly the holding of regular elections and the setting up of multi-party competition) began to be made into conditions attached to aid agreements. The consequence was that the already existing pattern of the establishment, in many cases, of partial, electoral democracies – rather than full liberal democracies – was extended.

9. Huntington (1991) did in fact identify globalisation as the primary cause of the third wave of democratisation. He failed, however, to provide a convincing account of the mechanisms whereby international factors or globalisation produce democratic transitions.

10. As of August 2003 the Bank's 'Governance' website defines its topic as: 'the traditions and institutions by which authority in a country is exercised for the common good. This includes (1) the process by which those in authority are selected, monitored and replaced, (2) the capacity of the government to effectively manage its resources and implement sound policies, and (3) the respect of citizens and the state for the institutions that govern economic and social interaction among them'.

11. A more recent, but very similar statement appears in the *Human Development Report* for 2002; e.g 'Over the past two decades there have been many new ways for people to participate in public debates and activities' (UNDP 2002: 5).
12. The quotations in this paragraph are taken from a manuscript by Peter Houtzager, the draft of the Introduction for the book *Changing Paths*. See Houtzager 2003.
13. Chandhoke's argument is, however, in line with Hilary Wainwright's: 'to be effective, international campaigns and networks need to be rooted in people's everyday lives' (2003: 32)
14. This is the theory that holds, following Weber and Schumpeter, that the complexity of the administration of a modern state means that the only realistic form of democracy is one which involves competition between elites.
15. This is what distinguishes the idea of 'public space' from Habermas's conception of the 'public sphere', as Avritzer (2002) explains at length.
16. See Schönleitner's extensive discussion (2004, ch. 2). As Schönleitner says, 'in Avritzer's own case studies of Participatory Budgeting in Porto Alegre and Belo Horizonte institutionalisation required the prior election of the PT into power, in other words, the establishment of PB required the transformation of political society (via elections) as a precondition for, not a consequence, of public deliberation' (2004: 43).
17. We use the work of Bourdieu to illustrate an overall analytical agenda that is shared by the contributing authors in this book, but not as a joint substantive theoretical framework. The concrete analyses of each chapter are obviously informed by diverse theoretical frameworks, including Bourdieu's notions of power.
18. Bourdieu's categories of economic resources may be supplemented with that of the ability to block economic resources through strike action.
19. There are indications that the Bharatiya Janata Party now also has such an institutionalised presence, at least in some parts of the country.
20. This, and the following comment are based on research in Delhi conducted by Neera Chandhoke and her colleagues from the Department of Political Science in Delhi University.

2
Decentralisation in Indonesia: Less State, More Democracy?[1]

Henk Schulte Nordholt

The miracle of the Titanic

After the Asian monetary and political crisis of 1997 and 1998, which was followed by a period labelled as 'reformasi', Indonesia is viewed by some observers as having entered a transitional phase from authoritarian rule towards a new democratic system of government in which civil society will play a more prominent role. This transition is, moreover, accompanied by a process of decentralisation that emphasises regional autonomy and is expected to bring democracy to the people while making government more transparent.

Others contest this optimistic perception and sketch a negative transition from 'order to disorder'. After decades of authoritarian centralist governance, attempts to introduce political and economic change seem doomed, in the face of bureaucratic sabotage, corrupt power politics, short-term opportunism, and the absence of a widely shared vision of the future. In the light of outbursts of ethnic and religious violence in various regions of the archipelago, regional resistance movements, the inability to restructure both the army and the economy and to curb collusion, nepotism and corruption, pessimists are inclined to classify Indonesia in the category of 'failing', or 'messy states'. In short, they predict further disintegration, which may eventually lead to the break-up of the nation-state.[2]

The trouble with the word 'transition' is that it suggests an irreversible and fundamental change from condition (or stage) A to condition B, and that these conditions are by and large static in character. This is outdated sociology. Although the term 'transition' can be used to indicate the current transfer from one authoritarian system to another, it does not capture the complexity of the historical processes that are creating contemporary Indonesia, nor does it offer the opportunity to trace changing continuities in Indonesian politics. Given that a 'new Indonesia' still seems far out of reach and that the present period is marked by a lot of stagnation, it seems, for the time being, wiser to use the more neutral term 'post-Soeharto Indonesia'. Ben Mboi, former governor of Nusa Tenggara Timor and (at the time of writing) advisor of the Minister of Interior, compared Indonesia in this respect with the Titanic. 'The only difference', he added, 'is that the Titanic sank, whereas Indonesia *keeps on sinking* all the time' (seminar at the Clingendael Institute, The Hague, June 2002).

Recently the process of decentralisation in Indonesia has been equated with a process of democratisation and the rise of civil society (Aspinall and Fealy 2003; Antlöv 2003; Syaikhu Usman 2002). These are, however, three very different processes. I will argue that a shift from centralised to a decentralised government is not synonymous with a shift from authoritarian to democratic rule nor does it automatically imply a shift from a strong state towards a strong civil society. The weakening of the central state does not automatically, in other words, result in more local democracy. On the contrary, decentralisation can under certain conditions be accompanied by authoritarian rule.

Two main factors can be held responsible for the political, economic, and social-cultural dynamics of the present period. First, the tendency toward decentralisation, with its widely varying effects in different regions. Second, attempts by the former political elite and the army to preserve the unitary state at any price. The outcome of the tensions between these centrifugal and centripetal forces, which is difficult to predict, will to a large extent determine Indonesia's future. These tensions should be seen in a wider historical context if we want to understand some of the complex dynamics in Indonesia.

The sudden demise of the strong New Order state came as a surprise to many professional Indonesia watchers. What seemed to be a solid and invincible regime turned out to be a fragile state, in which regional, religious and ethnic identity politics had become increasingly dominant. The collapse of Soeharto's regime in 1998, followed by a far-reaching policy of decentralisation, invites us to refocus our attention from the centre to the regions, and to abandon the concept of the strong state in favour of a model that offers room for a more fragmented polity. It would, however, be misleading to emphasise only discontinuities. Instead, I argue that both on the national and on the regional level we can identify 'changing continuities' that help to explain the problems connected with the implementation of decentralisation and the establishment of regional autonomy. It is necessary not only to find new concepts to describe the present situation in Indonesia, but also imperative to rethink established views on the New Order in order to identify the continuities that connect pre-colonial and late colonial patterns with contemporary developments.

The changing continuities I intend to explore are (1) the persistence of patrimonial ties and the denial of class in Indonesian politics; (2) the post-colonial nature of Indonesian politics in which boundaries between state, society and market are less clear than has been assumed; and (3) the historical role of regional elites and the way they use ethnicity to articulate their interests.

Rethinking analytical categories

New ways of looking at 'the state' are necessary in order to trace continuities in patrimonial patterns and to incorporate various arrangements that link formal institutions with informal networks. These undermine conventional distinctions between 'state, 'society' and, 'market'.

In his book on state formation in early Southeast Asia Tony Day (2002) makes the provocative argument that in order to trace the origins of modern Indonesian politics we should look back into the past. Family networks characterised pre-colonial political systems and continued to do so under Dutch colonial rule, despite the appearance of a rational bureaucracy. Likewise, bureaucracies were not purely Western implants but had local roots as well, while on the other hand ritual behaviour plays a prominent role in modern bureaucracies and political manifestations. Similarly, there are interesting parallels between the ritual character of elections during the New Order and large-scale royal rituals in pre-colonial Bali: both were intended to mobilise people and to master potential chaos, thus reinforcing the authority of the ruler (Pemberton 1986; Vickers 1991).

The New Order regime distributed large amounts of so-called INPRES (*Instruksi President*) money, suggesting that the president himself had personally decided to allocate funds for specific projects, while a substantial amount of state income was generated by informal means, which revealed the patrimonial character of the system. The armed forces relied on state revenues only for 30 per cent of their expenditure and depended for the remaining 70 per cent on their own sources of income. The army has therefore been characterised not as a hierarchically integrated organisation, but, instead, as an archipelago of semi-independent 'warlords'. In terms of violence there are, in this context, also continuities that predate the colonial period – although the impact of the (post) colonial state in terms of increase of scale should not be underestimated (Schulte Nordholt 2002). Protection against intimidation and violence involves the payment of informal taxes as well. Old notions of invulnerability are in this respect still relevant, but they do not in the first place refer to efforts by potential victims to protect themselves against violence and corruption, but to perpetrators who are allowed to act above and beyond the law.

A comparable system of informal taxation and 'bottom up' distribution of income characterised/s the Indonesian bureaucracy as well. Underpaid bureaucrats supplement(ed) their incomes with informal sources of income by selling licenses and levying personalised forms of taxation. The sheer lack of independent state institutions reinforced/s the reproduction of these patrimonial hierarchies.

The New Order was also part of a set of wider capitalist structures, which should be taken into account in order to understand mechanisms concerning the control of capital, production, labour and markets. The patron–client nature of patrimonial networks helped to obscure and deny issues of class. But New Order Indonesia did of course also produce rather clear-cut class divisions, reflected in an important distinction that can be made between those who live and work inside an air-conditioned environment and those who do not – a kind of 'difference of climate' (van Leeuwen 1997).

In many respects post-Soeharto Indonesia shows continuities with the previous period, even if the central leadership of the old regime has been weakened, making way for a considerable degree of factionalism and decentralisation of power. The extent to which 'civil society' has managed to organise itself in order to establish a more democratic system is questionable. Almost all political parties have a top down leadership structure and are primarily organised in order to mobilise support in exchange for the distribution of favours. Ideological debates are less relevant than the control of 'traditional' constituencies. Class distinctions in terms of 'climate' play an important role here as well. Most representatives of groups claiming to speak on behalf of 'civil society' have an air-conditioned middle class background. For them civil society is not automatically synonymous with democracy, because that would imply the power of the *massa* (from outside the world of air-conditioning). For a very brief moment in Indonesian history president Sukarno addressed and mobilised Indonesians as *rakyat*, co-patriots, but the New Order immobilised them and changed *rakyat* into *massa*, a potentially dangerous mob that needed constant surveillance (Siegel 1998). Many spokespeople who advocate the strengthening of civil society, share the fear of this same *massa*. Although Soeharto is gone, the language of his New Order is still spoken.

We may at this point tentatively conclude that it is misleading to see the New Order too much as an integrated set of institutions operating primarily apart from society, and having its origins in the late colonial period. Conventional distinctions between 'state' and 'society', 'state' and 'market', 'formal' and 'informal' relationships, and 'centre' and 'periphery' should be reviewed critically. Alternative perspectives indicate that the system operated predominantly along patrimonial hierarchies, which have their origin in earlier, pre-colonial, polities. Although power was concentrated in the centre, large sections of society were linked to the regime through a variety of informal ties and operated in its political system. Recent studies on Thailand demonstrate there, too, the extent to which the formal domains of politics and economy are interwoven with illegal economic activities and criminality in which bureaucrats, politicians, military, police, business-men and criminals maintain intimate relationships, and distinctions between their respective professions are often blurred (Pasuk *et al.* 1998; McVey 2000).

In a similar vein Barbara Harriss-White (2003) argues with respect to India that the *real* economy not only consists of state *and* market, and formal *and* informal arenas, but also that many informal arrangements – theft, corruption, tax evasion, privatisation of public property, – can be found within the formal and/or state sector. The characteristic of these sectors is not that they operate separately but that they are bound in a mutually protective embrace. And this is not the 'partnership' between state and market that is being advocated by the World Bank. Likewise the *real* state consists of a formal set of bureaucratic institutions that co-exists with a shadow state in which bureaucrats, businessmen, politicians and criminals interact on a regular basis. Although the formal state may at first sight look like a relatively small and weak set of institutions, the *real* state, which is characterised by the privatisation of public institutions and the institutionalisation of private interests, is a far-reaching and powerful octopus.

Against the backdrop of these considerations, it is time to turn to the 'regions' – which have been ignored in most New Order studies – to see how at the local level 'state', 'society', and 'market' were intertwined and structured along patrimonial lines and how things are changing in the post-Soeharto era.

Bringing the regions back in

Decentralisation is not a new phenomenon in Indonesia. The first legislation in this respect dates from one hundred years ago. In 1903 the urban European elites were allowed a limited measure of self-government. The law offered, however, next to nothing in terms of autonomy (Benda 1966: 241). Both the late colonial state and the New Order were not inclined to make any serious efforts in this respect.

While the first colonial measures were primarily aimed at urban areas, the following decades saw a transfer of a range of administrative functions to provinces and large districts. The decentralisation law of 1922 created new provinces, which had a fair degree of administrative autonomy. Apart from these new macro administrative units, in Java the so-called Ethical Policy of *'ontvoogding'*, or 'de-tutelisation', resulted at the district level in the establishment of councils in which the local elites were represented. These councils were conservative and functioned as bastions against nationalism (Sutherland 1979). Under colonial rule, decentralisation had nothing to do with democratisation and very little with the strengthening of civil society.

The reforms of the 1920s caused, nevertheless, a blurring of the lines of responsibility between European and native administrators which led to confusion and irritation. Eventually the communist uprisings of the mid-1920s in West Java and West Sumatra reinforced a conservative turn among the European rulers and from 1931 onwards colonial rule was re-centralised.

By and large, the colonial system was characterised by indirect rule, in which the conservative European administrative elite controlled a subordinate body of indigenous administrators. Moreover, European law was restricted to the European elite (and to some extent the Chinese), whereas the indigenous population was ruled according to 'their own' customary, or *adat* law. Moreover, the appointment of descendants of old dynasties as representatives of colonial rule reinforced the conservative character of indirect rule in the Outer Islands. This system was primarily intended to isolate the small nationalist movement within urban sectors by keeping the countryside and the areas outside Java under control of the traditional rule invented under colonialism.

During the Indonesian Revolution, the Dutch tried to revive pre-war plans for a federation of Indonesian states along provincial lines in order to isolate the Republican forces. The Dutch stimulated the establishment of regional rule by local aristocracies, as well, also in order to counteract revolutionary nationalists. This strategy failed. In 1950

Indonesia became a unitary nation-state, and the concept of federation became strictly taboo.

In reality, however, regional governments and military commands had a high degree of autonomy since the centre lacked the means to exert strict control. Due to pressure from the regions and especially the political parties which wanted to dismantle the monopoly of the post-colonial bureaucracy, far reaching reforms were formulated in Law 1 of 1957 regarding the decentralisation of provincial and regional government (Legge 1961; Malley 1999a). The law entitled provincial and district parliaments to appoint their own governor and district administrator, or *bupati*. For the first time power was transferred from appointed administrators to elected politicians and this measure invited the nation to participate in the state (Anderson 1983). An important side effect was the increase of the number of provinces from 12 in 1950 to 20 in 1958.[3] The fiscal side of the decentralisation measures, however, was highly centralist in character as a result of which many regions remained dependent on the centre.

Decentralisation did not get a chance to take root, because regional rebellions in Sumatra and Sulawesi against Jakarta, the proclamation of martial law, increased military power and, in 1959, the rise of authoritarian rule aborted this brief experiment. By Presidential Decree Number 6 of 1959, Law 1 of 1957 was abolished (Magenda 1989: 18).

At the end of the turbulent years between 1959 and 1974, during which the state regained its dominant position, Law 5 of 1974 formalised the supremacy of the centre over the regions. Although the law defined provinces and districts as 'autonomous' levels and elected councils were established in order to generate bottom-up representation, regional government consisted in practice of top-down execution of developmental interventions, initiated by the state, and accompanied by strict surveillance. Although provincial and district councils were entitled to nominate candidates for the position of governor and *bupati*, they were eventually appointed by the President and the Home Minister. These regional administrators were in fact agents of the centre. Law 5 of 1974 was accompanied by Law 5 of 1979 on village government, which not only made village administration uniform throughout Indonesia, but also reinforced the grip of the centre on local politics.

The appearance of development and order, and strict obedience to protocol, were as important as the channelling of large sums of routine and development funds from the centre to the regions, which made the system work. Due to an abundance of central resources – originating from oil exports and aid imports, later supplemented by foreign investments – regions depended heavily on the centre. The flows of money entering the regions resulted in the formation and reinforcement of state agencies, which penetrated deeply into local society (Schiller 1996). Parallel to a tight centralisation, there was a de-concentration of authority, which implied that central Ministries, like Agriculture, Public Works, and Religion, had their own representatives in the regions executing central policies at the regional level.

An even more powerful parallel state structure was formed by the military presence running from the centre, through the province, district, and sub-district down to the village level. Moreover, the military had entered the civil bureaucracy as well. In 1970 20 of the 26 provincial governors were recruited from the ranks of the military, while they still formed a majority – 14 out of 27 – in 1997 (Malley 1999a, Wihana Kirana Jaya and Dick 2001).

Despite their dependence on the central government, regional governments were relatively powerful in terms of local administration because they also offered employment and channelled government funds. This facilitated the reproduction of patrimonial patterns of rule at the local level, while it may be assumed that in general informal networks connected the interests of both local businessmen and bureaucrats.

The agony of decentralisation: 1999 and after

As outlined in the Introduction to this book, a wave of decentralisation has affected the structure of governments in many countries in the world over the last decades. The crisis of the Western welfare state, the collapse of socialist systems in Eastern Europe, and the end of the Cold War, which meant that the maintenance of authoritarian regimes in the Third World was no longer necessary, seemed to illustrate the failure of state-led politics. Organisations like the World Bank embraced the neo-liberal idea that decentralisation would stimulate both the economy and democracy. Democratisation was to be accompanied by the rise of a strong civil society, and they would together result in more efficient and transparent government at the local level (Malley 2003, Hadiz 2003b).

Decentralisation can be interpreted in three different ways (Dormeier-Freire and Maurer 2002): in terms of (1) the *delegation* of specific tasks while the centre retains its overall responsibility, which is comparable with the Law of 1974; (2) *deconcentration*, which refers to a relocation of decision making within a centralised state, which is reflected in the Law of 1957; and (3) *devolution*, which concerns the actual transfer of power to lower levels of government, and this was implemented in 2001.[4]

Looking back at the period 1998–2003 one may conclude that the most important reform measures were taken by the Habibie presidency (May 1998–October 1999). Apart from press freedom, the freedom to establish political parties, and free national elections, the Habibie government also pushed two important laws through parliament, in great haste, as a result of which a process of administrative decentralisation was set in motion.

The laws were primarily designed by bureaucrats while there was no feedback whatsoever from the regions. One month before the general elections in June 1999, the parliament – whose members, ironically, still belonged to the New Order era – agreed without much debate with the Laws numbers 22 and 25, which provided the administrative and fiscal framework of a process that seemed to change the very foundation of the unitary nation-state.

One of the main reasons why the government wanted to accelerate this process was to accommodate the anti-Jakarta sentiments in many regions outside Java while the still ruling Golkar party, which was on Java under political cross fire, tried to maintain its power bases in the outer islands by supporting regional autonomy.

The proposed two-year period of transition and implementation was even shortened to one and a half years, which implied that by 1 January 2001 the biggest administrative reorganisation in the history of the Indonesian state had to be completed.[5] A period of eighteen months was of course too short to get things done in a proper way, and this was a major reason for the resignation of Ryaas Rashid, the deputy minister who was responsible.[6]

In a sense the laws of 1999 revived the process of decentralisation that was stopped in the late 1950s, but they went much further. Because the new autonomy was located at the level of districts and municipalities, the power of the provinces was dismantled, while a process of political fragmentation was stimulated. Seen from this perspective decentralisation was a divide-and-rule strategy on the part of the centre, aimed at allowing for administrative fragmentation while maintaining fiscal control in the centre. This becomes clear when we focus on the differences between Law 22 and Law 25 (N. Schulte Nordholt 2003b).

Law 22 was made by the Home Ministry with the official intention of achieving a substantial devolution of power in order to bring government closer to the people and offer more transparency. Similar to Law no.1 of 1957, governors, *bupati* and *wali kota* are no longer appointed by the centre but are elected by regional parliaments. The regional political leaders are, therefore, back on stage.[7]

Apart from the fast and complex transfers of people, tasks and responsibilities, there is also an anxiety to create new provinces and districts. After 1999 the number of provinces increased from 27 to 33. Meanwhile people in Tapanuli, Cirebon, Madura, Luwu and Flores hope to achieve provincial status as well, though their chances are diminishing as time goes by. The number of districts increased from about 340 to more than 400 (Syaikhu Usman 2002, World Bank 2003), and the fission of districts has not come to an end. *Pemekaran*, or blossoming, is in this respect the new buzz word, referring to the expansion and development of autonomous districts.

Although the Home Ministry designed the far-reaching decentralisation that is now being implemented, at the time of writing the same Ministry wants to *reduce* the degree of autonomy granted to the regions (Hidayat and Antlöv, forthcoming). These plans met fierce opposition from APKASI, (*Asosiasi Pemerintah Kabupaten Seluruh Indonesia*), the pressure group of district administrations. The regions have also gained a formal foothold in the centre where they can oppose efforts to re-centralise government. In February 2003 the national parliament (DPR) decided to establish a Council of Regional Representatives (DPD) of 120 members that will become part of the National Congress (MPR) (*Jakarta Post* 17 February 2003).[8]

At first sight the role of the central government seems to resemble that of a 'night watchman state'. The few remaining responsibilities include national defence and security, foreign policy, fiscal and monetary matters, macro-economic planning, natural resources, justice and religion. Regions have autonomy with regard to public works, education and culture, health care, agriculture, transport, industry, trade, investments, environmental issues, co-operation, labour and, land (Ray and Goodpaster 2003). But in order to assess the nature of the current decentralisation it is important to look at the fiscal arrangements as well. Whereas Law 22 facilitates devolution of power, Law 25, made by the Ministry of Finance, is centralist in character. This implies that the central government maintains its grip on the main sources of revenue of the regions – 80 per cent of income tax, value added tax, import duties and export taxes, and foreign aid – while it still controls a sizable number of government enterprises. What we actually witness in Indonesia is a decentralisation of administrative power that is heavily subsidised by the central government.[9]

Professional optimism versus realistic pessimism

Since the process of decentralisation has by now been under way for two years we may draw a few preliminary conclusions. Professional optimism can be found among organisations with an institutional interest in decentralisation. NGO's like SMERU, and donor organisations like SfDM (Support for Decentralisation Measures), the Ford Foundation, Asia Foundation and financial giants like the World Bank actively support decentralisation and proclaim a firm ideological belief in its success. In the SMERU report, decentralisation is seen as a big administrative operation in which possible weaknesses can be improved (Syaikhu Usman 2002). The World Bank sees it as a huge financial operation – with the ominous title 'Big Bang' – which can be successfully managed (Lewis 2001; Hofman and Kaiser 2002; World Bank 2003). Such a technocratic approach erases questions about power struggles among competing interest groups (Hadiz 2003b).

The Asia Foundation and the Ford Foundation support decentralisation because it is supposed to strengthen democracy and civil society. Between the lines, however, one can find carefully phrased doubts and concerns about the outcome of the 'transition'. Although they profess their faith in the outcome of decentralisation, Hofman and Kaiser (2002: 7) state that after more than one year of decentralisation, much remains unclear as to what exactly has been decentralised and which administrative functions have been decentralised (World Bank 2003). Critical publications by authors without direct institutional involvement give voice to a more pessimistic attitude (Dormeier-Freire and Maurer 2002; Hadiz 2003a, b; Kingsbury and Aveling 2003; Malley 2003). And a brief list of unresolved issues justifies such an attitude of realistic pessimism.

World Bank experts have measured that *on aggregate* the regions receive enough revenues to cover the costs of their own autonomous administrative apparatus. This does not mean, however, that there is adequate funding for education, healthcare and poverty alleviation. Wihana Kirana Jaya (2001) remarks, moreover, that whereas Law 25 of 1999 reduces the vertical imbalance between centre and regions, it is likely to increase horizontal imbalances among regions. It is evident that resource rich regions can more easily survive than minus areas, because the richest region has 50 times more income than the poorest one. It is in this respect to be expected that new economic figurations will emerge in which rich areas will try to develop their own transnational networks, whereas poor regions will fall further behind and become increasingly isolated (World Bank 2003).[10]

A precise demarcation of responsibilities and claims between central government, province, and districts and municipalities does not yet exist. There seems to be a tendency for regions to issue their own regulations in fields not yet regulated by the central government, which may cause confusion and contention. There is also a general lack of administrative expertise, especially at the *kabupaten* level. Since most career paths headed towards Jakarta, bright young people were urged not to stay behind (Ismet Fanany 2003). Regional bureaucrats were used to wait and see what the centre would decide, but now they have to play a much more active role, without having been properly trained for it. Regional parliaments (DPRD), too, are slow in initiating legislation and have only a limited capacity for doing so. Also lacking are mechanisms to resolve conflicts between DPRD and the executive administrators, while members of the DPRD do not show much eagerness to represent their constituencies. Ryaas Rashid (2003) remarks in this context that DPRD are by and large controlled by party bosses who protect in the first place the special interests of their own party. There are indications that members of local parliaments prioritise substantial increases of their own salaries and travel budgets at the cost of education and health care (Dormeier-Freire and Maurer 2002; Syaikhu Usman 2002).

Because most regions are subsidised by the centre, regional governments tend to become spending machines (Ray and Goodpaster 2003). In general, financial management and accountability are weak, and money politics seem to prevail. There are widespread complaints that corruption has increased considerably since regional autonomy was implemented. Elections of governors and *bupatis* by provincial and district parliaments are generally accompanied by massive transfers of money, while budgets for development and construction projects are characterised by a substantial 'marking up' of 50–100 per cent that is divided among alliances of administrators and businessmen.[11]

In order to acquire additional funds regional administrations tend to burden their regions with extra taxes, while they pay little or no attention to environmental issues. Forests are under the authority of regional administrators who sell logging licenses, but there is a lack of inter-regional coordination regarding national parks and forest reserves (*Tempo* 17–23 April 2001). The Forestry Department has opposed the claim of districts to control forest reserves, and it seems that the environment will turn out to be the foremost victim of decentralisation (Pradnja Resosudarmo 2003).

Because there is a lack of coordinating power at a supra-regional level, decentralisation encourages inter-regional competition and conflict. One of the reasons why the leaders of Bangka-Belitung wanted to set up a separate province is that they did not want to share their mining revenues with the province and the other districts on the mainland. Conflicts between neighbouring districts along the north coast of Java about the demarcation of their fishing territories have regularly occurred. Elsewhere trade restrictions, which already existed under the New Order, are reinforced by new regulations (Ray and Goodpaster 2003). Measures that favour locals and exclude minorities may increase ethnic conflict.

It is revealing that in the writings of the 'professional optimists' the roles of the army and the police as important actors at the regional level are completely ignored. Both the World Bank (2003) and the Asia Foundation (2002) sketch in their reports an Indonesia without army, militias and organised crime. But to what extent can and will the army and police interfere in regional 'security' matters? It is common knowledge that big companies pay large sums of protection money to the armed forces. It seems that especially the army and to a lesser extent the police benefit from decentralisation, since more money is channelled to the regional level. Because its territorial structure is still intact, the army is willing to sell protection, and it can create a lot of insecurity if this offer is refused (Mietzner 2003.). Moreover, military involvement increases the violent nature of the shadow state at the regional level ('Current data' 2003: 22–32).

For those familiar with the literature on decentralisation in post-colonial states, the issues mentioned here do not come as a surprise. In a review on the subject Frerks and Otto (1996) conclude that the results of decentralisation overall are disappointing and far behind initial expectations. They refer also to reports by USAID and the World Bank from the 1990s, illustrating the structural amnesia of these institutions. A USAID report in 1995 on decentralisation identified a lack of planning, the failure to mobilise enough local resources, competition between local officials, and poor natural resource management as major problems. The World Bank stated in 1992 that a weak administrative capacity at the local level would lead to waste and corruption, while resources are arguably open to capture by elite groups at the local level (Frerks and Otto 1996).

Both the literature and the examples mentioned here illustrate that decentralisation does not necessarily result in democratisation, good governance and the strengthening of civil society at the regional level. Instead we witness a decentralisation of corruption, collusion and political violence that once belonged to the centralised regime of the New Order and is now moulded in existing patrimonial patterns at the regional level. We may expect that the continuity of these patterns will prevent the establishment of transparent rules, democratic procedures and control mechanisms. The district administrator, or *bupati*, plays a crucial role in this system. He receives most of the funds from the centre and controls the channels through which money is distributed. If he manages to cooperate with the chairman of the district parliament and leading businessmen, and if he is able to accommodate the military commander, he can rule his district and maintain his patronage network without encountering much opposition. Various people call the new autonomous regions in this respect 'little kingdoms', but do we know where the kings come from? Except for a few scholars (van Klinken 2002; Hadiz 2003a; Malley 2003) this question is by and large ignored in recent publications on decentralisation.

Regional elites, *adat* and ethnicity

Relationships between the centre of the state and regional elites have changed over time. In the late colonial period, a strong central state allied itself with aristocratic elites in the regions in order to establish a relatively cheap but stable form of indirect rule. Due to the protective colonial umbrella under which they operated, regional elites tended to become stronger. Hence a strong state does not necessarily exclude the existence of strong regional elites. It is important to go back to the colonial period in order to understand the connection between regional elites and ethnicity in present day Indonesia. Mahmood Mamdani (2001) has noted that African colonial systems were marked by contrasts between colonial overlords and local ethnicity, and between Western legal systems and local forms of customary law. This resulted in forms of indirect governance whereby regional ethnic elites acquired power that was framed in a discourse of customary law. Consequently large groups of the population were not allowed to become citizens in the new nation state. Instead they remained subjects of a post-colonial regime and this provided a weak basis for the development of a strong civil society. It is interesting to make a comparison with developments in Indonesia, where in many regions local aristocracies came to power during the colonial period. Customary law was an important mechanism of the colonial state for regulating local relations and keeping the ordinary people trapped in an ethnically ordered system.

Dutch colonial thinking conceptualised its role and rule in the Netherlands Indies – especially in the islands outside Java – in dualistic terms. These ideas, which separated European interests from native society, were materialised in the fields of economy, education and law (van Klinken 2003). In terms of law the Dutch created a corpus of knowledge about local customs, which not only separated natives from Europeans but also produced sharp divisions among the indigenous groups themselves. There was among ethically inspired Dutch administrators a genuine concern to respect and protect local cultures against the ambitions of the penetrating colonial state. This was, however, also part of a strategy of divide and rule that was intended to counter the spread of Islam, while it later served as a conservative 'medicine' against the 'virus' of nationalism.

Throughout the archipelago ethnic groups and boundaries were defined as a result of which fluid communities with flexible boundaries were now demarcated in rigid terms and located within fixed territorial structures (Schulte Nordholt 1994; Smith Kipp 1996). In many parts of the archipelago the Dutch administered these ethnic groups, or *adat* communities, through local aristocracies. And it was this colonial legacy that determined post-colonial relationships.

After independence the central state lost its grip on the regions, while societal forces started to penetrate into state institutions. As a result regional aristocracies faced competition from other groups in society that tried to mobilise mass support in order to reinforce their position. Moreover, aristocratic groups had to rely on their local power basis in order to survive. Hence, there was a correlation between a weak state and a threatened aristocracy. From the end of the 1950s onwards, central state agencies gained ground again while societal forces were gradually dismantled.

Burhan Magenda (1989, 1994) is one the few scholars who has pointed to the continuity of aristocratic rule in areas outside Java after independence. In his detailed study on the role of the surviving aristocracies in East Kalimantan, Nusa Tenggara Barat and South Sulawesi he shows that in the early 1950s the civil administrative corps of the Home Ministry, which was dominated by Javanese bureaucrats, allied themselves with regional aristocracies outside Java. Tied by common interests and fearing common enemies (leftist and Islamic parties) they were natural allies. The bureaucrats needed the aristocracies in order to rule the country and the aristocracies needed protection to counter local opposition. When in the 1950s political parties, and especially the modernist Islam party Masyumi, spread their influence throughout the archipelago, it was law 1 of 1957 that helped them to gain access to regional administrative structures.[12]

Apart from the bureaucracy, the army, which was predominantly staffed by anti-Islamic Javanese and Christian officers, formed another ally of the regional elites. The influence of the army increased considerably during the period of martial law (1957–63) when they suppressed the regional rebellions in Sumatra and Sulawesi in the late 1950s, and the

Masyumi party was dissolved. But the army had also its own agenda, which would limit the aristocracy's room to manoeuvre.

Although ethnicity was a topic of scholarly discussion during the 1950s, the dominant academic discourse was primarily focused on nation building, the role of political parties and the so-called *aliran* ('political pillars') on Java. As Ichlasul Amal (1992) has argued, this approach obscured to a large extent the importance of ethnic factors in shaping Indonesian politics. For instance, big national parties like PNI and PKI [Partai Nasional Indonesia, Partai Komunis Indonesia] were to a large extent predominantly Javanese parties, but majorities seldom define themselves in terms of ethnicity. One should also not forget that the first manifestations of nationalism in Indonesia had a strongly ethnic flavour because they were organised on a regional basis (van Klinken 2003).

Ideologically, ethnic identity refers to a timeless cultural essence, but it is formulated, framed, and contested within specific (post)colonial conditions. Under Guided Democracy (1959–65) political *cum* ethnic tensions increased rapidly in areas outside Java where the military had intervened. People felt as if they were cut off from participating in the nation-state while they resented the dominance of Javanese military in their region (Liddle1970; Kahin 1999). When from 1966 onwards the New Order replaced Guided Democracy there was a paradoxical euphoria in these areas (Ichlasul Amal 1992). The New Order was seen as liberating West Sumatra from Javanese occupation and restoring order in South Sulawesi, but it also marked the beginning of a long period of neo-colonial rule.

Compared to its colonial predecessor the New Order regime penetrated deeper into society and dominated local society to a much greater extent. Gradually processes of 'local state formation' took shape (Schiller 1996), without offering any prospect of regional autonomy. Despite the apparent dominance of the centre, which was moreover underlined by a strong military presence, regional elites showed a remarkable resilience and managed to survive. Apart from appointing (ex) military to strategic positions, the New Order recruited its local agents also from among the descendants of the old aristocracies. In many places the new regime and the old elites shared a dislike for leftist and Islamic movements while the old elite was used to finding its way into the new networks of patronage that linked regional hierarchies to the centre of the state and its rich resources.

By entering the state and adjusting smoothly to the new rules of the administrative and political game, many representatives of the regional elites created new niches for themselves where they could gradually expand their power, status and wealth (Magenda 1989, 1994; Ichlasul Amal 1992; Schiller 1996; Kahin 1999; Malley 1999a). Unable to control the military *aparat* of the regime, they could try to enter its civilian wing. While they showed their loyalty to the centre of the state by mobilising vast majorities for Golkar during the elections, they gradually managed to infiltrate and control the local branches of. this party. Depending on the attitude and interests of the networks of regional military commands, which were dominated by expatriate Javanese, members of the regional elite obtained access to key positions and profitable patronage networks of the state. In some instances local branches of Golkar were even brave and strong enough to withstand the appointments of governors and *bupati* by the centre, though due to its power, in most cases the centre was not interested in compromise, and as a result conflicts remained unresolved and grievances towards Jakarta increased (Malley 1999a: 92–3).

Officially ethnicity, religion, race and class were political no-go areas, which implied that public discourse about these topics was under close surveillance. Issues concerning religion and *adat* were monitored by state agencies, while the phenomenon of class was simply silenced. The national motto, 'Unity in Diversity', however, seemed to legitimise diversity. And it was precisely the interpretation of what diversity meant and who was in control of its meaning, that was to become a bone of contention during the late New Order period.

Rita Smith Kipp (1996) has analysed the ambiguous and contested nature of concepts like ethnicity, religion and culture in New Order Indonesia. She illustrates how since the colonial period the state has encouraged a process of 'dissociation', by which she means that there is no longer an overlap of religious and ethnic identities. Contrary to the old idea that national integration and increased contact between different groups would erode ethnic identities, government policy, migration and intensified competition for scarce resources had led since the 1980s to an intensification of ethnic consciousness.

The New Order believed that it could handle the variety of differences it had helped to create. Ethnic diversity was expected to diminish religious unity, while religion pluralised ethnic groups, and both ethnicity and religion denied class (Smith Kipp 1996: 261). The violent conflicts in the Moluccas, Central Sulawesi and West – and Central Kalimantan, which accompanied the demise of the Soeharto regime, demonstrate however that a monster had been created. Because the New Order had transformed Sukarno's popular nationalism with its mobilising potential into state monitored ceremonialism, ethnic identification seemed to become more powerful. Like nationalism, discourses based on ethnicity also imagine bonds of loyalty in terms of kinship and generate emotions, which persuade people to risk their lives and cleanse their territories from evil enemies.

Whereas many Indonesia watchers tended to identify the leading actors in these conflicts in terms of external provocateurs manipulated by key actors in Jakarta, Gerry van Klinken (2001, 2002) has pointed to the crucial role played by regional elites and the way they articulate ethnic identities. After the fall of the Soeharto regime the ruling Golkar party was seriously weakened, and both regional bureaucrats and party bosses had to reorganise their local power bases. No longer supported by the centre, they started to foster a local constituency in order to maintain (or to conquer) strategic positions in the regional administration and to gain access to regional economic resources. In order to explain and to legitimise their new role they presented themselves as 'traditional' leaders representing regional interests of their ethnic group. It is interesting to see to what extent old aristocracies did manage to play a decisive role under these new circumstances.

The rise of the strong state under the New Order was on the regional level accompanied by new alliances with descendents of the old aristocratic elites. Since they were incorporated in the state apparatus regional elites could distance themselves from their local constituencies. Thus the strong state could rely on privileged but dependent regional elites. We expect that under the present conditions, and in contrast to the 1950s, a weaker state will be paralleled by the rise of stronger regional elites.

In a preliminary effort at identification of Indonesia's current regional elites I suggest that we may distinguish three partly overlapping groups. The first is formed by families of bureaucrats with an aristocratic background who have managed to survive various regimes since the late colonial period. The second group consists of regional bureaucrats and party bosses who used to be the local operators of the New Order (Malley 2003; Hadiz 2003a). They make alliances with businessmen and local thugs in order to control the regional flows of money. Vedi Hadiz (2003b) observes such a regrouping of old predatory interests at the regional level.

Power at the regional level is in general still concentrated in the hands of politicians with a bureaucratic background – and reform measures are doomed to fail in the hands of bureaucrats and politicians who stand to lose power if they are implemented (Rohdewohld 2003). These politicians are, however, challenged by regional competitors who constitute the third group, which consists of members of local elites who want to establish a district of their own. Their success explains the rapid increase of the number of districts. Many of these people belong to the local aristocracy, have enjoyed higher education, made a career in Golkar, the Church or the army, and are able to lobby in Jakarta. Having secured local support from the parliament of the existing districts and the province, a delegation goes to Jakarta in order to convince Committee Two of the national parliament of the necessity to establish a new district. Among other things, it is required that the new district has enough natural resources and that the *aspirasi masyarakat* is strong. In general this *aspirasi masyarakat* is measured by the amounts of money that change pockets during a field visit by members of parliament from Jakarta. Such a campaign requires 1.5–2 billion Rupiah, which indicates that potential regional leaders expect to make large profits once they rule their new district through their network of loyal followers. Apart from receiving bribes, politicians in Jakarta are willing to support the creation of new districts because these may broaden the regional constituencies of their parties.[13]

Patrimonial patterns, democracy and state capacity

Despite the seeming discontinuity between the strong, centralised New Order state and the decentralised, fragmented nature of the post-Soeharto era, Indonesian politics has been marked by strong continuities of patrimonial patterns, which have their origin in pre-colonial times. These patterns are of course not static, because they have been affected by state-building processes as well as deeply influencing these same processes. A search for similar changing continuities at the regional level reveals that many of the problems in the relationship between decentralisation and democracy are rooted in the deeply entrenched nature of regional elites in Indonesia. During the colonial period the position of these elites was reinforced by a system of indirect rule, which emphasised ethnic distinctions and favoured *adat* law. The established elites have inherited Dutch colonial discourses on ethnic identity, and have been raised and trained under the New Order. They have access to central state agencies and rely on a local constituency which is mobilised though ethnic loyalties. The process of administrative decentralisation offers them the opportunity to expand and maintain regional networks of patron-client ties, combined with a continued fiscal dependency on the centre, which results in intense competition for strategic positions in the regional administration in order to acquire exclusive access to central funds and regional resources. Apart from funds from the centre they have also inherited a culture of political violence and criminality that found its origins in the New Order and is reinforced by the privatisation of state institutions at the regional level. Taken together regional leadership may take the shape of what John Sidel (1999) has called 'bossism', which operates in regional shadow regimes characterised by alliances of bureaucrats, party bosses, businessmen, military and criminals.[14]

The reproduction of patrimonial relationships within these shadow regimes is not an ideal breeding ground for democracy, but it reinforces the power of regional elites. It is to be feared that the system is still primarily driven by money politics and political violence, which prevent transparency and good governance. Commenting on the news that retired General Wiranto is one of Golkar's presidential candidates, Wimar Witoelar stated recently: 'If you're not a bad guy, you're not in control here. The elite is full of convicted people or about to be convicted people, or people who should be convicted...you name it...everybody's a crook.'[15]

If the core of the decentralising state is not only a source of money but also of corruption and criminality, what chances are there for local democracy to develop?[16] 'Less state' does not automatically result in 'more democracy', while the representatives of the 'civil society' who aspire to regional autonomy are not very democratic either. Based on a comparative analysis of developments in South Asia and West Africa, Crook and Manor (1998: 302) conclude that, instead of bringing fundamental changes, decentralization tends to reinforce existing political patterns at the regional level. And this seems to be the case in Indonesia as well.

Professional optimists, for whom decentralisation is synonymous with democracy, good governance and civil society, should know better. Based on such misconceptions democracy cannot be achieved. Facing Indonesia's insecure future the central question should not be about the extent to which decentralisation can be implemented and how fiscal arrangements should be refined, but on the conditions under which democratic institutions can be strengthened. In order to develop democratic control and to guarantee the rule of law, a certain 'state capacity' is required to overcome the persistence of old patrimonial patterns. Only if these conditions are created in the centre will decentralisation of democracy be achieved. As long as this is not the case there are at best incidental possibilities for a single-issue democracy (Törnquist 2001a) operating temporarily outside the corrupt institutions of the post-colonial state.

Notes

1. This article is a preliminary result of the KITLV research project 'Renegotiating Boundaries: Access, Agency and Identity in Post-Soeharto Indonesia' (see www.kitlv.nl) and has an explorative character. A more elaborate version of this chapter has been published in Schulte Nordholt (2003a). I would like to thank in particular Gerry van Klinken and the editors of this volume for their helpful comments.
2. Note in this respect the contrasting titles of the books edited by Kingsbury and Aveling (2003), and Aspinall and Fealy (2003).
3. More precisely: 10 provinces plus two special regions in 1950; see Legge (1961: 62–83).
4. The most far-reaching form of decentralization is, of course, privatization (Frerks and Otto 1996).
5. This implied that at least in theory more than 1000 government regulations and presidential decrees and instructions had to be revoked (Rifai Amzulian 2002: 33).
6. Actually the department of Ryaas Rashid was in operation as a relatively independent unit over a limited period of time, i.e. from April till August 2000 (World Bank 2003).
7. Part of the operation was a massive transfer of 2.1 million state employees – 50 per cent of whom are schoolteachers – to the regions. Since it concerned primarily a financial operation it did not imply actual mass migration (Rohdewohld 2003).
8. Efforts to recentralise government control are accompanied by a strong tendency within the PDI-P (Partai Demokrasi Indonesia-Perjuangan) to strengthen the grip of the party headquarters in Jakarta over its regional branches. Several conflicts occurred when during the elections of governors and *bupati* local party branches were forced to support candidates who were favoured by the headquarters in Jakarta.
9. The central government keeps 75 per cent of all these revenues, and distributes 25 per cent to the regions in the form of a general grant (DAU, *Dana Alokasi Umum*), 90 per cent of which goes to the autonomous regions while the provinces receive 10 per cent. In 2001 in total Rp60.5 trillion, or US$6.1 billion flowed from Jakarta to the regions. The criteria for the distribution of funds among the variety of districts are complex, depending on the relative size of the population, the poverty rate, geographical conditions and price indices.
   The contentious provinces Papua and Aceh received special autonomy (respectively Laws Nos 18 and 21/2001), granting Aceh 80 per cent of oil and gas revenues, and Papua 80 per cent of its mining revenues and 70 per cent of revenues from oil and gas. It is ironic that in the case of both Aceh and Papua autonomy was granted to the *province* instead of the districts. For one would expect a strong rebellious and ethnically homogeneous province to break away from the nation-state. Both provincial administrations are still dominated by old Golkar elites, however, who control the flows of money, while at the time of writing in 2003 the army is waging a war in Aceh.
10. This does not necessarily mean that Indonesia will fall apart into a Balkanized archipelago of small states. The example of the recently formed resource rich province of Bangka-Belitung (the islands southeast of Sumatra) shows that

loyalty towards Jakarta increased considerably when autonomy was granted (Minako Sakai 2003).

11. The World Bank (2003) refers in this respect to the surprisingly great number of newly elected *bupati* who are not affiliated with majority parties in their region, and admits that substantial amounts of money that have been transferred from the center apparently disappear.

12. Especially on Java, Bali and parts of Sumatra the communist party (PKI) succeeded in gaining influence.

13. *Far Eastern Economic Review (FEER)* 29 May 2003; presentation by dr. Jacqueline Vel on decentralization in Sumba at the Annual Meeting of the KITLV, 24 May 2003.

14. See for similar developments in Thailand see Pasuk *et al.* (1998) and McVey (2000).

15. www.voanews.com 27/2/03.

16. Decentralisation does not stop at the regional, or *kabupaten* level. Law 22/1999 abolished also Law 5/1979 on village government, which has serious implications for the way local government is organised. Antlöv (2003) has pointed to the importance of democracy at the village level through village councils (*Dewan Perwakilan Desa*), while White and Gutomo Bayu Aji (2000) emphasise the relevance of this institution as a training ground for democracy, because the majority of the population is unfamiliar with democratic procedures and processes (cf. Kana *et al.* 2001). Acciaioli (2002) shows that *adat* plays a more prominent role at the local level. Political changes at the village level involve complex conflicts over access to land which are phrased in terms of *adat* (von Benda Beckmann and von Benda Beckmann 2001). *Adat* also seems to reinforce ethnic identities and the exclusion of outsiders. In Bali a stronger emphasis on local *adat* facilitated the birth of a new and aggressive village police, or *pecalang*, consisting of young men who redirect traffic during rituals, lynch thieves and cleanse neighborhoods from foreign migrant workers (Degung Santikarma 2001). The revival of *adat* rule in Bali reinforced also a consciousness of territorial autonomy, which recently led to a series of border conflicts between adat villages. Village democracy based on *adat* faces, in other words, particular constraints and is, moreover, relatively powerless *vis-à-vis* higher levels of government.

3

Bossism and Democracy in the Philippines, Thailand and Indonesia: Towards an Alternative Framework for the Study of 'Local Strongmen'

John T. Sidel

Introduction

Over the course of the past several years, increasing academic, journalistic, governmental, and NGO attention has been devoted to the problems of local 'money politics' (*politik uang*) and 'gangsterism' (*premanisme*) in regencies, municipalities, and provinces around the Indonesian archipelago. The election of regents (*bupati*), mayors (*walikota*), and governors (*gubernur*) during this period is said to have been heavily swayed by monetary inducements on the one hand, and threats of violence, on the other, with local businessmen and leaders of criminal rackets playing a prominent role on or off stage. Newly assertive local assemblies (Dewan Perwakilan Rakyat Daerah or DPRD) are said to be dominated by businessmen, gangsters, and their minions, or machine politicians susceptible to their influence. The enactment and implementation of new laws and regulations by these DPRD, moreover, are likewise described as decisively shaped by the interplay of competing interests of rival business and criminal cliques, rather than by the broader interests of the local population. Meanwhile, accounts of communal violence in provinces as varied as Central Kalimantan, Central Sulawesi, and Maluku have stressed the leadership role of 'local elites' in mobilising local communities – or armed gangs within local communities – for inter-religious or inter-ethnic violence. After half a decade of democratisation and decentralisation in Indonesia, a consensus has emerged among observers that 'local elites' constitute a major obstacle to the economic, political, and social advancement of the country.

In this context, it is hardly surprising that scholars and activists working on local politics in Indonesia have begun to turn to writings on manifestations of this new phenomenon in Indonesia as long found in other parts of Southeast Asia and elsewhere in the world, most notably the work of Joel Migdal on so-called 'local strongmen'. Indeed, although the academic literature on local brokers, patrons, and clients was rich and varied in the late 1960s, 1970s, and early 1980s, over the past decade the point of departure for the study of 'local strongmen' in Africa, Asia, and Latin America has narrowed down considerably to Joel Migdal's (1988, 2001) writings on this topic.[1] Migdal's work is included in the reading lists of countless undergraduate and graduate courses and provides an analytical framework that numerous scholars have – knowingly or otherwise – relied upon and/or reproduced in their study of sub-national politics in many parts of the world.

Against this backdrop, the aim of this brief chapter is both to criticise Migdal in a systematic fashion, and to offer an alternative framework for understanding patterns of 'local strongmen', using Southeast Asian examples – the Philippines, Thailand, and Indonesia – to suggest the explanatory power of this framework. First, a brief sketch of Migdal's arguments. Migdal seeks to explain why 'local strongmen' have, through their success at 'social control', often effectively 'captured' parts of Third World states: 'They have succeeded in having themselves or their family members placed in critical state posts to ensure allocation of resources according to their own rules, rather than the rules propounded in the official rhetoric, policy statements, and legislation generated in the capital city or those put forth by a strong implementor' (Migdal 1988: 256).

His explanation for this observed phenomenon consists of three interrelated arguments. First of all, Migdal argues, local strongmen have flourished in what are described as 'weblike' societies, which 'host a mélange of fairly autonomous social organisations,' and in which 'social control' is effectively 'fragmented'. This supposedly distinctive pattern of fragmented social control, it is claimed, often crystallised in the course of colonial rule and integration into the world capitalist economy, most notably in the entrenchment of large landowning classes. In short, due to the weblike *structure of society*, local strongmen enjoy significant influence and leverage over state leaders and local bureaucrats in what Migdal describes as a 'triangle of accommodation' (Migdal 1988: 238–58). Secondly, local strongmen come to exercise social control by delivering key components for the so-called 'strategies of survival' of the local population. By this account, the strongmen not only enjoy legitimacy and support among the local populace but also exist essentially to satisfy this constituency's needs and demands for their services. Thus authors inspired by Migdal tend to frame their discussions in terms of 'personalism,' 'clientelism,' and 'patron–client relations' and to portray local strongmen as occupying roles as patrons who provide personal benefits to needy clients and followers in their bailiwicks. Thirdly and finally, Migdal argues that local strongmen's success in 'capturing' state agencies and resources impedes or compromises the efforts of state leaders to implement various policies. Local strongmen, overall, limit state autonomy and capacity, causing state weakness 'in effecting goal-oriented social changes' (Migdal 1988: 9) and contributing to 'ungovernability' and 'disorder.' Insofar as successful industrialisation and growth strategies depend heavily on coherent, effective state policy formation and implementation, local strongmen thus constitute obstacles to economic development in the Third World.

This chapter offers an account of 'local strongmen' in Southeast Asia which is strikingly at odds with Migdal's arguments. As illustrated in the pages below, the contexts in which local strongmen thrive are shaped at least as much by the nature of *the state* as by that of society. Local elites, it is argued, may be less 'traditional' – and oligarchies less enduring – than is often assumed; in fact, they typically emerge as much from within the state as from 'society'.[2] For all the supposed 'weakness' of the state, it is in fact the very – in Migdal's terms, 'weblike' – structure of *the state* which creates the conditions for the emergence, survival, and success of local strongmen.

Equally, this chapter takes issue with the stress on 'clientelism' and 'personalism' and the suggestion that the political culture, predispositions, and particularistic demands of local populations essentially cause, legitimate, and bear responsibility for local forms of despotism. As the cases cited below suggest, the *supply* of local strongmen does not necessarily reflect popular *demand*; people do not, in other words, simply 'get the government they ask for' (and thus deserve). Finally, this chapter argues against the notion that local strongmen impede capitalist development, revealing instead their capacity to facilitate and benefit from the expansion of market relations and the process of industrial growth in their bailiwicks.

In sum, the discussion of local bosses in the Philippines, Thailand, and Indonesia below offers a counterpoint to the dominant account of local strongmen in the Third World as provided by Migdal and other authors who have drawn upon his work. The alternative framework suggested by the analysis below is one which is not only more descriptively accurate with regard to the nature of local strongman rule in the Philippines, Thailand, and Indonesia, but also more illuminating with regard to explaining the pattern of variation observed across the three cases. Thus the chapter does not simply include Indonesia among a growing number of instances of 'bossism' – in addition, it provides an explanation for the subtle but crucial differences between the 'bossism' found in the Philippines, Thailand, and Indonesia. These differences should be of considerable interest to scholars, policy-makers, and activists working to promote democratisation – as well as decentralisation – in Southeast Asia and other regions of the world.

The Philippines: clientelism, oligarchy and a 'weak' state?

Of all the countries of Southeast Asia, the Philippines offers the most obvious case of local strongmen through which to re-examine the scholarly literature sketched above. Scholars and other commentators have long emphasised both the predominance of patron–client relations and the persistence of a landowning elite in the archipelago. Elections – local, congressional, and national – in the Philippines have long been dominated by local politicians and 'political clans' known to enjoy not only political longevity but also economic pre-eminence – if not a monopolistic position – within their respective municipal, congressional, or provincial bailiwicks, through landownership, commercial networks, logging or mining concessions, transportation companies, and/or control over illegal economic activities.

Yet this pattern of local strongman rule cannot be said to reflect the strength and endurance of 'patron–client relations' and a 'landowning elite' in Philippine politics.[3] Widespread electoral fraud, vote-buying and violence have long played a decisive role in elections, and high re-election rates for incumbent legislators and local officials belie the fiction that bi-factional competition between rival patron–client networks has allowed constituents to exercise effective influence over politicians. In addition, the size and importance of large private landholdings have been much exaggerated, as has the extent to which landownership ever provided a truly *independent* economic base for the exercise of political power. Moreover, many of the entrenched politicians and magnates in the country have derived their power and wealth not from private landownership but from state resources and commercial capital, and many of those entrenched politicians and 'landed élites' who have accumulated large landholdings did so after – rather than before – assuming elected office. Finally, concentrations of landownership have *not* in fact corresponded with the political longevity of elected officials: some of the most enduring politicians and political clans are found in rural bailiwicks notable for an absence of large landholdings or in urban areas.

In fact, the entrenchment of local bosses in the Philippines reflects neither the strength of patron–client relations nor the rule and resilience of a landed oligarchy, but rather the peculiar institutional structures of the state. In particular, the subordination of a poorly insulated state apparatus to *elected* municipal, provincial, and national officials in the American colonial era (1900–41) contrasted sharply with the bureaucratisation and insulation of colonial states elsewhere in the region and combined with the onset of what might loosely be termed 'primitive accumulation' to facilitate the emergence of bossism in the Philippines in the early 20th century. While the Spanish colonial regime had delegated certain local powers to native officials elected according to highly restricted suffrage requirements and closely supervised by Spanish parish priests, American colonial rule in the Philippines from 1901 until the outbreak of World War II essentially expanded the structure of private control over the local coercive and extractive agencies of the state 'upwards' through the subordination of a national state apparatus to provincial- and national-level elected officials. Elections to municipal office, based on highly restricted suffrage and freed from the intervention of ecclesiastical authorities, were first held in 1901, followed by those for provincial governors (1902), representatives to the national Philippine Assembly (1907), an American-style bicameral legislature (1916), and a Commonwealth presidency (1935). Elected municipal mayors retained their Spanish-era discretionary powers over local law-enforcement, public works, and taxation, winning complete independence from parish priests and full authority to appoint municipal police forces. While elected governors enjoyed somewhat similar law-enforcement and taxation powers at the provincial level, representatives to legislature gained control over a hastily constructed and rapidly Filipinised national state apparatus. Within their own districts, legislators exercised effective discretion over the disbursement of pork barrel funds for public works and the appointment of Constabulary commanders, district engineers and superintendents of schools, provincial fiscals, treasurers, and assessors, judges of the court of first instance, and local agents of the Bureau of Lands. In Manila, meanwhile, these legislators likewise exerted influence over the awarding of contracts, concessions, and monopoly franchises, the appointment of ranking officials in national government agencies, and the allocation of loans by the Philippine National Bank. Finally, with the election of a Commonwealth president in 1935, these local executives and national legislators were subordinated to a directly elected national executive. This distinctly American form of late colonial administration contrasted sharply with the processes of state expansion, bureaucratisation, and centralisation ongoing in this period elsewhere in Southeast Asia. The subordination of municipal, provincial, and national agencies of the state apparatus to elected officials combined with the onset of primitive capital accumulation and the expanding role of the colonial state in the economy to facilitate the emergence and entrenchment of *bosses* in a variety of localities and at different levels of state power in the colonial era. The term 'bosses' here refers to local brokers who enjoy an enduring monopolistic position over coercive and economic resources within their respective bailiwicks: long-term mayors who ran their municipalities as their private fiefdoms, congressmen and governors who built up political machines and business empires that spanned entire districts or provinces.

As the independent Republic inaugurated in 1946 essentially reconstructed the institutional legacies of American colonial rule, bosses have continued to thrive in the Philippines to the present day. While close electoral competition and frequent turnover have endured in some localities, bosses have emerged and entrenched themselves in countless municipalities, cities, congressional districts, and provinces. Throughout the Philippines, one can find localities where one politician – or one family – has held office and built up a monopolistic position in the local economy over the course of many years.

Research on local bosses in different parts of the Philippines reveals the following patterns of local variation. First of all, local bosses have succeeded in entrenching themselves when and where the 'commanding heights' of the local political economy have lent themselves to monopolistic control, most notably illegal activities, nodal commercial/transportation chokepoints, public lands, heavily regulated crops and industries. Secondly, where such monopolistic control over the local economy has hinged on state-based derivative and discretionary powers, single-generation gangster-style bosses have relied heavily upon superordinate power brokers, whose backing has underpinned their emergence, entrenchment, and survival, and whose hostility has spelled their downfall or death. Thirdly, where, by contrast, monopolistic control over the local economy has rested upon the construction of a solid base in proprietary wealth outside the realm of state intervention, bosses have withstood the hostile machinations of superordinate power brokers and successfully passed on their bailiwicks to successive generations in classic *dynasty* form.

Today, local bosses thrive in a wide variety of settings, and without relying upon large landholdings or patron–client relations as the essential underpinnings of their rule. Control over elected office provides access to a broad array of state resources and prerogatives, from control over public land to discretion over law-enforcement to authority over construction contracts and monopoly franchises. Violence and intimidation, vote-buying and electoral fraud work in tandem with the mobilisation of local machines for self-perpetuation in office. Thus fishing magnates and bus company owners in the Visayas, smugglers in Sulu, and rulers of urban slum squatter settlements in Metro Manila have entrenched themselves in their bailiwicks for decades at a time. Even in provinces like Cavite and Cebu, suburban growth zones filled with industrial estates, golf courses, residential subdivisions, and tourist resorts, local bosses have used their considerable discretionary powers – over zoning ordinances, construction contracts, and police forces used for busting unions and clearing land of 'squatters' – to oil their political machines by serving as gate-keepers and facilitators to Manila-based and foreign investors.

In sum, the example of bossism in the Philippines does not in fact confirm the arguments of Migdal and others concerning local strongmen. Neither the strength of patron–client relations nor the endurance of a landed oligarchy offer compelling society-based explanations as to why local bosses have emerged and entrenched themselves in various localities around the archipelago. Instead, the analysis above suggests that it was the distinctive pattern of (colonial-era) *state* formation which prefigured the prevalence of local bosses in the Philippines. As for the conventional wisdom that landed élites and local strongmen have obstructed economic growth in the Philippines, the evidence in fact suggests otherwise. It was under an authoritarian regime far more centralised and autonomous from societal influences than its predecessors that the Philippine economy experienced dramatic decline in the late 1970s and early 1980s, and it has been in large measure through the efforts of local bosses that growth zones in provinces like Cavite and Cebu have attracted Manila-based and foreign investors since the restoration of competitive electoral democracy after 1986. Overall, local bosses in the Philippines have been described above as far less paternalistic, rooted in society, and detrimental to capitalist development than previously argued or assumed. Instead, they have emerged and entrenched themselves in large part through violence and guile, thanks to enabling state structures and institutions, and as active promoters of capital accumulation and industrial growth.

Bossism in comparative perspective: Thailand

Overall, the Philippine case suggests that bossism reflects a fairly common conjuncture in state formation and capitalist development: the subordination of the state apparatus to *elected* officials against the backdrop of what might loosely be termed 'primitive accumulation'. 'Primitive accumulation' here refers to a phase of capitalist development in which a significant section of the population has lost direct control over the means of production and direct access to means of subsistence, and been reduced to a state of economic security and dependence on scarce wage labour; and in which considerable economic resources and prerogatives remain in the 'public' domain. Taken together, these last two conditions signal both the susceptibility of many voters to clientelistic, coercive, and monetary pressures and the centrality of state offices and state resources for capital accumulation and control over the 'commanding heights' of local economies.

This argument linking bossism to democracy and 'primitive accumulation' finds considerable support in a comparative analysis of bossism's manifestations throughout Southeast Asia. Broadly speaking, the only other country in the region where local bosses have achieved power and prominence analogous to what has been observed in the Philippines is, curiously, Thailand. What is it about Thailand that has made it so hospitable to local bossism in recent years?

Under military rule and 'the bureaucratic polity' in Thailand until the 1970s, the institutional constraints upon embryonic manifestations of local bossism were significant. The steady growth of rice cultivation since the mid-19th century did provide ample opportunities for capital accumulation through control over the expanding circuitries of production and distribution, and a provincial economic èlite accordingly did emerge, based in landownership, moneylending, milling, marketing, and transportation as well as such illegal activities as gambling and smuggling. A pattern of what James C. Scott has identified as 'market corruption' thrived, with pliable or predatory local agents of various central government ministries open to the 'purchase' of their discretionary and regulatory powers over the local economy. Yet these local government officials were only available, as it were, for temporary rent rather than permanent sale, and at prices open to competitive bidding, as decisions with regard to appointment, promotion, removal, and transfer were made by Bangkok-based bureaucrats rather than up-country bosses.

By the 1970s, however, the social forces generated by the Vietnam War boom in Thailand began to combine with the internal contradictions of army rule to shift the locus of national-level power away from the military establishment and towards previously ceremonial and impotent parliamentary institutions. While an initial period of unprecedented openness in 1973–76 led to a brutal right-wing backlash against the most vocal proponents of democratisation, the intensity of factional rivalries at the highest echelons of the army derailed efforts to reconstruct a military-dominated 'bureaucratic polity' and delivered increasing political leverage and legislative authority into the hands of parliament in the 1980s. Thus, although an appointed Senate and threats of a *coup d'état* left considerable power in military hands well into the 1980s and 1990s, Bangkok's agro-business, banking, commercial, and industrial magnates began to view parliament as an essential avenue of influence and re-channelled their resources accordingly. While Bangkok-based magnates commanded tremendous financial resources, only province-based businessmen enjoyed links to large blocs of voters in the country's overwhelmingly rural constituencies, and parliamentary seats promised influence over (or inclusion among) cabinet ministers, central ministries, and local agents of the Thai state. With the vast majority of parliamentary (multiple-seat) constituencies located in *rural* areas, it is thus no surprise that by 1990, nearly half of all Cabinet members were provincial businessmen.

Against this backdrop, by the mid-1980s, observers of Thai politics had begun to comment on the growing manifestations of local bossism, most prominently with reference to what have come to be known as *chao pho* (or *jao poh*), Thai 'godfathers' of a distinctly *mafioso* variety.[4] These *chao pho* are identifiable through the multiplicity and monopolistic quality of their economic activities within loosely defined territorial bailiwicks, in terms of accumulation of proprietary wealth (agricultural land, real-estate properties, mills, processing centres, factories; shares in banks and industrial firms), acquisition of state-derived concessions, contracts, and franchises (e.g. logging, mining, public works, transport), and involvement in illegal rackets (e.g. drug trade, gambling, smuggling). These *chao pho* have achieved great prominence and power through their successful service as – or provision of – vote brokers (*hua khanaen*) in elections, delivering parliamentary constituencies, or regional clusters of constituencies, to Bangkok-based patrons, local clients, or themselves on election day, through a combination of coercion, vote-buying, and electoral fraud. These *chao pho* have also become notorious for their control over the local tentacles of the state, most notably its coercive apparatuses, and their ability to achieve effective local monopolies over the organisation of (state and extra-state) violence within their bailiwicks, for use in capital accumulation, electoral manipulation, and enforcement of illegal rackets.

Compared to manifestations of local bossism observed in the Philippines, the contemporary Thai variant is distinctive in two key respects. Firstly, the transfer of effective control over the state apparatus to *elected* officials came *relatively late vis-à-vis* the process of capitalist development, with

enormous Bangkok-based financial, agro-business, and industrial con-
glomerates and up-country magnates with province- or region-wide
empires already entrenched and equipped with ample resources for
electoral competition. Thus prominent Bangkok bankers and industrialists
have themselves assumed political party leadership posts or otherwise
engineered alliances with regional clusters of *chao pho*, and provincial
businessmen have in some cases exercised *chao pho*-like influence over
multiple constituencies or even provinces.

Secondly, the subordination of the state apparatus to a parliament
drawn from multiple-seat constituencies and without proportional
representation has facilitated the emergence of a highly fluid system of
political parties held together largely by patronage networks (regional and
national) and personal ties and coalition governments stitched together
through multi-party Cabinets. Under such a system, it has been difficult
to build a truly nation-wide political party greater than the sum of its –
local – parts. Thus *chao pho* exercising control over several constituencies
have found it relatively easy to install themselves or their stooges in the
Cabinet and thereby to wield considerable influence over the internal
affairs of key central ministries and their local line agencies. The distinctiveness of this configuration in contemporary Thailand is apparent
when compared to the highly decentralised state and presidential
system in the Philippines, with its multi-tiered pattern of municipal,
congressional, and provincial bosses.

In short, in contemporary Southeast Asia, bossism has begun to take
root beyond the Philippines over the past ten years. In Thailand, bosses –
known as 'godfathers' or *chao pho* – have emerged with the entrenchment
of electoral democracy since the 1980s, yet, unlike the Philippines, in the
context of a more industrialised economy, a more centralised bureaucracy,
and a European-style parliamentary system, with local executive powers
remaining in civilian bureaucrats' hands and military generals retaining
a measure of national influence through an appointed Senate and other
forms of political and economic intervention. At the same time, the case of
Thailand confirms the broader argument that it is the subordination of
the state to elected officials, rather than the strength of 'traditional élites'
and clientelistic demands in society, that constitutes the crucial precondition for local bossism.

Indonesia: local mafias, networks and clans

In contrast with the pattern of bossism observed in the Philippines and
Thailand, a distinctively different form of local power has begun to

crystallise, expand, and entrench itself in Indonesia in recent years. During the three decades of the Soeharto era (1966–98), the Indonesian state was tightly centralised and insulated from centrifugal and societal constraints on the internal circulation and machinations of its officials. Although pseudo-parliamentary bodies at the district, provincial, and national levels were regularly elected on a five-year cycle, their effective powers and prerogatives were severely limited. Electoral competition was confined to three parties, Golkar, the United Development Party (PPP), and the Indonesian Democratic Party (PDI), with Golkar enjoying tremendous advantages – and persistent majorities – as the government's political machine, and PPP and PDI restricted to minor supporting roles. At the district and provincial levels, local executives were essentially imposed by the Ministry of Internal Affairs and vested with powers that dwarfed those of the elected assemblies, while at the national level a supra-parliamentary body stacked with carefully selected appointees convened on a quinquennial basis to 're-elect' Soeharto and his anointed vice-president. A multi-tiered hierarchy of military commands mirrored the structure of local government, and active and retired officers were appointed not only to reserved seats in the regional assemblies and the national parliament but also to nearly half the governorships and regencies in the country. Active and retired military officers staffed countless other local and national government positions and, at least until the 1990s, dominated the leadership of Golkar, which operated as a centralised and 'closed-list' dominant party throughout the New Order.[5]

The implications of this organisation of state power were obvious: the possibilities for the emergence of 'local strongmen' were highly restricted. Officials at all levels of the state hierarchy were highly responsive to demands and directives from 'above', as their assignments and promotions depended entirely on appointments determined in Jakarta. As one study of the Soeharto government's family planning programme noted:

> When a governor is approaching the end of his five-year term of office and wants a second term, his achievements are evaluated by a national team, who scrutinize family planning in particular. If the province has a poor record in family planning, the doors are generally closed to a new appointment for the governor. Periodic evaluations of the performance of provincial officials therefore serve as an inbuilt incentive to ensure that the program has produced demonstrable results (Selo Soemardjan and Kennon Breazeale 1993: 65).

Regular rotations of governors, as well as district-level and provincial Army commanders, in and out of localities, prevented these middle-ranking civilian and military officials from building up local fiefdoms independent of the centre. Conversely, small-town businessmen and other local powerbrokers were impeded from exerting direct discretion over state personnel, resources, and regulatory powers. Local government officials offering special favours and facilities to private parties 'for a price' did so essentially as 'retail outlet' distributors and collectors for the national ('wholesale') centre in Jakarta, with promotions and assignments contingent on delivery of regular 'franchise renewal' fees (Malley 1999a: 300–1). As provinces and districts enjoyed only minimal powers of legislation and taxation and depended heavily on Jakarta for revenues, centrally appointed governors and regents essentially exercised discretion over the enforcement of national laws and regulations and the distribution of state revenues and resources (contracts, jobs, subsidies) on behalf of the centre.[6]

Against these relentlessly centripetal forces of the New Order's strong centralised state, at least two mitigating circumstances exerted residual centrifugal influence and created state-based niches for 'local elites'. First of all, clusters of entrenched local interests emerged within the Indonesian state itself. For example, the very organisation of presidential – and, more generally, civilian – control over the Armed Forces depended heavily on a strictly enforced policy of retirement for all military officers at 55 years of age and their reincorporation into the state in civilian positions of local and national authority. While the highest-ranking retiring Army officers were awarded cabinet posts, governorships, and seats in the national parliament as their 'retirement packages', low- and mid-level retiring officers were allotted posts in district-level and provincial assemblies and Golkar branches, and other available sinecures *in their home provinces, and often in the very localities where they had served as active officers.* Thus even as the regular rotation of regents and governors, and district and regional military commanders, worked to maintain control over key local posts in the hands of Jakarta, some observers noted the emergence in the 1980s of 'local mafias' from among lower- and middle-ranking military personnel serving – *and then retiring* – in various provinces of the archipelago:

> [T]hey have the opportunity to build powerful long-term local bases in the regions, first as representatives of the Center, later as real-estate speculators, fixers, commission-agents, local monopolists, and racketeers. These long-term prospects, meaning retirement in the regions, are

helped by local alliances, including marriage connections (themselves or their children), business partnerships with local elites, and personnel manipulations through former subordinates within the active military. As 'old hands,' such military men are in a strong position to inveigle or obstruct 'new broom' officers sent in from the Center. Essentially, we are speaking of the formation of *local mafias*, which often have their eye on such 'civilian' political positions as bupati, provincial secretary, and even governor ('Current Data' 1992: 98; emphasis added).

Such state-based provincial- and regency-level 'mafias' were by no means confined to military officers alone. In the 1970s, for example, the generous flow of development funds from the central government during the oil boom allowed local aristocrats who held key government posts – *bupati* (regent), *sekwilda* (regional secretary) and *ketua* DPRD (head of the regional assembly) – to emerge as owners of plantations, fishponds, logging concessions, cement factories, private banks, construction companies, hotels and tourist resorts. As one observer of South Sulawesi during this period concluded:

> It was hard to find any *bupati* or high-ranking official in the governor's office who did not own profitable clove plantations or salt-water fishponds or both...Officials owning large areas of productive land represented the continuation of a long established pattern in which aristocratic families owned land and invested some of the money they received from landowning in trade. But it also reflected the new economic climate of the New Order which enabled nobles who were also government officials to commercialize their landholdings (Ichlasul Amal 1992: 179).

Meanwhile, in the 1980s and 1990s the processes of economic growth, industrialisation, and social-political mobilisation in Jakarta and in major provincial cities facilitated the emergence of *preman* (gangsters) belonging to the para-statal group *Pemuda Pancasila* (Pancasila Youth) or otherwise linked to the regime. These gangsters enjoyed control over various criminal rackets and provided much-needed muscle for strike-breaking, repression of opposition protests, and election-related services in the late Soeharto years.[7]

Thus even as Jakarta regularly rotated regents, governors, regency-level (*dandim*) and regional (*pangdam*) military commanders in and out of localities throughout the Indonesian archipelago, these centrally appointed officials often found it convenient to reach accommodations with entrenched provincial, regency-level, and municipal 'mafias' nestled in local government offices, regional assemblies, and Golkar and Pemuda Pancasila branches. Given their role in the everyday affairs of local government and in the delivery of votes for Golkar in the 5-year election cycle, they were well positioned to partake in the distribution of government resource flows (subsidies, contracts, jobs) and to influence the enforcement of government regulations to their own advantage. Thus the central government's 'Inpres' programmes for the financing of primary schools, health clinics, markets, and other public facilities in localities around the country created countless opportunities for petty pilfering, padding of payrolls, and fixing of contracts, even as the diversification of trade patterns, business operations, and industrial activities in the provinces facilitated the proliferation of 'wild taxes' (*pungutan liar*) for the facilitation of business operations by local officials.[8] Not all the proceeds were simply 'kicked upstairs' to higher officials: entrenched provincial- and regency-level 'mafias' benefited as well.

Meanwhile, below the sub-district level of the centralised New Order bureaucracy, state power at the lowest administrative level – the village or *desa* – rested in the hands of elected officials with local roots and local interests. Under Dutch colonial rule and in the early post-independence period, village headmen were elected for life, and this arrangement was retained by the Soeharto regime until 1979, at which point new legislation was introduced which limited the village headman (*kepala desa*) to an eight-year term in office and to a total of two terms. While village elections (*pilkades*) and the management of village affairs were overseen by appointed civilian sub-district officers (*camat*), and military presence and surveillance reached down into the village as well, a local elite firmly rooted in the village economy flourished over the course of the New Order. The *kepala desa*, after all, presided over two consultative bodies – the *Lembaga Ketahanan Masyarakat Desa* (Village Social Defense Council) and the *Lembaga Musyawarah Desa* (Village Consultative Council) – whose members he appointed with the approval of the *camat*, and oversaw the staffing and machinations of a bewildering variety of village-level state and para-statal organisations. Indeed, the density of the state at the village level was remarkable. As the author of one village study noted in the mid-1990s: 'It is not unusual for a village to have two hundred official posts in a village bureaucracy of twenty organisations, each with a sign in front of the village office' (Antlöv 1995: 7).[9]

Control over the office of *kepala desa* guaranteed privileged access to state resources and discretion over state regulatory powers in the economy.

From the Dutch colonial era onwards, village headmen in many villages in Java and elsewhere were awarded control over communal or salary lands (*tanah bengkok*) for the duration of their tenure, and in some cases these tracts of land were more sizeable than the private land owned by the wealthiest local landowners. Over the course of the 19th and 20th centuries, the office of headman in many villages was often held by a single family or group of families over several generations, whose control over large tracts of communal or salary land helped to finance the purchase of private land and diversification into other economic activities as well. Under the Soeharto regime, these large landowners benefited greatly from the government's efforts to raise agricultural productivity, as their control over the office of *kepala desa* gave them discretion over the flow of government subsidies for agricultural inputs (e.g. HYV seeds, fertilisers, pesticides), credit facilities, and infrastructure. Thus the New Order era saw village headmen and their families pioneering local investment in agricultural machinery (e.g. tractors, combine harvesters), processing facilities (e.g. rice mills), transport (e.g. buses and trucks), and a variety of capital-intensive agricultural (e.g. prawn farms, fishponds, sugar plantations) and mercantile activities as well as construction and real estate speculation. By investing in education for their children, moreover, these village-level elite families developed supra-local networks, through marriage, school affiliation, and opportunities for government employment. Small wonder that observers noted the increase in vote-buying in village elections during this period: much was at stake in the contest for the office of *kepala desa* (Husken 1994; Maurer 1994).

Thus the imposition of centralised authoritarian rule and the implementation of New Order government programmes were mediated by the interests of local elites who controlled the lowest rung of the administrative hierarchy and commanded considerable economic resources at the village level. The *kepala desa* and the cluster of personal and familial interests they represented used their positions as intermediaries – enforcers of local order, dispensers of state resources, vote brokers for Golkar – to enhance their strategies of political entrenchment and private capital accumulation. Studies of government programmes ranging from rural electrification to intensification of agricultural productivity to family planning consistently revealed that these village elites played a decisive role in the allocation of government resources and the enforcement of government regulations at the local level. *Kepala desa* were responsible for brokering the maintenance of village cooperatives (KUD or Koperasi Unit Desa), the leasing of village land to agro-business concerns, and the re-zoning of the village for real-estate 'development'.Together with regents (*bupati*) and sub-district officers (*camat*), the *kepala desa* enjoyed such discretion over the flow of state resources that some studies estimated a 'loss' of twenty percent of village development funds in transit from the regency to the village itself (Antlöv 1994: 91).

In short, the highly centralised and authoritarian nature of the Soeharto-era state made it impossible for 'local bosses' to emerge, survive, and flourish in Indonesia up through the turn of the century. Local aristocracies in Java and the Outer Islands, Muslim scholars operating vast networks of Islamic schools in the archipelago, and customary (*adat*) institutions in a number of provinces impressed some observers with regard to the strength and density of Indonesian society, yet no 'local strongmen' surfaced from among these clusters of social forces. Instead, at the lower rungs of the Indonesian state, loose networks, 'mafias', and clans emerged, growing from within the state rather than emerging organically from Indonesian society. As Michael Meeker has noted in a different context:

> Each governor, sub-governor, and subordinate officers was after all always more than a singular, isolated individual. He was a father of children, a master of a household, a relative among relatives, a friend among friends, a partner among partners, and a patron among clients. That is to say, each took his place in a world of nonofficial as well as official associations. So each was the representative of a discipline of interpersonal association as father, master, relative, friend, partner, and patron. *And given that each was the subject of a discipline of interpersonal association, insofar as they were members of the official class, would it not also follow that adherence to such a discipline would also shape the ethics of families, households, patronage, kinship, partnership, and patronage?* (Meeker 2002: 145–6).

In short, if even a centralised, authoritarian state was inevitably 'penetrated' and 'captured' in some way by local elites, the very form and extent of local elite power was defined by the nature of the state, in both its overarching national structures – centralised, authoritarian – and its micro-institutional foundations (e.g. early retirement of Army officers, provincial and regency-level assemblies, village-level elections and state land allocations). It was thus the organisation of state power – rather than society – in Indonesia which made it so difficult for full-blown 'local strongmen' to emerge during the Soeharto era.

With the transition to regular competitive elections in 1999, however, conditions approximating those found in the Philippines and Thailand have come into force in Indonesia, greatly widening the possibilities for the accumulation of power by mafias, networks, and clans in localities around the archipelago. With competitive elections in 1999 came the transfer of state power to those capable of mobilising and capturing votes and thus elected offices. With the decentralisation legislation of the same year came the simultaneous devolution of control over the dispensation of state resources and the enactment and implementation of state regulations. Overall, power was shifted 'downwards' and 'outwards', from within a centralised bureaucracy firmly rooted in Jakarta to elected members of assemblies in regencies, municipalities, and provinces around the archipelago.

Scholars of Indonesian politics were quick to pick up on the rapid rise to prominence of local powerbrokers previously limited in access to and control over state power. In North Sumatra, for example, one scholar concluded:

> the newly salient political actors have tended to be small and medium-level entrepreneurs who are at least partly dependent on state projects and contracts; professional politicians with links to the old New Order parties; or activists who have latched onto organizations such as the Association of Muslim Students (HMI), the National Council of Indonesian Youth (KNPI), the Indonesian Nationalist Student Movement (GMNI) and the Indonesian Christian Students Movement (GMKI), from which the New Order regularly recruited new apparatchiks and fixers. No less important are those who acted as the regime's local henchmen through organizations such as Pancasila Youth (Pemuda Pancasila) (Hadiz 2003a: 124–5).

Of 22 *bupatis* and mayors elected in North Sumatra, six were local business moguls, many active in construction, 'demonstrating the growing attractiveness for local business people of wielding direct control over the state apparatus. The majority of the remainder have bureaucratic backgrounds, indicating continuity with the New Order' (Hadiz 2003a: 125).

With democratisation and decentralisation, such local powerbrokers were given unprecedented opportunities to 'capture' state offices and agencies. Careful research on local politics in one regency in the neighbouring province of Aceh, for example, has revealed the entrenchment of a 'timber mafia', which enjoys considerable influence in the local assembly and in the various local offices of the bureaucracy. Through their influence, this network of logging interests ensures that 'district politicians dependent on local support do not threaten their business operations. In many cases local business elites influential in local legislative bodies work to ensure that decentralised district administrations create new formal decisions regarding the management of local resources that favour their interests and those of their business partners from outside the region' (McCarthy 2002b: 882):

> At the apex of the network are four key business figures, predominantly from a particular Alas clan (*marga*). These figures dominated Southeast Aceh politics, and even the *Bupati* was enmeshed in this network. Those who upset this group would be excluded from the webs of patron-client relations running Southeast Aceh....
>
> Key figures there, allegedly including the *Bupati*, are enmeshed in a social order that extends to forestry staff working for the National Park, police (*Polres*) and army personnel (*Kodim*), local government officials, the judiciary and local religious leaders (*imam*). Irrespective of the precise formal position within the state of those playing various roles, the links among businessmen, intermediaries, brokers and villagers lie outside the formal structure of the state (McCarthy 2002a: 93–4).

The emergence and entrenchment of such 'local mafias' has also been evident in much less remote and rural settings. In the city of Medan, for example, the municipal assembly is said to be dominated by rival *preman* (gangster) groupings, some of which enjoy close links to cliques of retired Army and police officers. The mayor is a local businessman who won office in large part through vote-buying and violence, and in condominium with these 'local mafias' in the city (Ryter 2000).

In some parts of the country, moreover, local 'mafias' and 'networks' have also emerged under the leadership of local aristocracies and of the avowed representatives of religious and ethnic communities, who have played prominent roles in the mobilisation of violence in communal conflicts around the archipelago. The role of traditional Islamic teachers (*ulama* or *kyai*) in mobilising votes – and since 1999 winning seats in local assemblies – is one obvious example, most notably in the East Java and *pasisir* (north coastal) strongholds of Nahdlatul Ulama (NU). Since 1999, numerous incidents of violence and intimidation – election-related and otherwise – have been attributed to the youth wing (Ansor) and civilian militia (Banser) associated with NU, whose members are drawn from NU *pesantren* ('traditional' Islamic boarding schools) and help to enforce the authority of local religious leaders (Endang Turmudi 2004). A recent study of local politics in eastern Indonesia has revealed a broader pattern: *pam swakarsa* (civilian militias) linked to rival groupings of *tuan guru* (Islamic teachers) are described as holding sway over many parts of Lombok, even as community patrols originally assigned to police local customary law (*adat*) on Bali have evolved into thuggish enforcers of the PDI-P, which dominates politics on the island.[10] Rival Christian and Muslim 'mafias' of politicians, businessmen, clerics, and gangsters have clearly been at the heart of the inter-religious violence in Ambon and elsewhere in Maluku (Klinken 2001), as have their counterparts in the Central Sulawesi regency of Poso (Aragon 2001). The rival sultanates of Ternate and Tidore are likewise reported to have emerged as alternative poles in local factional politics – and inter-religious violence – in North Maluku (Smith Alhadar 2000, Tamrin Amal Tomagola 2000), even as the leaders of new organisations claiming to represent 'the Dayaks' of Central Kalimantan have evolved into major powerbrokers in the electoral arena, and in the 'ethnic cleansing' of Madurese immigrants from the province (Klinken 2002).

Overall, it is clear that the past several years have witnessed the rise to power and prominence of local 'mafias', 'networks', and 'clans' around the country in tandem with the shift to competitive elections and the devolution of considerable state powers to elected regency-level, municipal, and provincial assemblies. It is also abundantly clear that something rather different from the pattern of local 'bosses' in the Philippines and Thailand has crystallised in Indonesia: local power does not seem to be monopolised by individual 'strongmen' or 'dynasties'. Instead, economic and political power at the regency-, municipal, and provincial levels in Indonesia appears to be associated with loosely defined, somewhat shadowy, and rather fluid clusters and cliques of businessmen, politicians, and officials. As the author of one particularly rich study of local politics in a Central Java regency concluded:

> After three years in office, a new *modus vivendi* based on negotiation and deal-making appears to be evolving between the bureaucracy and the legislature. The system serves as an avenue for political players to maximise their access to resources and enhance their political standing. Each tries to outdo the others, because they all realize that victory in the fight for strategic positions depends on being able to mobilise financial resources and build a popular support base (Amrih Widodo 2003: 190).

Even where such power is associated with forces deeply rooted in society – local aristocracies, customary institutions, religious school networks – there seems to be a pronounced tendency towards the diffusion of power within a set of families rather than concentration within a single leader or lineage. Only at the village level is there some evidence of cases of enduring monopoly over state office (*kepala desa*) and economic resources (*tanah bengkok*, brokerage services, construction contracts) in some localities, and even here power-sharing arrangements, contestation between rival families and factions, and high turnover appear to be the rule (Antlöv 2004).

How then can we explain the decidedly looser, more nebulous and less monolithic pattern of local networks, 'mafias', and 'clans' in Indonesia, as contrasted with the more narrowly concentrated and sharply defined entrenchment of 'bosses' and *chaopho* in the Philippines in Thailand? Migdal's work would suggest that the answer must lie in a weaker and more fissiparous Indonesian *society*, in which power is diffused and fragmented rather than concentrated in individual 'strongmen'. Yet an alternative response more in line with the analysis of the Philippines and Thailand above is suggested by close analysis of the micro-foundational structures of the – now more fully electoralised and decentralised – Indonesian *state*. That is, in sharp contrast with the direct elections – and unrestricted powers – of mayors, governors, and congressmen in the Philippines, and parliamentarians (MPs) in Thailand, the system of elected offices found in Indonesia is much less hospitable to the concentration of power in the hands of a single 'boss' or 'dynasty'. To date, governors (*gubernur*), mayors (*walikota*), and regents (*bupati*) have been elected not directly by the residents within their localities, but instead by the elected members of their local assemblies (DPRD), who also enjoy broad legislative powers thanks to decentralisation. Would-be provincial, municipal, or regency-level 'bosses' and 'dynasties' are thus kept in check by the institutional obstacles to the concentration of local powers in single hands, which alongside the strength of local assemblies include a highly centralised political party system and law-enforcement apparatus.

Even at the village level, where *kepala desa* are directly elected, the 1999 legislation has imposed important checks: tenure is restricted to a maximum of two (10-year) terms, and Village Representative Bodies (*Badan Perwakilan Desa* or BPD) based on direct election by village residents. These village councils now play a central role in the determination of village-level regulations, the allocation of village budgetary funds, and the monitoring of the performance of the *kepala desa*. The BPD is even empowered to initiate proceedings for the dismissal of the *kepala desa*, although the decision itself rests in the hands of the regent (*bupati*).[11] The emergence of 'local bosses' in Indonesia is thus severely constrained by the very organisation of state power at the local level, with neither strong local executive positions nor locally powerful national parliamentary seats, as available sites for the accumulation – and monopolisation – of power (as in the Philippines and Thailand). In this context, the planned shift to directly elected regents (*bupati*) and governors (*gubernur*) in Indonesia over the next few years might well be expected to facilitate the emergence of Philippine- or Thai-style 'bosses' in some localities, albeit ones still hampered by the remaining institutional obstacles cited above.

Conclusion: 'local strongmen' in Southeast Asia revisited

In contrast to Migdal, the Southeast Asian cases outlined above provide ample support for much more careful analysis of state structures in addressing the question of 'local strongmen' in the Third World. As seen in the Philippines and Thailand, a pattern of local bossism has emerged and prevailed when and where the state apparatus is subordinated to elected officials at a relatively early stage of capitalist development which we can gloss as 'primitive accumulation', with the differences between the two cases corresponding to the constellation of elected offices and the timing of 'democratisation'.

Against the backdrop of these variegated configurations of state structures and diverging patterns of local 'strongman' rule, *sub-national* variation in local bosses and 'mafias' does in fact reflect the landscape of what Migdal and others refer to as 'society'. Yet here again the notion of 'strong societies' does not conform to the available evidence: enduring local bosses in the Philippines and Thailand and local mafias in Indonesia are found not so much in bailiwicks where private wealth is concentrated in very few hands (e.g. plantation belts) but more often in localities notable for diffused private economic power and distinguished by the central role of *the state* in the economy. The above-noted case of the 'timber mafia' in Southeast Aceh is paradigmatic: the forests in question lie on state lands. As scholars of local politics in the United States and Southern Europe have noted, local state 'strength' rather than 'weakness' may in fact underpin boss rule. Thus one study of the Christian Democrat (Democrazia Cristiana or DC) party machine's endurance in Palermo concluded: 'The monopolisation of economic resources in the hands of the DC is possible because of the absence of an autonomous resource base at the local level and the consequent dependence of the local economy on the resources of the state' (Chubb 1982: 215). Conversely, the strength of the dominant social class may in fact constrain boss rule: thus in the Philippines, mayors in most major provincial cities serve as brokers for a cluster of local business interests, rather than as entrenched bosses in their own right.

In terms of the linkages between these 'local strongmen' and the people who reside in their bailiwicks, the preceding pages have suggested a more 'supply-side' response than the 'demand'-driven conventional wisdom exemplified by Migdal. To be sure, the broad mass of the population in much of Southeast Asia lives in conditions of economic deprivation and insecurity, and local bosses and mafias have served as patrons to countless needy – and grateful – clients over the years, amassing personal followings whose loyalty may help to under-gird the local foundations of their rule. Yet, as noted above, national-level state structure and local political economy, rather than popular 'demand' for patronage, appear decisive in determining the 'supply' of local strongmen in a given setting. Moreover, as suggested by their use of violence, vote-buying, and fraud in elections, reliance on state agencies and powers (including those of the police) in accumulating wealth, and involvement in criminal activities, local bosses and mafias – as these evocative terms themselves suggest – are far more predatory than paternalistic, more coercive than clientelistic in the treatment of their putative constituencies. Overall, these 'local strongmen' work to achieve positions of local monopoly, in which the terms of exchange between 'patron' and 'client' lean heavily in their favour, and in which control over economic and coercive resources facilitates the preservation and manipulation of the scarcities and insecurities experienced by the local populace.

Finally, the pages above have cast considerable doubt on the commonly held notion that 'local strongmen' stand as both hallmarks of backwardness and obstacles to capitalist development. As noted in passing with reference to the case of suburban industrial zones in the Philippines, local bosses have in fact served as the hand-maidens of economic growth, facilitating land conversion and labour repression and reaping huge profits as real-estate brokers and construction moguls. As suggested above, 'local mafias' in Indonesia have likewise overseen industrial growth in cities like Medan and natural resource extraction in forested and mineral-rich localities around the archipelago. The 'local strongmen' so often disparaged as the enemies of development appear instead above as the unacknowledged front-line agents of capitalist development.

Against the arguments of Joel Migdal outlined and criticised above, this paper has suggested an alternative framework for the analysis of 'local strongmen', one which pays much closer attention to the opportunities and constraints for the accumulation and monopolisation of local economic and political power which are provided by the macro- and micro-structures of the state. As the preceding pages have shown, this framework helps to explain not only when and where 'local strongmen' emerge and entrench themselves, but also the diverging forms which 'local strongman' rule assumes in different institutional contexts. In this analysis, the paper has been ruthlessly, polemically, and perhaps excessively, 'state-centred'.

Indeed, both the strengths and the limitations of this alternative framework for the analysis of 'local strongmen' are evident in the case of emerging forms of local 'mafias', 'networks', and 'clans' in Indonesia since the onset of competitive electoral politics in the country in 1999. While this pattern of local machine politics closely corresponds to the distinctive structures of the Indonesian *state*, it also reflects certain – non-Migdalian – features of what should be acknowledged as a genuinely 'strong' *society*. That is, if, unlike Migdal, this paper has suggested that 'local strongmen' of various stripes should be understood essentially as extensions of states rather than representatives of societies, then it might be hoped that constraints – and forms of resistance – to strongman rule should also be expected from within the *societies* in which they are found. Thus the virtually 'pure' cases of bossism observed in the Philippines and Thailand are ones in which, for the most part, only other would-be bosses – and, as noted in passing above, city-based bankers and businessmen – constrain local bosses' entrenchment and exercise of power. This configuration is understandable against the backdrop of societies in which the 'vertical' pattern of boss rule is not mitigated by countervailing 'horizontal' solidarities and forms of 'social capital'. Neither in the Philippines nor in Thailand do we find evidence of the strong community, class, ethnic, and religious identities found in Indonesia (or, for example, India). In neither case do we find much in the way of pre-electoral social mobilisation along the lines of the Indonesian (or Indian) struggle for independence. In neither case do we find 'nationalist' impediments to the direct exercise of class power by businessmen (especially those of 'Chinese' ancestry) as seen in more statist economies like Indonesia (or India).

Against this backdrop, it is hardly surprising that the various obstacles and objections to local boss rule in the Philippines and Thailand observed in recent years pale in comparison to the myriad forms of local popular mobilisation against local 'mafias', 'networks', and 'clans' seen in Indonesia since 1999, and the much more complex, collective, and contentious pattern of local electoral mobilisation in the country.[12] Thus if we adopt 'bossism' as an alternative framework for understanding patterns of variation in 'local strongman' rule, we must also look beyond the bosses and the states in which they are embedded, and examine much more closely the societies from which challenges and constraints to their rule are imposed. For the fruits of democratisation and decentralisation to be more fully enjoyed and more widely shared in countries like the Philippines, Thailand, and Indonesia, a different kind of 'strong society' than that described by Migdal – or that lionised by many avowed supporters of democratisation – should be applauded, assisted, empowered, and mobilised.

Notes

1. In the later book, Migdal's assumptions and arguments with regard to 'local strongmen', while slightly qualified, remain essentially unchanged.
2. On this point, see Michael E. Meeker (2002), especially pp. 28–31, 144–7 and 185–226.
3. These arguments are defended and elaborated in John T. Sidel (1999).
4. See James Soren Ockey (1992), Ruth McVey (2000) and Daniel Arghiros (2001).
5. See John MacDougall (1982) and Michael S. Malley (1999).
6. On this point, see for example, R. A. Richards (1978).
7. On this phenomenon, see, for example, Loren Ryter (1968).
8. See, for example, Sudarno Sumarto, *et al.* (1998).
9. In the village in West Java where Antlöv conducted his fieldwork, for example, there were 178 state offices in a *desa* of 1,600 households (Antlöv 1995: 144).
10. The Perils of Private Security in Indonesia: Guards and Militias on Bali and Lombok (Jakarta/Brussels: International Crisis Group, 7 November 2003).
11. Undang-Undang Republik Indonesia Nomor 22 Tahun 1999 Tentang Pemerintahan Daerah, Pasal 11.
12. See, for example, Anton Lucas (1999), Douglas Kammen (2003) and Anton Lucas and Carol Warren (2003).

4

Can Public Deliberation Democratise State Action?: Municipal Health Councils and Local Democracy in Brazil

Günther Schönleitner

Within the debate about decentralisation, democratisation, and the role of civil society in bringing about effective democratic government, participation has been widely advocated as a way of making governments more accountable and public services more responsive to user needs and preferences. Moreover, in recent years public deliberation has been proposed as an instrument of strengthening democracy. Calls for such arrangements are largely based on normative arguments or assumptions. Local governments would be willing, or can be compelled, to share a part of their power with civil society actors; these are assumed to be separate and autonomous from the state, yet engaged in public affairs and willing and capable of exerting 'social control' over state action. Deliberative arrangements are supposed to allow for decision-making by force of the better argument rather than power politics, providing appropriate channels for deepening or consolidating democracy from the bottom up. However, there is limited empirical evidence on the determinants and outcomes of deliberative participation. Therefore I turn these assumptions into questions.

First, why would governments give up power and what if they do not? Under what political conditions can we expect deliberative partici- pation to enable civil society to influence public decision-making and effectively control state action? Secondly, does deliberative participation require civic virtues or a 'Tocquevillean' civil society, and what if these are weakly developed? Thirdly, what institutional formats are required for effective deliberation, how are these likely to come about, and under what conditions can they contribute to consolidating democracy? I examine these questions in the context of Brazil, a highly decentralised country but not yet fully consolidated democracy, that has enshrined participation in the 1988 Constitution and incorporated participatory arrangements into the formal structure of the state. Although Participatory Budgeting (PB) has attracted most international attention, it is deliberative sector councils that have proliferated all over the country since 1990. These councils are functional bodies of joint decision-making of local government and civil society in a range of policy areas. In 1999 there were 27,000 municipal councils, that is on average almost five per municipality;[1] over 4000 of them were municipal health councils (Avritzer 2000: 71).

The chapter is based on a comparative study of four cases that were selected by crossing two variables: the political commitment of local governments to participation, and the 'civicness'[2] of the local community. I chose two middle-sized towns in Northeast Brazil (Camaragibe, Camaçari), and two in the southern state of Rio Grande do Sul. The latter are Italian (Caxias) and German (Santa Cruz) immigrant communities with high levels of associational activity, while both north-eastern cases show relatively low levels of civic organising.[3] In both regions I selected one municipality run by the leftist Workers' Party (PT) and another governed by centre-right parties. Popular participation has long been a hallmark of PT that has used it as a tool to disrupt entrenched patron–client schemes, while clientelism has been a longstanding political practice among traditional rightist parties.[4] I focused on the health sector because this is where decentralisation coupled with civil society participation was first implemented. Thus the outcomes are already more clearly visible.

The chapter is divided into six sections. The first part discusses the theoretical argument that 'deliberative public spaces' provide a missing institutional link for bottom-up democratisation. It questions the assumption that civil society is an inherently pro-democratic force and points to the highly demanding conditions needed for deliberative decision-making. Section two examines the extent to which institutional designs helped redress the inequalities that hamper effective deliberation. It shows that local formats varied according to the distribution of bargaining power; hence local designs could not offset inequalities that derived from these very patterns. The third section develops a framework for analysing the participatory performance of the councils on a continuum between 'hegemony' and 'deliberation'. It identifies government commitment and the patterns of political inclusion as the key determinants; in the fourth part this framework is applied to and confirmed by our four cases. The fifth section examines the local 'public spheres' and their interaction with the polity. It challenges the neo-Tocquevillean view arguing that political agency, state action, and ideologies were important for whether or not the 'public sphere' became an effective democratic force. The final part outlines how the interaction between informal clientelism and formal representative and deliberative institutions may affect the prospects of democratic consolidation. It argues that deliberative democracy presupposes the functioning of representative democracy; it is therefore an outcome rather than a catalyst of democratic consolidation.

Deliberative public spaces: the missing link for democratic consolidation?

Recently attempts have been made to ground deliberative participation into democratisation theory. Avritzer (2002) conceives of such arrangements as 'deliberative public spaces' that link 'the public' (civil society) and political society; they constitute bridges between a societal sphere of cultural innovation and a polity populated by traditional political actors with ambiguous stances toward democracy and continued undemocratic practices. Public spaces are supposed to transfer new democratic practices from the societal level to political society, thus consolidating democracy. Avritzer builds his essentially normative approach on a critique of both democratic elitism and transition theory that fail, he argues, to explain the functioning and breakdown of democracy in Latin America. The elite-masses dichotomy of the former leaves rational decision-making to elites while limiting the role of the masses to choosing between competing elites. Transition theory does allow for the possibility of undemocratic elites and pro-democratic mobilisation and collective action, but limits the role of mobilised masses to negotiating with elites whose practices are still seen as the key to democratisation. Moreover, Avritzer argues, transition theory neglects the obstacles to democratisation posed by Latin America's hierarchical and particularistic political culture. The 'hybridisation' between emulated modern institutions and traditional informal institutions (e.g. clientelism) makes it impossible to dissociate politics from particularism. The tension between autonomy and dependency, universality and exceptionalism, equality and privilege has strong anti-democratic consequences that cannot be dealt with by electoral competition and representation alone.

Building on Habermas' concept of the 'public sphere' as an 'intermediary structure between the political system...and the private sectors of the lifeworld and functional systems' (1996: 373) Avritzer seeks a third path between democratic elitism and participatory democracy. Yet Habermas does not provide a framework for public deliberation outside liberal democratic institutions. Avritzer criticises this failure 'to connect reason and will formation' and attempts to link both by advocating *institution-alised* forums of face-to-face deliberation where contentious issues can be politically addressed and alternative practices brought from the societal to the political level. These forums and the administration need to be linked through mechanisms of *accountability*, preserving the space for administrative complexity, but challenging the exclusive access of experts to decision-making (2002: 49–50). The underlying assumption is that there is a fundamental difference in political attitudes and practices between civil society and political society, the former being seen as the source of democratic renewal and the latter as the source of authoritarianism and clientelistic domination. Avritzer underestimates the likelihood of congruent values and practices in society and polity.

As Putnam argues, 'elite and mass attitudes are in fact two sides of a single coin, bound together in a mutually reinforcing equilibrium.... It would be surprising if elite and mass attitudes were not congruent. A situation of authoritarian elites and assertive masses cannot be a stable equilibrium' (1993: 104). Avritzer agrees with Putnam that incongruent attitudes are a source of instability and tension that 'may endanger democracy itself' (2002: 6). Therefore he advocates deliberative spaces to transform elite practices. Putnam's assumption of congruent attitudes leads to the determinism of path-dependent vicious or virtuous equilibria, and the inability to explain how these came into being (Boix and Posner 1998: 687). Avritzer's assumption of incongruent attitudes requires the postulate that elite and mass attitudes remain unaffected by existing channels of interaction, preventing their eventual convergence into a stable equilibrium. Both positions are problematic.

Avritzer actually maintains the elite–masses dichotomy but inverts their roles in the democratisation process. Not elites competing for the masses' votes promote democracy but civil society bringing innovative democratic practices to an ambiguous political society. This requires 'deliberative public spaces' as transmission belts between society and the polity beyond electoral competition. However, as Dryzek points out, in using the idea of the public sphere as a normative concept, one has to be careful to apply critical standards rather than simply assuming that it is praiseworthy (2000: 23). Avritzer recognises that elites *and* masses have an instrumental relation to democracy, but he is probably too optimistic about the societal end of political culture. Bottom-up democratisation via deliberative public spaces may not materialise due to congruent attitudes and practices. It is also conceivable that pressures for democratic renewal flow in the opposite direction. Political society (e.g. committed governments) rather than the public sphere may act as the driving force in attempts at changing the prevailing political practices. Avritzer advocates *institutionalised* public spaces without explaining how such institutions would come about. Who are the 'democratic engineers' and why and how do they shape deliberative institutions? Finally, even if there are incongruent attitudes in the sense of a democratic public sphere and authoritarian elites, the mechanism of public deliberation may not deliver the hoped-for transformations.

Deliberation is a discursive process in which free and equal participants arrive at collective choices through public reasoning, argumentation, and persuasion. For liberal democrats democracy is about aggregating given, unchangeable preferences prior to the political process, while deliberative democrats believe in the transformation of preferences through political interaction. Arrow's (1963) impossibility theorem has shown the arbitrariness and instability of voting mechanisms. Thus liberal democrats call for 'minimal democracy' limited to the selection of rulers rather than policies, while deliberative democrats advocate non-voting mechanisms of democratic will-formation aimed at consensus. Yet deliberation too is subject to the social choice critique. Processes of argumentation and reflection are prone to strategic calculations, deception and manipulation; and deliberative arrangements rely also on voting if consensus is unattainable. Dryzek (2000: 49) replaces consensus with the more realistic aim of 'reasoned agreement', but this too opens the door to bargaining, strategy, and manipulation.

Partly these problems may be overcome by appropriate institutional design. The dilemma is that 'one must postulate either a benign *deus ex machina* to design the institution in question, or have the process of choice about structure subject to all the instability and arbitrariness that social choice theory has identified'. Moreover, 'it is not clear what normative criteria institutional design should be trying to achieve' (Dryzek 2000: 44). Restrictions of preferences and options may provide another shield against Arrowian problems. Some theorists argue that deliberation itself 'eliminates preference orderings which cannot be [publicly] defended' (Dryzek 2000: 43). As actors need to argue in terms of public interest, they become subject to the 'civilising force of hypocrisy' (Elster 1998: 12) or genuinely acquire 'public spirit' (Dryzek 2000: 47). Other authors advocate exogenous restrictions. According to Gutmann and Thompson (1996) participants must subscribe in advance to the principles of reciprocity, publicity and accountability, as well as to values and norms such as mutual respect, cooperation, 'civic integrity', and 'civic magnanimity' (acknowledging the moral status of opposed positions). An established need for exogenous restrictions implies that the viability of public deliberation depends on the presence of these values and norms in the respective polity or, at least, among the deliberative public. Even if deliberation does create these virtues where they do not exist *ex-ante*, some sort of political agency would have to establish deliberative institutions and to persuade actors to participate in the first place.

The biggest threat to effective deliberation is inequality. Wright and Fung argue that deliberative arrangements may in various ways be subverted into domination from inside: (1) Participants may generally represent better-off citizens or dominant groups. (2) Even with balanced representation, the better off may use superior resources, information, rhetoric etc. to advance collective decisions that unreasonably favour them. (3) Powerful participants may seek to exclude issues that threaten their interests. (4) If deliberative arrangements seriously challenge the power and privileges of dominant elites, they may be dismantled (1999: 18f) or otherwise disempowered. Thus deliberative arrangements need to meet standards of *procedural* equality, like equal access to agenda setting and decision-making, equal treatment in a fair 'contest of reason' etc., and *substantive* inequality. The latter implies 'equal opportunity of political influence', which entails a passive aspect, namely free and uncoerced participation in decision-making, and an active dimension of 'equal opportunity to influence others' (Knight and Johnson 1997: 292ff). Bohman (1997) suggests 'the social capacity to initiate public deliberation' about one's concerns as the 'floor' of deliberative equality, and the ability of powerful actors to abandon, or remove issues from, deliberation as its 'ceiling'.

Brazil's policy councils combine elements of deliberation *and* representation. This adds another dimension to the problem of inequality. The councils are a version of what Cohen (1997) calls 'associative democracy', a form of governance in which secondary associations assume a joint regulatory role for solving functionally specific problems. This demands the representation of all stakeholder interests and the integration of marginalised groups into policy-making. As the poorest are likely to be less well-organised or unorganised they may remain excluded from deliberation among collectively organised interests. In such cases Cohen calls for 'public powers' to encourage the 'organised representation of presently excluded interests' (1997: 426). Yet this presupposes the political commitment of those who command 'public power' to integrating those excluded. Moreover, Gutmann and Thompson warn against 'balkanising' citizens into many distinct groups, and the parochialism that may result (1996: 154).

Deliberation requires representatives to justify their actions not only to their constituency but also to the rest of the deliberative assembly and the general public. This tension is difficult to solve. Gutmann and Thompson stress that 'in a deliberative forum each is accountable to all. Citizens and officials try to justify their decisions to all those who are bound by them and some of those who are affected by them' (1996: 128). Deliberation widens the scope of accountability to a broader 'moral constituency' (Gutman and Thompson 1996: 144), transcending geographical boundaries, classes and interest groups. If representatives are accountable only to their own group they leave others (perhaps the majority) without representation, limit their legitimacy as collective decision-makers, and may undermine deliberation itself. If they are accountable to the wider public, constituencies may resent the 'inattention' of their representatives to their specific needs and interests.

Finally, the extent to which the inclusion of disadvantaged groups into deliberative arenas has a democratising impact on the public sphere or the polity remains unclear. Arguably, it can have adverse effects. Deliberation may absorb the time and resources of civil society leaders away from other activities such as mobilisation, protesting, campaigning etc. It also may neutralise the comparative political advantage of the poor (their numbers) while exposing them to deliberative inequality. Gutmann and Thompson believe that 'to the extent that the political struggle takes place on the basis of deliberation rather than of power, it is more evenly matched. . . . Moral appeals are the weapons of the weak – not the only weapon, to be sure, but one that by its nature gives them an advantage over the powerful' (1996: 133). They seem to assume that deliberation and moral appeals can neutralise adverse power dynamics.

In sum, public deliberation is likely to be caught in several dilemmas that are difficult to solve. How can the need for consensus be relaxed without opening the door for strategy and manipulation? How can the need for deliberative equality be reconciled with economic and political inequality in society, or how can the latter's effects be neutralised without making the deliberative forum politically irrelevant? How can group representation become compatible with deliberative accountability? How can we bring about 'associative democracy' without risking 'balkanisation'? Is the inclusion of civil society through state-sponsored public deliberation at all conducive to democracy? And how can democratising institutional designs arise in semi-democratic or authoritarian polities?

Deliberative inequality and institutional design

Deliberative democracy requires institutional designs that redress deliberative inequalities. To what extent has the institutional framework of the CMS delivered such corrections? Brazil's health councils are an essential component of the Unified Health System (SUS) that has decentralised and unified public health care. The councils were designed by federal legislation as permanent and deliberative collegiate organs with representations of the respective government, service providers, health professionals, and users. Their competency is to 'act in the formulation of strategies and the control of the implementation of health policies at the corresponding instance, including in economic and financial aspects' (Brazil 2000: 42). The users were granted 'parity' in relation to all other sectors, i.e. at least 50 percent of the seats. Federal resource transfers became contingent upon the council's existence (among other requirements), which largely accounts for the dramatic proliferation of the councils after 1990.

The federal legislation has delegated the councils' organisation and norms of functioning to statutes to be approved by the councils themselves. Carvalho celebrates this as an 'advance in the autonomy of the councils' (1995: 62). Yet, this delegation is extremely problematic, for the same reason why *electoral* institutions are normally designed at the constitutional rather than local level. It is hardly desirable to have the rules of democratic will formation subjected to 'institutional competition' across jurisdictions, according to local power dynamics. If the CMS are to be instances of democratic control it is problematic that the primary targets of their control function, local governments, can exert considerable influence in shaping the rules that govern the very mechanisms supposed to control them. These rules include the composition, selection procedures, chair, specific competencies, internal procedures, etc. Thus institutional design is both an independent and a dependent variable for participatory performance. It is independent (from a *local* perspective) because the *federal* legislation has established certain principles that cannot be changed by local factors, and created incentives and sanctions to which local actors need to adapt. *Local* designs are both independent and dependent variables. They are independent because they determine key aspects of deliberative equality such as access and agenda setting etc. that shape the outcomes of deliberation. However, local designs are also dependent variables because their corrective capacity is shaped by the interactions of local actors that are subject to the same inequalities that affect deliberation and which institutional design is supposed to redress.

The case selection has given us four distinct patterns of bargaining over institutional design and significant variations in the resulting rules. In *Camaçari* (low civicness, low political commitment) local governments dominated the institutionalisation of the CMS. Although crucial steps of rule setting occurred under leftist or centre-left governments, there are no records of strong and sustained pressure from civil society aimed at shaping the rules. Both these governments sought not only to mobilise but also to control and co-opt civil society; the subsequent rightist administrations continued this tradition. On the CMS, government dominance and weak bottom-up pressure produced the least equalising design of the selection. The Statute allowed the health secretary to chair the CMS, to appoint its executive secretary, and to control agenda setting. The councillors were nominated by organisations whose representation was rigidly defined in the Statute, which maintained an essentially arbitrary composition that favoured a government majority. The 'user bench' included a representative of the legislature and two business associations allied to the government. Moreover, the government's unrestrained use of leverage over other actors (based on bureaucratic authority, jobs, contracts, provision and withdrawal of favours etc.) harmed deliberative equality.

In *Camaragibe* (low civicness, high political commitment) leftist governments have promoted political transformation from above. The now incumbent mayor (PT) built on a small 'cell' of more civic-minded civil society leaders, initiated a process of civic education, and largely 'engineered' new participatory formats for state–society relations. The institutionalisation of the CMS was the first step in this political project, which was reflected in its relatively equalising design. Local legislation defined the composition in terms of segments among which the non-governmental councillors were to be elected in joint assemblies of all interested organisations. Each user organisation could have either a councillor or a deputy but not both, so as to maximise the number of represented organisations. Neither the delegates to electoral assemblies nor the councillors they elected were allowed to have 'bonds' (especially of employment) to the town hall or the legislature. The council's chair came to be elected in rotation between the four segments. The council appointed its executive secretary, and government control over agenda setting was reduced.

In *Caxias* (high civicness, high political commitment) significant mobilisation and pressure from the 'popular movement' influenced the institutionalisation and design of the CMS in 1992, but caused confrontation and stalemate within it until 1996. Political transformation from the 'bottom-up' brought a committed government to power in 1997, which allowed the CMS to shift from confrontation to participation. A host of new participatory institutions surrounded and consolidated a CMS with a relatively equalising design. The union and neighbourhood movements largely occupied the user bench. The unionists were elected by joint assemblies of their segment, and the neighbourhood representatives in assemblies of all associations in a health district. The same rules of selection applied to all the segments represented on the CMS that comprised more than one organisation. The chair was to be elected from among the users or the professionals. This institutional framework equalised the 'opportunities of political influence' between the 'popular movement' and previously dominant groups like doctors and private providers.

In *Santa Cruz* (high civicness, low political commitment) the institutionalisation of the CMS was associated with intense political bargaining between the union movement and reluctant local governments. The CUT[5] unionists put through the election of the non-governmental councillors and forced the executive to share power when a new inexperienced government came into office. They forged a cohesive user alliance with the support of the local university and established a majority through a mix of articulation, mobilisation and transgression of prevailing rules. The unionists seized control over the selection process and eliminated the business associations from representation on the user bench. In 1997 they achieved that the chair was to be elected by the councillors, which democratised control over the agenda. However, the unionists also created inequalities within the user camp through their ability to threaten 'dissidents' with exclusion. This clearly violated 'freedom from coercion' – a core requirement of deliberative equality. Yet, it was exactly the formation of a cohesive 'bloc' that enabled the users to develop, pass, and implement their own occupational health programme, and thus to surpass Bohman's 'floor' of deliberative equality.

In all cases some 'exogenous restrictions' on preferences were introduced. In PT-run towns these filters favoured the participation of poorer user segments while excluding business associations, employer unions etc. As Knight and Johnson argue, in order to foster substantive equality it may be necessary to generate procedural inequalities such as the acceptance of unequal (preferential) treatment when disadvantaged groups are incorporated into deliberative arrangements (1997: 304). The election of councillors ensured that this did not simply give preferential access to political allies of the government. In Camaragibe these filters also banned party politics from the CMS. In the cases with low government commitment institutional or *de facto* restrictions tended to focus on representatives' 'alignment' with the political project of those capable of imposing access filters. This may also have given preferential access to representative user organisations, as in Santa Cruz, but the objective was the construction or maintenance of majorities. This implied a loss in individual autonomy due to ideological attachment and the use of leverage in contradiction with 'passive' substantive equality.

The need for collective action is an indicator of deliberative inequality (Bohman 1997). It may be a necessary reaction to the use of power rather than reasoning within a deliberative forum. But collective action also causes inequality as long as it relies on building majorities in order to overcome political obstacles to deliberation posed by powerful participants. The relation between majority and minority is one of inequality. Individual preferences are constrained by group loyalties, compromise, and often hierarchies needed to defeat their opponents. Thus collective action is about aggregation rather than deliberation; it implies a search for majorities rather than the best argument, in which strategy and manipulation abound. Thus, if the most powerful actors on the CMS, local governments, are not committed to power sharing and deliberation, the council necessarily shifts to an aggregative, hegemonic logic. This was the case in Camaçari and Santa Cruz, but also in Caxias before 1997.

Deliberation requires that governments act like equals among equals. This is not easy even in cases with committed governments. Deliberative processes shift power to those with better argumentative skills, regardless of their representativity. Institutional formats have responded in various ways to the problem of unequal resources and capabilities, but none of them could actually establish reasonable equality in the capacity to propose. This kind of inequality cannot be simply solved by institutional design. Hence, in all four cases there have been strong calls for training schemes. Yet, there are clear limits to such efforts, not least because there is a relatively rapid turnover of councillors. Moreover, training schemes can hardly compensate for weak or lacking primary or secondary education of exactly those most representative of poorer user segments. The need for specialist training could 'self-select' to the council people who are more educated but less representative, which highlights the trade-off between equality of capabilities and representativity.

Does deliberative equality require the councils to become forums of people with comparable specialist knowledge, or can different forms of knowledge be brought together in a complementary, co-operative way? Pellizzoni concludes that 'the effects of differences among forms of knowledge cannot be overcome...by sitting experts and laymen around a table and instructing the former to justify their actions. Persuading non-experts is not the issue, nor is turning them into experts.... Understanding depends on the construction of mutual recognition which, by means of joint management of problems, redefines the division of epistemic work, the connection among competencies – with respect to these problems and not in abstract' (2001: 82). Shifting from the 'myth of the best argument' to a focus on 'mutual recognition' and social co-operation may avoid the 'elitist' path of expert committees. But such an approach reinforces the need for both political conditions and civic capabilities favourable to cooperation based on a plurality of reason.

Public space between hegemony and deliberation

The councils may operate as spaces for the argumentative definition of collective preferences; as arenas of struggle for the power to enforce aggregated preferences; or they may combine both to varying degrees. Therefore, in practice the councils move along a continuum between two paradigms:hegemony and deliberation. I have discussed deliberation above. But how can we conceive of hegemony? Gramsci most frequently uses the concept 'to denote a form of social and political 'control' which combines physical force or *coercion* with intellectual, moral and cultural persuasion or *consent*' (Ransome 1992: 135). Hegemony has a dual character. It implies 'domination' in relation to antagonistic groups, and 'intellectual and moral leadership' exercised over a 'cohesive and purposeful alliance...of social groups and their aspirations'. A hegemonic 'bloc' needs to transcend 'the particular self-interests of its component parts' (Ransome 1992: 136). Both coercion and persuasion can be used not only towards opposed groups but also to establish and maintain cohesion *within* hegemonic groups.

Power is the key factor determining a council's position on the continuum. If powerful actors do not renounce their power over others as a means for shaping collective decision-making, deliberation can hardly be sustained. Both the force of the better argument and the possibility of reasoned agreement succumb to the logic of power and imposition. 'Self-reproducing practices and strategies'[6] by the powerful are likely to trigger responses of resistance and collective action with the rest of the participatory forum threatened by exclusion from influence over decision-making. Antagonistic groups are likely to resort to aggregation and majority building rather than public reasoning, engaging in strategic rather than communicative action. The exercise of power is, of course, determined to a great extent by underlying social cleavages and inequalities. A move towards hegemony is likely to indicate that deliberative inequality within the council has surpassed Bohman's 'ceiling' and 'the process of communicative action must be substantially shaped by struggles between asymmetrically advantaged groups' (Stewart 2001: 46). Thus, in the hegemonic paradigm, participation on the councils is characterised by instrumental action and strategies by groups that aim at maximising their own influence upon decision-making while minimising that of opponent groups.

Is deliberation only possible in a utopian power-free space? Let us clarify what we understand by power. Commonly the concept is used to describe situations in which social actors (power holders) are able to induce or force others to act, or prevent them from acting, in ways that advance the formers' interests. These are conceptions in terms of 'power over' or domination, with an essentially instrumental character. Hannah Arendt contrasts this with 'social power' or 'power to' that resides in 'the human ability not just to act but to act in concert' (in Lukes 1974: 3). She conceives of power in terms of concerted and communicative action. For Habermas 'the communicatively produced power of common convictions originates in the fact that those involved are oriented towards reaching agreement and not primarily to their respective individual successes' (in Stewart 2001: 39). Thus Stewart distinguishes power as domination, referring to 'reproduced asymmetric social relations', and power as concerted agency, understood as 'expressive of communicative interaction' (2001: 50).

Applied to our continuum we expect *domination* to push the councils towards the hegemonic, and *concerted agency* towards the deliberative, paradigm. What distinguishes concerted agency from aggregative collective action and strategy is that the former is aimed at producing common convictions or agreements, while the latter seeks to accumulate 'power over' in order to establish hegemony or counter-hegemony. Concerted agency 'can only occur on the basis of some intersubjective framework which specifies the relevant experience(s) as typical of an entire group' (Stewart 2001: 54). Thus, deliberation tends to occur *within* such groups that, in their external interactions, may engage in struggles for, or resistance of, the exercise of 'power over'. 'Hegemonic' councils are likely to be internally polarised and deliberation may occur within opposed subgroups. 'Deliberative' councils tend to be de-polarised and deliberation is more likely to take place at council level. Polarisation refers to the council's division into two or more antagonistic subgroups. This typically results from power struggles over competing interests, and the agents of polarisation are likely to be political actors.

'Hegemonic' and 'deliberative' councils tend to differ in the patterns of politicisation, that is, the ways in which actors define issues and interests in political terms, and how they try to mobilise political support to pursue them (see Törnquist 2002a). Politicisation has three dimensions: (1) the issues and interests brought to the political arena, (2) the actors putting them on the agenda, and (3) the ways in which these actors are politically included into the participatory forum. 'Single issues and/or specific interests' are likely to be linked to autonomous associations, networks, cause-oriented movements, or pressure groups (Törnquist 2002a: 15). This pattern tends to predominate with 'deliberation'. On the other hand, 'ideologies and/or collective interests' tend to be pursued by 'parties based on societal conflict', 'large sector-based unionism', and/or state actors. This pattern is more likely to be associated with 'hegemony'. The key characteristic of the latter category of actors is that they command or compete for state power, or advance projects and agendas for the polity as a whole. I refer to them as 'political society'[7] to be contrasted with 'civil society'.

The third dimension of politicisation is the way in which actors are included into political participation, and how they relate to each other in political arenas like the CMS. Drawing on Mouzelis (1986) I distinguish 'integration' and 'elitist incorporation'. Integration means political inclusion based on relatively autonomous movements, networks, and associations capable of acting spontaneously and in collective or concerted ways. Elitist incorporation refers to political elites actively encouraging the inclusion of less well-organised popular organisations and/or individuals into participatory forums. If we apply this dichotomy to our continuum, we get four cells with distinctive patterns of political inclusion and participation. With *hegemony cum integration* we probably see well-organised collective actors bound together by political ideologies and structures of organisation and integration under the leadership of parties or unions, i.e. political society. With *hegemony cum elitist incorporation* we expect state actors to dominate and control the inclusion of non-state actors by means of clientelism and other forms of 'power over'. Again, political society is in the driving seat. With *deliberation cum integration* we probably find deliberative forums populated by well-organised collective actors that act autonomously though capable of spontaneous concerted action. Party politics and ideologies are likely to recede into the background. With *deliberation cum elitist incorporation* we expect the state to actively encourage the inclusion of relatively weak popular organisations as part of a project of civic education and emancipation. Party politics and ideology tend to recede and the government grants relative autonomy to civil society actors.

The role of 'political society' can vary dramatically. While party allegiance and ideologies are vital for galvanising group identities in times of hegemonic struggles, they tend to become obstacles when councils shift from political to technical debate, and discuss health policy rather than the politics of health. Yet, 'deliberative' councils need not be apolitical. The criterion is to what extent they are geared towards discussing competing health care models (which *are* essentially political) in programmatic terms, or serve primarily as stages for party-political tactics and confrontation (often at the expense of public health concerns). Thus, in the deliberative paradigm, we expect political society to play a less salient role on the CMS, and its relationships to other participants will tend to move towards autonomy and emancipation. The four case studies fit surprisingly well into the cells described above. In towns with uncommitted governments the CMS tended to operate in the hegemonic paradigm: the uncivic/uncommitted case (Camaçari) under government hegemony cum elite incorporation, the civic/uncommitted case (Santa Cruz) under a user-led hegemony cum integration. The PT-governed cases showed no clear hegemonic patterns and tended towards deliberation, but differed in terms of bottom-up integration (Caxias) vs. top-down emancipatory incorporation (Camaragibe). Table 4.1 shows the positions of the cases in the four cells.

It is difficult to 'measure' the exact position of a council on the hegemony-deliberation continuum. But we see fundamentally different patterns if we look at the councillors' perceptions, in 2001–02, of the autonomy of the CMS *vis-à-vis* the local government, and the council's influence upon the formulation of health policy. Table 4.2 shows that both the councillors of the 'deliberative' case (Caxias, Camaragibe) and those in Santa Cruz (user-led hegemony) strongly *disagreed* with the view that the CMS had little autonomy, while a majority in Camaçari *agreed* with this statement. If we look at the user segment alone, nine of ten user representatives in Camaçari agreed that the CMS had little autonomy. In Caxias and Santa Cruz the perception of the users was

Table 4.1 CMS by pattern of political inclusion and tendency on the hegemony-deliberation continuum

	Hegemony	Deliberation
Integration	Santa Cruz	Caxias
	Civic/uncommitted government	Civic/committed government
	User-led hegemony based on consent and threats	Relative autonomy, concerted agency
Elite incorporation	Camaçari	Camaragibe
	Uncivic/uncommitted government	Uncivic/committed government
	Government hegemony based on leverage and coercion	State-granted autonomy and emancipation

Table 4.2 Councillors' perception of CMS autonomy

Municipality		The CMS has little autonomy, it mostly does what the executive wants			Total
		Agree	Disagree	Don't know	
Camaçari	Count	10	9		19
	%	52.6	47.4		100.0
Caxias	Count	10	19	2	31
	%	32.3	61.3	6.5	100.0
Santa Cruz	Count	4	18		22
	%	18.2	81.8		100.0
Camaragibe	Count	3	15	3	21
	%	14.3	71.4	14.3	100.0
Total	Count	27	61	5	93
	%	29.0	65.6	5.4	100.0

almost identical with that of the whole council, while in Camaragibe a slightly smaller share of users (62.5 per cent) disagreed with the statement that the CMS had little autonomy. Table 4.3 shows a similar pattern. The councillors indicated the strongest influence in Camaragibe, followed by Santa Cruz and Caxias, and the lowest in Camaçari. The users alone had a strongly more negative view in Camaçari, while their colleagues in the other towns hold similar or slightly more positive views than the councils as a whole.

Table 4.3 Councillors' perception of CMS influence on municipal health policy

Municipality		\multicolumn{5}{c}{To what extent has the CMS influenced the current municipal health policy?}
		Entirely	Significantly	A little	Not at all	Total
Camaçari	Count	1	8	8	2	19
	%	5.3	42.1	42.1	10.5	100.0
Caxias	Count	6	14	10	1	31
	%	19.4	45.2	32.3	3.2	100.0
Santa Cruz	Count	2	17	3	1	23
	%	8.7	73.9	13.0	4.3	100.0
Camaragibe	Count	10	11	1		22
	%	45.5	50.0	4.5		100.0
Total	Count	19	50	22	4	95
	%	20.0	52.6	23.2	4.2	100.0

The politics of participatory governance

To what extent and how have political factors such as government commitment, the exercise of power and different forms of politicisation shaped the participatory process in the tension between hegemony and deliberation? In *Camaçari* a relatively authoritarian government was reluctant to engage in power sharing and deliberation. It exploited existing inequalities and exercised power over other participants in order to maintain control over decision-making. Polarisation and power struggles between the government/provider group and a part of the user representatives led to the aggregation rather than transformation of preferences, majority imposition rather than persuasion, and strategic rather than communicative action. These strategies involved manipulating access and composition, bypassing the council, exerting leverage, strategic use of information, imposing rules, etc. Political society (state actors) rather than civil society dominated the council, aimed at minimising the influence of opponent groups whose ability to initiate deliberation on issues of their concern was limited indeed. The 'opposition' felt relatively powerless. It was unable to forge a cohesive counter-hegemonic bloc because of horizontal distrust caused by several users' vertical bonds to government and politicians, and the local CUT's failure to exert the required leadership.

In *Santa Cruz* participation on the CMS was historically characterised by the hegemony of local governments seeking to exclude politically opposed user organisations such as the unions of CUT. These unions embarked on constructing a counter-hegemonic alliance, which eventually established its own hegemony based on both 'consent' and 'coercion' among and over the rest of the unionist camp and other user associations. Political society was the driving force: first the government, then the unionists with strong links to PT. Aggregation rather than deliberation was the dominant game; and polarisation between the user bloc and the government/ provider group led to intra-group deliberation within the hegemonic bloc rather than the whole council. The relationship between the antagonistic groups was based on strategic rather than communicative action. Yet, despite the users' majority, it was power sharing and negotiation rather than imposition that characterised their interaction with the government, which by its very nature was too powerful to be dominated by the user-led CMS.

In *Camaragibe* the government was committed to popular participation as the key to its strategy of political transformation from above that sought to include the poor and their organisations into the political process in ways that broke with clientelism. This 'emancipatory populism' mobilised 'the people' directly in order to bypass/disrupt the longstanding collusion between community leaders and clientelistic politicians. It incorporated citizens and leaders into participatory forums without co-opting them. The government sought to make participation credible through transparency, sharing responsibility, and negotiating rather than imposing. The council's move towards the deliberative paradigm was associated with depolarisation, the retreat of party politics, the salience of civil society rather than political society, but also a predominance of fragmented and parochial interests. In general, participation was based on communicative rather than strategic interaction, although neighbourhood representatives occasionally resorted to community mobilisation to push special interests. Decision-making tended to rely on negotiated agreements rather than consensus.

In *Caxias* the council's tendency shifted from hegemony to deliberation after PT came to power in 1997, committed to power sharing and deliberation. However, the establishment of autonomous concerted agency was difficult, due to a 'parent–child' relation between the government and the council, deriving from the previous counter-hegemonic alliance that bound together users, professionals and leftist activists now in government. The government did not attempt to dominate the council, and there was little or no polarisation, alliance building, or intra-group deliberation. Communicative rather than strategic interaction characterised the process of participation. Nevertheless, many councillors felt that their participation was formal and they did not effectively share in the joint formulation of policies. However, this 'paradox' had less to do with government reluctance than with a certain relaxation of user participation due to political loyalties to their allies in the government and relative satisfaction with the performance of health provision.

Camaçari and Santa Cruz show that the government's exercise of power as domination or concerted agency and the patterns of political inclusion were important factors for explaining government hegemony or user-led hegemony, respectively. Santa Cruz also showed that forced power sharing is not enough for a shift to deliberation. This requires real commitment to 'concerted agency'. Camaragibe and Caxias were both ruled by PT for which deliberative participation was a crucial part of its political strategy, but the civic context varied. In Camaragibe the political inclusion of civil society actors relied on incorporation through 'emancipatory populism', while in Caxias it was based on integration and bottom-up political transformation. Yet, neither of them fully reached the deliberative ideal due to 'balkanised' agendas or relaxed intensity of participation resulting from user satisfaction and/or political loyalty. Although decision-making was generally based on argumentative processes, disagreement was often solved either by negotiation or majority voting rather than consensus. In Camaragibe negotiated agreements did not prevent some civil society actors from resorting to grassroots mobilisation in pursuit of parochial interests.

The councils occupied a certain position on the continuum in their overall functioning, but to some degree they may move back and forth between hegemony and deliberation depending on the nature of the decisions, actors and interests. Even on an overall hegemonic council a move to deliberation is possible if an issue is politically little contentious, or the actors are less interested or less informed. On overall deliberative councils decision-making may shift to an aggregative, hegemonic logic if strongly contentious interests are at stake on which the actors have clear, relatively inflexible and articulated positions (although this may imply a high political price). Delegating issues to commissions may also narrow the scope of deliberation. These commissions can either become instruments of specialist authority in order to deal with complexity or forums of bargaining and negotiation to solve conflicts. As government commitment is crucial, the councils are clearly sensitive to political change. The overall tendency of the council changed only in Caxias. The CMS of Santa Cruz did not change its hegemonic tendency, but only the dominant alliance. The council of Camaragibe did not yet change its overall tendency, but if an uncommitted government should come to power it is likely to shift to government hegemony rather than civil society-led hegemony due to fragile horizontal ties and weak capability of alliance building.

The variations in the councillors' perception of the CMS's influence upon local health policy can largely be explained by the extent to which local governments were prepared, or could be forced, to share power. However, it was also shaped by the nature of actors' grievances and demands, the perceived gap between their needs and actual service provision, and the resulting intensity of participation. If user satisfaction is high, both demands and participation may weaken, and user influence may be lower than expected if we look at power sharing alone. In our cases the users perceived the council's influence to be strongest in Camaragibe, followed by Santa Cruz, and to a significantly lesser degree in Caxias. They indicated the weakest influence in Camaçari. This is in line with the patterns of power sharing, except in Caxias. Here the perception of relatively low influence reflected also relaxed participation resulting from high satisfaction with health services, and partly also from the political proximity between the government and many users and professionals.

Table 4.4 shows the satisfaction of both the user segment and all CMS councillors with health provision under 'full local management'; Table 4.5 shows their perceptions of who benefited most from munici-palised health care. Satisfaction was very high in Caxias, and a majority felt that the poor benefited most. The same is true for Santa Cruz, but there the users were engaged in a hegemonic struggle, which prevented them from relaxing their participation. In Camaragibe a majority was happy with access but most users were discontent with quality; a majority of users and councillors saw the local government as the big beneficiary. In Camaçari a slight majority of users perceived the results of 'full local management' to be negative or indifferent in terms of both access and quality, while most of them saw the local government, private providers, and individual politicians to benefit most from municipalisation.

The case studies have also confirmed that participation on councils with both hegemonic and deliberative tendency was constrained by inequality in technical capabilities and expertise. The councils were primarily forums of information exchange, demand making, and denouncing, rather than policy formulation. Civil society actors' control function was constrained by limited access to information and specialist knowledge. Their 'deliberative' influence[8] upon policy formulation was greatly reduced as they lacked the technical skills for being aware of available policy options and drafting their own proposals. Thus it was

Table 4.4   Councillors' satisfaction with health services under local management

How do you evaluate the results of the 'full local management' of health care concerning the access to an the quality of services?

		Camaçari		Camaragibe		Caxias		Santa Cruz	
		CMS	Users	CMS	Users	CMS	Users	CMS	Users
ACCESS	Positive	11	4	14	6	27	15	20	8
	%	61.1	44.4	66.7	75.0	90.0	100.0	87.0	80.0
	Negative	3	3					1	
	%	16.7	33.3					4.3	
	Indifferent	4	2	3	1	2			
	%	22.2	22.2	14.3	12.5	6.7			
	Don't know			4	1	1		2	2
	%			19.0	12.5	3.3		8.7	20.0
QUALITY	Positive	10	4	12	3	23	11	19	7
	%	58.8	44.4	57.1	37.5	85.2	84.6	95.0	100.0
	Negative	3	3	2	2	2	2		
	%	17.6	33.3	9.5	25.0	7.4	15.4		
	Indifferent	4	2	2	1	1		1	
	%	23.5	22.2	9.5	12.5	3.7		5.0	
	Don't know			5	2	1			
	%			23.8	25.0	3.7			

Source: author's questionnaire

frequently not the strength of their arguments that enhanced the councillors' influence, but the political clout they had, for instance, through a user-led hegemony in Santa Cruz or the government's political imperative of 'emancipatory populism' in Camaragibe.

The public sphere: source of democratic renewal?

Government commitment, patterns of political inclusion, and institutional design were important factors. But what accounts for them? How can we understand, for instance, the different ways in which user representatives in Camaçari and Santa Cruz responded to local government's reluctance to share power and engage in serious deliberation? Do the councils just reflect the prevailing dynamics of state–society relations? Let us look more closely at the characteristics of the 'public sphere' and its interaction with the polity. In examining local public spheres we have to answer three questions. What are the attitudes and practices of local civil societies with regard to the public domain? How

Table 4.5 Beneficiaries from the municipalisation of health according to councillors/users

| | Who benefited most from municipalisation? | | | | | | | |
| | Camaçari | | Camaragibe | | Caxias | | Santa Cruz | |
	CMS	Users	CMS	Users	CMS	Users	CMS	Users
Municipal government	14	9	16	5	13	4	13	7
%	73.0	90.0	72.7	55.6	41.9	25.0	61.9	77.8
State government	3	1	2		5	3	3	
%	15.8	10.0	9.1		16.1	18.8	14.3	
Federal government	1		6		6	4	2	
%	5.3		27.3		19.4	25.0	9.5	
Individual politicians	6	5	1	1	2			
%	31.6	50.0	4.5	11.1	6.5			
Public providers	3	1	5	2	5	5	2	
%	15.8	10.0	22.7	22.2	16.1	31.3	9.5	
Private providers	9	7	6	4	1	1	3	1
%	47.4	70.0	27.3	44.4	3.2	6.3	14.3	11.1
Health professionals	2	1	6	3	8	5	2	
%	10.5	10.0	27.3	33.3	25.8	31.3	9.5	
Particular user groups	5	1	8	4	12	4	4	1
%	26.3	10.0	36.4	44.4	38.7	25.0	19.0	11.1
The poor	7	1	10	4	17	9	16	8
%	36.8	10.0	45.5	44.4	54.8	56.3	76.2	88.9

Source: author's questionnaire. Multiple responses were possible

do these attitudes and practices translate into patterns of civic engagement and participation once deliberative public spaces are available? And how does political society shape civil society's attitudes and practices?

Although Putnam and Avritzer disagree on the likelihood of incongruent values and practices between elites and the masses, they do share a bottom-up approach expecting more democratic potential in more civic settings. For Putnam citizens in a civic community, 'though not selfless agents, regard the public domain as more than a battleground for pursuing personal interest' (1993: 88), and 'citizens..., like their leaders, have a pervasive distaste for hierarchical authority patterns' (Putnam 1993: 104). Civic communities demand more effective public services and act collectively to get them (Putnam 1993: 182). Avritzer expects democratic innovation to emerge more likely from the public sphere, although he recognises that some support is needed from sectors of political society. Such political actors are prepared to give up part of their power in favour of institutions that incorporate citizens and try to establish a new relationship between state and society (2002: 170). However, both Putnam and Avritzer fail to capture the role of political society in shaping the prospects for the public sphere to become an effective pro-democratic force. They also neglect the possibility, and sometimes the necessity, of top-down transformation of a public sphere still caught in clientelism.

The standard neo-Tocquevillean account of civil society-centred transformation stresses the importance of civic associations as a school of democratic values, tolerance, cooperation and civic engagement. Participation in associations is perceived as a check on, and counterweight to, state power. Membership even in non-political associations creates the skills necessary to engage in political participation, and this participation in turn brings about effective democratic governance. However, our four case studies suggest a somewhat differentiated pattern. First, there is *no automatic translation of vibrant community into civic engagement with the polity*, as the case of Santa Cruz attests. The German settler community is one of the world's largest centres of tobacco production based on contract farming arrangements integrating small growers and multinational processing industries. Its vibrant associational life was historically aimed at maintaining German cultural identity and substituting for lacking state services rather than transforming the polity. Vibrant community life has co-existed with 'hierarchical authority patterns' on the part of political society; and political engagement and participation have not matched the vibrancy of associational activity.

Until 1996 politics was effectively an elite affair and (even since then) the patterns of civic engagement have hardly followed the neo-Tocquevillean script. The local (German) elite, politically organised in PPB (the heir of the military regime's ARENA), ruled the town for 20 years before 1997. They embodied insulated elitist technocracy rather than participatory politics. Due to compulsory voting we are unable to use voter turnout for measuring political participation; but in terms of party membership Santa Cruz does not stand out. According to Schmidt *et al.* (2002),[9] only 7.7 per cent of the electorate are party members.[10] Most citizens 'distrust political agents, parties and institutions; have median interest in politics, prefer democracy to dictatorship, and exhibit relatively low levels of political information. They participate very little in activities of the municipal executive and legislature, and vote according to the personal qualities of candidates rather than those of their parties or ideologies' (Schmidt 2003: 50). Santa Cruz has not been a stronghold of clientelism but a rather self-reliant society with a 'do-it-yourself' approach to the public domain. Due to relative economic prosperity fewer people than elsewhere depend upon government favours. But the exchange of favours for votes has existed nonetheless; and the programmatic profiles of most parties in Santa Cruz have not differed much from those in less civic areas. In sum, we largely find Brazilian 'normality' despite outstanding levels of civic activism. 'Civic energies' were diverted away from the polity. The user hegemony on the CMS does not reflect a general pattern of an assertive, politically engaged civil society. Rather, it reflects the determination of a small group of unionists who learned to trust each other, built a cohesive alliance, and skilfully used political opportunities and legal loopholes in order to advance their project.

The second contradiction to the neo-Tocquevillean account is that *the nature and roles of emerging public spheres in uncivic settings depended crucially on the government's attitudes and policies towards civil society.* Both Camaragibe and Camaçari are uncivic communities embedded in traditional vertical bonds and hierarchical social structures. During the early 1980s leftist militants and Catholic Church activists helped organise these poor communities in neighbourhood associations, self-help groups, mothers' clubs, etc. Leftist unionists also managed to 'conquer' the labour unions in Camaçari hitherto considered *pelegos* (elite co-opted). These religious and political value suppliers sought to instil horizontal co-operation and solidarity in a social fabric thoroughly pervaded by clientelism. Partly as a result of these efforts, both municipalities elected leftist mayors in 1985 and 1988, respectively, but state-society relations would evolve in very different trajectories.

Camaçari has been Bahia's industrial powerhouse ever since a large petrochemical complex was created by the military regime in the 1970s. In 2001 Ford implemented a large assembly plant on its territory. Camaçari has high rates of poverty, yet it is rich in municipal tax revenues that it earns from the local industries. This has caused fierce local political competition in which two episodes of leftist government ended in disaster (exacerbated by a hostile state government that withheld constitutional transfers in order to punish a local government opposed to it). In 1986 Caetano, a leftist militant, was elected after he had helped organise about 100 neighbourhood, women's, and youth associations. What Caetano had built from the bottom-up he destroyed from the top-down: an autonomous civil society. Once in power he 'aligned' and instrumentalised a civil society that could never establish its autonomy. Today he admits that the 'popular movement' was 'already born with the philosophy of a dependent movement'. The following rightist administrations (interrupted by another hapless centre-left term) under Tude, a follower of Bahia's 'strongman' Antonio Carlos Magalhães, continued the politics of tutelage and alignment, transforming civil society into a political battleground. He undermined associations perceived as 'opposition' by actively encouraging 'aligned' rivals with easier access to public resources. Tude's government was a mixture of modern technocracy and patronage. Many associations were seen to 'belong' to certain city-councillors. Pervasive vertical bonds to clientelistic politicians fragmented civil society and hampered horizontal collective action. The choice between being friend of the powerful or facing the consequences left little room for autonomous participation. The performance of the CMS mirrored these patterns of state-society relations and state action, and the 'deliberative public spaces' could do little to transform them.

Camaragibe is a poor 'dormitory town' on the outskirts of Pernambuco's state capital Recife. It saw the rise of leftwing politicians resulting from a local power vacuum after the town's political independence from its neighbouring municipality in 1982. These politicians embarked on a gradual process of leadership-driven political transformation. After Mayor Santana (PT) came to power in 1996 he introduced several councils and a version of PB enabling citizens and communities to achieve improvements through collective action and mobilisation rather than particularistic ties to politicians. This undermined clientelistic city-councillors and traditional community leaders 'addicted' to favours and privileges. The executive encouraged new leaders by having the people elect delegates for PB. Clientelism came under considerable pressure, but the process suffered several setbacks due to weak and fragmented horizontal ties. The administration had to change the rules repeatedly to avoid the subversion of deliberative forums by particularistic interests. PB contributed to the demise of the neighbourhood federation and failed to bring about a 'reinvention' of civil society. Many new leaders were prone to the same old practices; clientelistic allegiances continued, and many citizens tended to focus on particularistic and parochial concerns. People still look up and down social hierarchies rather than to their fellow citizens for solving problems. The difference is that they now see a government that encourages collective rather than particularistic solutions, and creates institutional channels for it. Continued committed leadership is crucial for a long-term process of civic education. The CMS has not yet suffered a serious backlash due to councillors who are strongly committed to participation and citizenship. But with the possible election of an uncommitted government the normative consensus on deliberation could break down.

Thirdly, the case of Caxias shows that *bottom-up political transformation through democratic public spheres is possible. But this is likely to require a vibrant civil society intermeshed with and politicised by progressive parts of political society. The transmission belt between society and the polity is then the electoral mechanism rather than deliberative public spaces*, which can only function reasonably well once a committed government has come to power. The functioning of electoral competition as a means of democratic transformation has to precede the full operationalisation of deliberative spaces, which makes them an unlikely tool of democratisation. What distinguishes Santa Cruz and Caxias is that in the latter case leftist activists managed to penetrate grassroots associations connecting them to party politics. The unifying appeal of their ideology helped create an effective electoral alliance between the working and lower middle classes, and the balance of power began to shift. This did not happen in Santa Cruz probably because it is a municipality whose 'backbone' is still the rural economy. A different class structure meant that the conservatism of rural communities weighed more strongly in local politics. Leftist activism in Santa Cruz started only in the 1980s. But even there some electoral-political transformation had to take place (the defeat of the power elite around PPB and the election of a 'populist' mayor in 1996) before the union coalition could strengthen its grip on the CMS forcing the government to share power.

Caxias is a prosperous centre of Italian immigration. It started as a settler society based on small farming, but quickly evolved into a regional industrial centre. The (Italian) elite has had vested local interests and was long divided between UDC (a rightist coalition) and PMDB (the 'official' opposition to the military's ARENA). Civil society was historically organised around the church, also with the purpose of maintaining cultural identity, and promoting co-operation and sociability. Yet, the drive to political engagement and interest representation emerged earlier and more strongly than in Santa Cruz. Communist activists started to organise the neighbourhood associations in the 1960s. During and after the dictatorship the local Church inserted itself strongly into civil society training community leaders. Around 1990 PT and the communist PC do B took over the unions; yet these lost force due to liberalisation and industrial restructuring. PT militants also politicised the neighbourhood associations whose federation UAB aggregated some 55,000 people. Although UAB and the unions were part of the 'Popular Front' that came to power in 1997, they maintained relative autonomy. The government raised the number of sector-policy councils to 24 and carefully designed a PB scheme so as not to harm the neighbourhood associations by eliminating their intermediary role in favour of citizens' direct participation; in effect PB strengthened the associations. Both PB and the councils curbed the particularistic tendencies of city councillors and clientelism largely disappeared. Yet, the participatory experience of the CMS and other 'deliberative public spaces' is an expression of these wider processes of societal and political transformation (in tandem) rather than having caused them in any significant way.

Incongruent attitudes between civil society and political society may not be as frequent as Avritzer suggests. The only clear case of elite-society dissociation was Camaragibe where democratic transformation has been a difficult top-down process. Only in Santa Cruz could we see a clear deviation of the participatory patterns on the CMS from the macro dynamics of state-society relations. Thus the CMS had a transformative character both in Camaragibe and Santa Cruz but hardly so in Camaçari and Caxias (which were cases of congruence and conformity). In Santa Cruz the CMS was an arena for bottom-up transformation against the odds of an otherwise little assertive or politically engaged civil society. In Camaragibe it was one of several instruments of a government-induced transformation of attitudes and practices at societal level. Thus the arrow of democratic renewal did not always point in the direction expected by Avritzer.

Putnam's notion of congruence and determinism has not been confirmed either. As Wood argues, the democratic promise of social capital 'often remains on the horizon until connected to explicitly democratic political organising' (2001: 262–3). All cases point to the crucial role of two big absentees in the Putnamian version of the neo-Tocquevillean account: the ideational content of social ties and networks, and political agency both by governments and parties or unions. When it comes to civic engagement, community ties play different roles depending on whether they embody ideas and values aimed at political transformation rather than sociability or the capture of patronage. Political agency was crucial for shaping the ways in which civil society related to the public domain. There have been pre-dispositions for 'integration' or 'incorporation' deriving from historical endowments of 'civicness', structural conditions, and different levels of deprivation. But it was state agency that accounted, for instance, for the variations in the form of incorporation between 'clientelistic authoritarianism' (Camaçari) and 'emancipatory populism' (Camaragibe).

The importance of political agency is good news insofar as it breaks with the deterministic notion of entrenched path-dependent equilibria. It is bad news in the sense that it is difficult to envisage structural explanations for pro-democratic political leadership in uncivic, clientelistic settings. How does it emerge and how can it be replicated on a more general basis? Avritzer is too dismissive of the democratising potential of reforming representative democratic institutions. He neglects the point that the prevailing constitutional rules are a source of continued clientelism. Brazil's political and electoral institutions systematically encourage the fragmentation of the party system, undermine politicians' loyalty to parties, and personalise election campaigns. A reform could do much to discourage clientelistic politics, improve the functioning of deliberative arrangements, and reduce the burden on them of having to transform political society against the working of a powerful adverse incentive structure.

Institutional interaction and transformation

The democratic potential of deliberative public spaces depends not only on attitudes and practices at the levels of society and polity but also on the interaction of these institutional innovations with the overall institutional template. As Dryzek points out, 'introducing additional stability-promoting institutional rules is not cumulative; the interaction of different rules that induce stability in isolation may together induce greater instability'. It is therefore difficult to 'predict the effects of any combination of institutional innovations' (2000: 44). The introduction of new, or redesign of prevailing, institutions is bound to destabilise existing settlements (Knight 1992). Indeed, deliberative arrangements are intended to do exactly that. They are therefore likely to be contested. This contestation takes place in the context of institutional hybridism in which vertical particularistic ties conflict with horizontal bonds of class-based representation, co-operation, and collective action. Trading privileges rather than general problem solving is at the heart of clientelistic politics. Although clientelism may involve 'elements of collective organisation and identity' (Gay 1998: 14), co-operation becomes difficult to sustain as various clienteles compete with each other for patronage. This has strong fragmenting effects. Patrons command, or intermediate access to, resources the clients want to share in. Clients are supplicants and patrons are donors, which leaves little room for demand making based on rights and citizenship.

Clientelism interacts with formal institutions of democratic representation. This is the starting point of Avritzer's argument and a major rationale for deliberative arrangements. Clientelism corresponds with Brazil's constitutional order of strong executive and weak legislature, dysfunctional electoral institutions, and a weak, fragmented party system. This leads to personalised, non-programmatic electoral competition rather than the aggregation of broad class-based interests. There are thus strong institutional incentives for using clientelism as a political strategy. Local legislatures regularly function as centrepieces of clientelistic systems. Yet, clientelism also disempowers the legislature. In order to sustain client networks city councillors often rely on government-controlled powers and resources, which they can access only by becoming clients themselves of the executive. This is why so many mayors in Brazil have comfortable majorities in the legislature despite highly fragmented party systems. The legislators compete as clients for patronage, and as patrons for clients; they need to gain influence over neighbourhood associations and other CSOs by co-opting community leaders. Although clientelistic allegiances divide and weaken the associations, they are important for increasing the reach of client networks, helping patrons to maximise electoral returns.

Deliberative arrangements interact with representative institutions by reducing the legislature's power over budgeting. City-councillors find it hard to reject a budget worked out with the participation of thousands of citizens. Both in Caxias and Camaragibe the chambers tried to block budgets in order to enforce their right to introduce amendments (which are core tools of particularism) but they had to back down under public pressure. As citizens' demands are publicly processed under transparent rules, PB disrupts the legislators' role as inter-mediators of particularistic demands. Therefore, PB has far more potential of transforming clientelistic politics than sector-policy councils. Nevertheless, there are also tensions between the legislature and the councils. Uncommitted governments often use the legislature for bypassing or pre-empting the councils, especially when they have a majority in the legislature but face difficulties to get council approval. What are the implications of the weakening of the legislature? A focus on deliberative arrangements risks marginalising legislative representation rather than reforming it. This empowers the executive and increases further the dependency of deliberative arrangements on government commitment. Moreover, clientelistic city councillors may resort to 'compensation strategies' trying to subvert deliberative forums.

Clientelism may subvert deliberative arrangements by providing an institutional alternative to the 'contest of reason'. For instance, in Camaragibe several PB delegates in the first year selected priorities according to their own particularistic interests rather than those of their communities. Hence, the government gave the population the right to vote on the delegate list and any citizen could suggest additional projects. Yet, some delegates subverted the system by mobilising the community strategically and selectively in order get their projects elected. Thus, the local government took over the task of mobilisation. Even so, delegates and city councillors mobilised voters from outside, which is not allowed but difficult to control. Some elections were contested on the 'ethics commission', but the actors involved conspired to maintain them.

Deliberation may undermine deliberation. There is an unresolved tension between the councils that deal with sector policies and PB that is concerned with public investments in any sector within a specific geographic area. This may result in contradictory decisions. In Caxias and Camaragibe such conflicts led to government-backed renegotiations between CMS and the respective community, but this tension potentially does harm the credibility of deliberation. Another problem is policy co-ordination between deliberative councils. There is again the danger of sectorally fragmented and contradictory decision-making. This has been felt most strongly in Caxias with its 24 sector councils, prompting the government to take steps towards integration and harmonisation through a 'forum of municipal councils'. The challenge is how sector-specific and geographic deliberation can be made compatible with integrated, long-term, and municipality-wide planning.

Conclusions

The case studies challenge simple notions of bottom-up transformation and suggest a complex interaction of a 'causal triangle' between political commitment, civicness, and institutions that shapes the participatory performance and democratising potential of deliberative spaces like CMS. Only a positive interaction of all three dimensions is likely to make deliberation work. Government commitment is the key factor that determines a council's tendency on a continuum between hegemony and deliberation. The former is associated with polarisation, strategic interaction, and the aggregation of preferences; the latter with de-polarisation, communicative interaction, and the transformation of preferences.

Yet, it is government commitment combined with patterns of civic organising that shapes the outcomes of participatory interaction on the CMS. With weak horizontal ties, the political inclusion of societal actors tends to be based on 'incorporation', either through clientelism/authoritarianism or 'populist' emancipation, depending on the exercise of power. With strong and politically activated horizontal ties (i.e. with ideational contents based on 'political' values) the form of inclusion is likely to be integration. Again, this can lead to hegemonic struggle or concerted agency, depending on the government's political project. The outcomes of hegemonic struggles depend on the nature and strength of civicness, the local power distribution, institutional factors, and political opportunities. They can lead to government hegemony, civil society counter-hegemony, or stalemate.

Supportive institutional design needs to redress deliberative inequality, insure against volatile political commitment, and encourage civicness. To the extent that these institutions are defined locally, their 'corrective' capacity depends upon local political commitment and/or the strength of bottom-up networks. Local designs are therefore dependent variables subject to the same inequalities they would have to offset. With weak political commitment and weak civicness institutional formats that protect public deliberation and safeguard reasonable deliberative equality can only originate from benevolent central governments. Outside agencies may also have to enforce deliberative rules and decisions.

Deliberative participation is embedded in rather than autonomous from local power dynamics, which it is meant to transform. Deliberation depends upon a peculiar power constellation that remains fragile, especially if not bolstered by strong horizontal forms of civic and political organising. Effective deliberation presupposes conditions most likely to be found in already more democratic polities. This suggests a 'hierarchy' between representative and deliberative democracy. Conventional means of 'aggregative' politics and electoral transformation are logically prior and superior. Only with power-political obstacles removed can public deliberation contribute to deepening democracy. Democratic consolidation can hardly be achieved by prescribing deliberative 'add-ons' to the prevailing institutional matrix. Any serious attempt to overcome 'institutional hybridism' must address the malfunctions of the country's core political institutions of representative democracy.

Notes

1. IBGE, www1.ibge.gov.br/ibge/presidencia/notícias/1704munic.shtm (17/04/2001)
2. By 'civicness' I mean the characteristics of civic organising and the attitudes and practices of civil society actors towards the polity. I took membership in associations as a proxy for civicness. Putnam's (1993) other three measures are hardly applicable to the Brazilian case. Newspaper readership would be distorted by varying literacy rates. Electoral turnout is inappropriate because voting is

compulsory. 'Preference voting' is a specific Italian institution. In Brazil voting is generally highly personalised.

3. Two data sets by Brazil's statistics agency (IBGE/PNAD 1988 and IBGE/PME 1996) demonstrate variations in associational life, one across six states, and the other across metropolitan regions. They confirm that the South is most and the Northeast least 'civic': in Rio Grande do Sul we find an average membership rate of 15.27, more than three times the rate of Bahia and Pernambuco, the states of our north-eastern cases (PNAD 1988, quoted in Arretche, 2000: 287). A study on 'regional development, political culture and social capital' in Rio Grande do Sul (UFRGS/IFCH 2001) shows that Santa Cruz and Caxias belong to this state's micro regions with the highest rates of membership in associations.

4. The case selection aimed at theoretical insight rather than being representative of Brazil's over 5,500 municipalities. While seeking variations in government commitment and civicness, I sought to keep other variables as constant as possible: comparable size; a government that was re-elected in 2000; and the highest degree of decentralisation of health care ('full local management') etc. The latter resulted in the selection of relatively good performers in the health sector. I suspect, however, that the combination of weak civicness and uncommitted government is the pattern most frequently found in Brazil.

5. CUT is a leftist union federation with political links to PT and the communist PC do B.

6. Benton, (1981), quoted in Stewart (2001: 44)

7. I use the term 'political society' in a broader sense than Gramsci, who equates political society with state actors (Ransome, 1992: 138).

8. Influence was 'measured' by their subjective perception and the government's concessions to them.

9. These figures are based on the state electoral authority (TRE).

10. This is much less than the regional average of the Rio Pardo valley (12.3) and only slightly more than the national average (around 5 per cent).

5
Historical Hurdles in the Course of the People's Planning Campaign in Kerala, India

P. K. Michael Tharakan

The Indian state of Kerala has become well known for human development and democratisation, based on what Amartaya Sen has called 'public action'. Most recently, the effort at democratic decentralisation and a massive Peoples' Planning Campaign (PPC) has been looked upon as Asia's equivalent of the successful participatory budgeting in Porto Alegre. Below the surface, however, serious problems have occurred in Kerala. This review of the experience draws attention to the discrepancy between, on the one hand, the expectations that a radical programme for social change would take root within extensive civil society-based movements and compensate for the previously limited mobilisation of marginalised sections of the population, and, on the other hand, the historically generated party-politicisation of associational life. The People's Planning Campaign was conceived as a 'top-to-bottom' programme with the expectation that it would take root within civil society and thereby be turned into a 'bottom up' programme for social change. This expectation of favourable synergies between left-oriented parties and social movements has not proven valid. Instead clientelistic party-politicisation of civil society and limited mobilisation of marginalised social groups have emerged as historically rooted hurdles in the course of deliberative planning in Kerala.

The chapter first introduces the institutional context and the roots and character of the Peoples' Planning Campaign, so as to establish a framework against which to review the experience. The remainder of the chapter focuses on the problems of politicisation and popular mobilisation.

The institutional framework

In 1992, the Indian national parliament passed the 73rd and 74th Amendments to the Constitution. These Amendments came into force in 1993 and gave a clear mandate to devolve increased power to local governments, both in the rural and urban areas. The 73rd Amendment in particular was undertaken in the light of the experience of village-level local bodies called the *Panchayat Raj* Institutions (PRIs). These institutions had been long established, but it was felt that they had to be strengthened and that it was important to enshrine some of their features in the Constitution itself. A separate 11th schedule was added to the Constitution, listing 29 subjects that could be devolved to local government. It was left to the state legislatures, however, to pass further facilitating legislation to devolve more powers, authority, functions, finance and so on to the local bodies whereby they could be elevated to the status of Local Self Governing Institutions (LSGIs).[1]

The state of Kerala passed the Kerala *Panchayat Raj* Act 1994 pertaining to rural areas, within the directions of the 73rd Amendment, superseding the earlier two-tier system of district council and village-level *panchayats*. Elections to the new three-tier *panchayats* and two-tier urban administration were held in September 1995 (Raphael 2000: 311).

By the mid-1990s there were major political changes in Kerala. The Left and Democratic Front (LDF), led by the Communist Party of India (Marxist) (CPI-M), had been successful in the 1995 local elections and then won the state assembly elections, thus regaining government powers from the United Democratic Front (UDF), the rival political formation. An earlier LDF government had introduced the two-tier district council system that had been dismantled by the 73rd Amendment under the outgoing UDF government (Ramachandran 1988). The new LDF government accepted the three-tier system but tried to empower the LSGIs within a broad scheme for democratic decentralisation and mass participation in planning from below. One important reason was the need for politically focused popular mobilisation.

These ideas were not entirely new to Kerala. There was already an established tradition of discussion and debate on issues and possibilities of decentralisation, particularly within the left political spectrum. The well known Marxist theoretician and political leader, E. M. S. Namboodiripad (1978, 1989, 1992a,b,c, 1994), had been a particularly important contributor. Noted economist, K. N. Raj (1984, 1992; *et al.* 1993) had also put forward economic arguments in favour of decentralised planning and development.

In addition, there had been many local-level experiments. These were indispensable as a basis for the new large-scale scheme of decentralisation and local development planning (Isaac with Franke 2000: 53–77). The experiments included projects in a northern Kerala village called Kalliassery (Isaac *et al.* 1995a, b; Tharakan 1996), regional initiatives in a national campaign for total literacy (KSS n.d.; Tharakan 1990), attempts at group farming in paddy agriculture (Government of Kerala 1989), a group approach for locally adapted and sustainable agriculture (Pathiyoor *et al.* 1990), and the people's resource mapping programme (Chathopadhyaya *et al.* 1999). In some of these experiments, the well known people's science movement the *Kerala Sasthra Sahithya Parishat* (KSSP) (Zachariah and Sooryamoorthy 1994; Isaac and Ekbal 1998) was crucial and gained vital experience along with voluntary organisations like the Centre for Science and Technology for Rural Development (COSTFORD), as well as certain official agencies.

The LDF government decided to initiate a major effort at decentralisation by integrating various political, economic and practical questions. First, a Committee on Decentralisation of Power (popularly known as the Sen Committee) was appointed to recommend suggestions regarding legislation to empower the LSGIs, promote their smooth functioning and facilitate the necessary administrative changes. In accordance with these recommendations, an Administrative Reforms Committee would then suggest a comprehensive overhaul of the administration while one State Finance Commission first carried out detailed analysis of resource mobilisation by LSGIs, and then a second considered long-term suggestions for decentralised planning.[2] Secondly, a People's Planning Campaign (PPC) was initiated whereby a substantial share of the planning funds, around 35–40 per cent, was to be devolved through annual budgets to LSGIs, giving them not only the right to make decisions regarding local development, but also the financial backing to implement such decisions.[3]

The character of the reforms in comparative perspective

The PPC was initiated through an approach paper prepared by the Kerala State Planning Board (KSPB). The paper and thus also the PPC was officially approved by the government on 14 July 1996 (SPB 1996). The new efforts were widely reported and attracted considerable attention both inside and outside Kerala. Thinkers of different persuasions were attracted by the concept that democracy might be strengthened through popular participation at the local level.

On a general level, this fitted well with the new interest world-wide in a more decentralised pattern of governance, irrespective of political system. In almost all attempts in this direction, localised decision-making supported by social movements and civil society organisations seems to have been crucial, or at least has been thought to have been so (World Bank 1999; Bond 2000b). Participatory planning in terms of empowering people to make decisions regarding problems that they encounter locally had become one of the reigning paradigms in development circles (Chambers 1994), and interest in 'bottom-up' decision-making had cut across policy divides.

Some of the advocates of these ideas, however, wanted to distribute authority not only to local institutions but also to structures outside the state. In this context, the new efforts in Kerala were different. The campaigners pointed out that decentralisation and participatory planning might instead be a strategic response to the incursion of neo-liberalism (Fung and Wright 2003b: 5–42) – and defend whatever was left of Kerala's well-known model of human development, (CDS/UN 1975; Jeffrey 1992; George 1993; Tharakan 1998). The new Left Government did not just make speeches, but also followed through by undertaking a massive scheme that was to cover 990 village *panchayats*, 52 municipalities, 3 city corporations, 152 block *panchayats* and 14 district *panchayats* (Isaac with Franke 2000: 77). The campaign was expected to facilitate and ignite 'the creativity and the social logic of a movement' and thus transform the planning process to become 'an instrument of social mobilisation'. The result would be the 'creation of a new civic culture' that by way of 'an integrated, democratic vision' would alter 'the bureaucratic departmental approach to development' (Isaac with Franke 2000: 12, 9, 11). Quite against neo-liberal ideas, the PPC would thus strengthen the role of the state and deepen the roots of democracy by empowering public institutions and practices at the local level.

The Kerala campaign was along the same lines as the experiments in Brazil and South Africa, which are addressed in the chapters by Schönleitner and Stokke and Oldfield in this book. According to the comparative analysis by Patrick Heller (2001: 131–63), participatory budgeting from 1989 in Porto Alegre is most comparable with the experiments in Kerala in the sense that it was introduced by an electoral alliance headed by a social movement based party, the Workers Party (*Parti dos Trabalhadores*, or PT); it focussed on popular participation in economic and development planning and in the monitoring of projects; it was based on neighbourhood associations; and it undermined the interests of clientelistic politicians in budgetary allocation.[4]

Enough time has now passed since the PPC was launched in 1996 to undertake an evaluation. So far, however, most of the critical discussion has not been very fruitful. In late 2003, for instance, at the time of this writing, a controversy has arisen regarding the political character of the campaign and the relationship between decentralisation and planning. Among others, this controversy has actively engaged persons from the leftist persuasion who take different positions. Newspapers and popular journals in Kerala are flooded by allegations and counter-allegations about prominent personalities and organisations closely associated with the PPC. The main allegation against protagonists of PPC is that they were too closely associated with foreign scholars and too ready to accept financing for studies and training from foreign sources, and so opened up possibilities of 'smuggling' in globalisation and anti-left persuasions.

The historical roots of popular mobilisation

Aside from the institutional and political basis of the PPC, that we have already discussed, the most important precondition for the PPC was Kerala's long history of participatory forms of democratisation.[5] A brief analysis of this history is thus essential in order to understand the PPC. As early as the 18th century, the centralised princely states that emerged in this region required the support of intermediary landholders and superior tenants, in favour of whom the succeeding monarchical regimes made policies. These policies led to the commercialisation of agriculture and agricultural processing, which opened up possibilities for sections of backward Hindu castes as well as non-Hindu communities to amass wealth (see Raj and Tharakan 1983). This also helped them to acquire literacy and modern education through which they were able to gain important positions in society (Tharakan 1984). The resultant contradictions between their newly gained economic ascendancy and their limited social status within the existing caste society were negotiated through socio-religious reform movements (Tharakan 1992). The mobilisational power of these movements sharply declined, however, in the wake of the world economic depression of the 1930s, which caused sharp economic polarisation among their caste or community based constituencies (Jeffrey 1975, 1981; Houtart and Lemercinier 1978).

In the northern part of Kerala this kind of development did not take place with the same strength. Here the suppression by the colonial government of a widespread rebellion by predominantly Muslim poor peasantry (Panikkar 1989) forced the leadership of the Nationalist

Movement to avoid espousing openly the cause of the poor peasantry and landless agricultural labourers.

Into the gap that resulted from the decline of the social reform movements in the south of Kerala, and the conservatism of the Nationalist Movement in the north, Socialist and eventually Communist groups emerged, upholding demands of the poor peasantry and landless agricultural labourers. Later, riding on the crest of a widely felt demand of almost all sections of the peasantry for comprehensive land reforms, and the equally widespread demand of the Malayalam speaking people for a United Kerala, the Communists came to power in the very first Kerala Assembly Elections in 1957. Once in power they introduced comprehensive land reforms – implemented in 1970, after various delays and obstructions (Tharakan 1982; Herring 1983). Soon afterwards, legislation was passed ensuring minimum wages for almost all organised and unorganised sectors of labour, and a public distribution system (with wide coverage) for supplying essential goods at 'fair' prices was introduced (George 1979; Sathyamoorthy 1985; Oommen 1993).

These reforms gave the poorest sections better access to essential services and goods, and therefore widened the coverage of the 'Kerala Model of Development'. But significant sections of the poor were left out from direct benefits: some of the *Dalit* population who did not qualify for benefits of land reform provisions granting one tenth of an acre for landless agricultural labourers, the Tribal people, and the traditional marine fisherfolk, and particularly women from all groups.[6] With the implementation of comprehensive land reforms, there was no immediate unifying slogan around which these sections of Kerala society could be mobilised. In addition, in the 1960s the two major political parties of Kerala, the Communist Party of India (CPI) and the Indian National Congress (INC), had each split at the national level as well as in Kerala. From this point on there were two communist parties, the larger CPI-M and the smaller CPI, and a whole set of Congress related parties. The resultant factions had to resort to coalition politics with parties of different persuasions to gain and remain in power; thereby lessening their ability to mobilise the poor as compared with before (Tharakan 2000: 98–102, Kunhaman 2000: 103–6).

Successive governments in Kerala tried several programmes of participatory development. The 1987 LDF ministry, for instance, promoted new efforts at group farming in paddy agriculture and a campaign for total literacy (Isaac and Kumar 1991; Franke and Chasin 1994; Törnquist 1995). None of them succeeded, however, in mobilising all sections of Kerala society, which was by now divided on a party or coalition basis as well as along caste and community lines. Economic stagnation, growing unemployment and a financial crisis also plagued the state up to the early 1990s (George 1993). Subsequently the liberalisation of the Indian economy and globalisation posed major threats to the Kerala Model of Development.

The basic assumptions about civil society and marginalised people

A requirement for a fair but critical review of the campaign is to recall the PPC-designers' original intentions and expectations – in order to be able thereafter to discuss whether the factors that they *thought* would make the campaign successful really were effective in practice.

These intentions and expectations must be understood in the context of the common view among Kerala analysts that there are in the state significant social movements, civil society organisations and social capital (see, for example, Heller 2001). As already indicated, the long drawn-out process of democratisation in Kerala resulted in the emergence of social reform movements, the Nationalist Movement and the Communist movement in addition, later, to the KSSP. Observers assumed, therefore, that Kerala society had an active 'associational life' marked by a high level of social capital.

While discussing civil society organisations in Kerala, however, Isaac and Heller (2003: 85) also spelt out certain negative aspects, including their widespread party-politicisation. Writing in the introduction to T. M. Thomas Isaac's work on the theory and practice of people's planning (Isaac 1997), the senior Nationalist and Communist leader E. M. S. Namboodiripad himself stressed the non-party, non-religious nature of the mobilisation for development. Namboodiripad called for the convergence of people of different political viewpoints for developmental activities as early as 1989 (Namboodiripad 1989).[7]

Yet, one may wonder why the PPC organisers thought that civil society organisations negatively affected by party-politicisation would be able to co-operate on the basis of trust. Their main answer was that '[i]nstead of taking civic culture as historically determined and given, the People's Campaign approaches it as shaped by the nature of civic and political engagement. Many of the unique features of state–society synergies in Kerala have been facilitated by nature of such engagement, driven by lower class mobilisation' (Isaac with Franke 2000: 11).

While the previously mentioned initiatives of the 1987 LDF ministry with popular participation were not deemed to 'form part of a larger political strategy', its leading party, the CPI-M, was by 1996 assumed to have acquired a 'coherent strategy', the centrepiece of which was 'decentralisation with mass involvement' (Isaac with Franke 2000: 318). This was expected to help undermine 'the bipolar compartmentalisation of Kerala politics' and that 'the resulting dialogue' would 'facilitate a further advance of the Left in the State' (Isaac with Franke 2000: 52).

In brief, it was the associational networks and autonomous civil society organisations rooted in 'class and mass organisations' that were expected to enable the PPC to act as a transformative social programme, to broaden the 'Kerala Model' and include previously marginalised groups. This, therefore, is the basis against which the performance of the PPC will now be reviewed.

From political to party-political civic movements

Since the campaigners assumed that it would be possible to facilitate and support one particularly fruitful form of civic engagement, there is a need for an historical analysis to see whether the kind of 'civic and political engagement' that has gone on in Kerala has *actually* facilitated the emergence of civil society organisations that could have strengthened the functioning of the PPC.

The character of civic and political engagement in Kerala is mainly based on the growing consciousness among the underprivileged that their individual and collective rights are a result of collective struggles for access to basic services (Tharakan 1998: 161). This consciousness and these struggles, in turn, produced a widespread popular base for further mobilisation. As a result, political activity in Kerala evolved as local level collective demands and needs that were aggregated and articulated through political and legislative bodies to higher levels of decision-making.

This kind of politicisation led to the strengthening of the democratisation process through empowering lower social and economic groups to demand basic services as their rights. It strengthened the political will of the governments that came to power in independent Kerala to supply such services to the comparatively underprivileged sections of society (see Rouyer 1987: 453–70). This resulted in the implementation of a more far-reaching and effective agrarian reform in Kerala than elsewhere in the country (Herring 1983, Raj and Tharakan 1983: 31–90).

Dreze and Sen (1995) have put this slightly differently by attributing the achievements of Kerala to 'public action'. Public action definitely emanated from organised efforts of people at the lower socio-economic levels in Kerala society. This in turn was facilitated by earlier mobilisation on the part of social reform movements and political movements, and the leftist movements in particular. The leftists, including the undivided CPI, were able to assert their political hegemony in Kerala (even challenging the position of the Indian National Congress) by helping to articulate the demands of the labouring poor and integrating these demands within a broad demand for comprehensive land reform that appealed to various segments of the Kerala farming community (Tharakan 1982; Raj and Tharakan 1983). What is important in these developments is that CPI was able to assert its hegemonic position by initiating and riding on the crest of two powerful movements: one for comprehensive agrarian reforms and the other for United Kerala.[8]

The emergence of the undivided CPI in Kerala society was thus facilitated by the earlier activities of social reform movements. At least in southern Kerala, these activities not only effectively challenged the hierarchical caste system in which the social dynamics of the region were imprisoned (Isaac and Tharakan 1986; Tharakan 1992, 1998), but they also helped to establish secular concepts (Mathew 1989). As already indicated, it was only in the 1930s, when the world economic depression had affected Kerala and resulted in widespread economic polarisation within caste or religious based communities, that their ability to mobilise all sections of the population became more limited (Jeffrey 1975, 1981, Houtart and Lemercinier 1978). The Left gradually replaced the organisational structures created by social reform movements or the Congress, and created new organisations. Several trade unions, organisations of the unemployed, student organisations, youth movements and women's associations were created, most of them under Leftist influence (see Cherian 1999: 511–46, Gopalankutty 1989, 1999: 547–90). But when these organisations were transformed or created anew under Leftist ideological orientation, there was counter-action by non-leftists, mainly the Congress, to create or to energise their own organisations.

On the one hand, it is thus true that there was a genuine and broad movement base behind the victory in 1957 of the undivided CPI in the first unified Kerala Assembly Elections. On the other hand, however, the state inherited not only autonomous civil society organisations, but also several factions of trade unions, student organisations and women's associations. These owed allegiance not only to Communists and Congress but also to different groups within the respective camps and to the numerous political parties that eventually appeared.

After some time – first during the successful attempt to destabilise the new Communist led government but primarily after the additional party divisions in the mid-1960s – these civil society organisations could not play the role that might have been expected of political but autonomous civic associations. This was because the increasingly politicised organisations demonstrated a certain inflexibility in their postures and rhetoric, reflecting the clientelism that had developed within the parties with which they were affiliated. Such civic organisations have turned out to be 'front' organisations of clientelistic political parties. After every election, such civil society organisations and parties mainly become engaged in distributing the spoils of power. In Kerala from 1977 onwards, the two political coalitions under which most of the mainstream parties are still grouped together have rotated their positions as ruling party or opposition, ensuring a certain evenness in such distribution.

If we for a moment return to history – well before the divisions within the original CPI in the 1960s – it is correct to conclude, however, that the Communist Party closely resembled a social movement in content and style. Its growth was facilitated by social reform movements and the nascent Congress movement. In fact, many of the Communist leaders had a long background within the Congress. They espoused popular demands, eventually integrating them under two unifying slogans that appealed to all sections of people of Kerala: 'for a comprehensive land reform' and 'for a United Kerala'. It was only when the parties or movements wanted to compete for and assume a hegemonic position in regional politics, and various divisive parties were formed, that they opted for the kind of increasingly clientelistic forms of party-politicisation of associational life that have generated present problems. These problems were further enhanced when the parties gained access to state resources that could be distributed along partisan lines. Meanwhile, moreover, the socio-religious reform movements also degenerated, thus making things even worse.[9]

The People's Planning Campaign and the party-politicised civil society

Given these historical circumstances, therefore, the assumption behind the PPC that civil society organisations, social movements and autonomous associations would take over the initiative for decentralisation and carry it forward seems to have been mistaken. What were the consequences?

Very few attempts have been made to analyse empirically the actual working of the PPC or to make a critical appraisal in relation to the character of the civil society that it was to be based on. Most of what has been published by local newspapers has been isolated incidents that have either proclaimed successes or failures – depending on the side that the investigator supported. (This tendency itself demonstrates how the deep party-polarisation of attitudes prevents the development of a generally accepted public space where such issues can be discussed.)

In one of the few good case studies, however, John and Chathukulam (2003) have carried out an insightful study of a *panchayat* during the PPC. To begin with they find that the efforts to prevent decline in cultivated land and production of main agricultural crops did not succeed even under the PPC – and that this was partly because of the party-politicisation of the farmers' organisations. Farmers' groups like *Padasekhara Samithi* (paddy field level committees), as well as the CPI-M's, CPI's and INC's farmers' organisations, failed to address questions regarding production and to ensure the timely release of subsidies. They also failed to promote co-ordination of the various agencies involved in agricultural production. In a focus group discussion, the agricultural workers' union under the leadership of CPI-M and CPI reported that they were 'unwilling to cultivate land by themselves even if it is found necessary in the *panchayat*, except with the help of strong institutional support' (John and Chathukulam 2003: 12). This institutional support was found lacking. In fact, the members of the elected *Panchayat* Committee did not seem to give productive investments high priority but continued to prefer redistributional, welfare or infrastructural measures. This same study was also unable to indicate that there had been any positive influence on the outcome of the projects because of local level synergy based on 'social capital' (John and Chathukulam 2003: 1–24). The researchers found no support for the assumption that civic consciousness, reciprocity and trust would be generated and turned into 'economic assets'.[10] John and Chathukulam (2003: 14) conclude that 'there has not been any qualitative change in the projects compared to the other rural development schemes'. This is in sharp contrast to the expectations of the PPC that the newly created local level organisations as well as older mass and class organisations would make a spectacular difference in the execution of projects.

One may also reconsider the reported inability of mass and class organisations affiliated with state and national political parties to contribute corrective measures. This may be because their affiliations as well as their mobilisational practices are of a vertical nature, thus making them less well equipped to handle local problems of production and even of welfare. Such questions become relevant in the light of the failure in the same village of the farm labour organisation affiliated with the CPI-M to get even fifty persons for a sit-in before the *panchayat* office to demand cultivation of all fallow lands (John and Chathulkulam 2003: 12). This thus raises doubts about the idea, supported by Patnaik (2004), that decentralisation would allow such organisations further to advance the 'class struggle'.

As already indicated, the weaknesses attributed to organisations affiliated with state or national political parties may also hold for newly created local associations like paddy field level committees or *Padasekhara Samithi*. Actually, these organisations may very well be ensembles of diverse party-political and caste and community interests. It is evident, in short, that Kerala society has deep fissures created by clientelistic party affiliations, while there are also reports that caste and community interests are reappearing in manifold ways. In Kerala society, polarised as it is by clientelistic political party coalitions, it is difficult for local level organisations by themselves to rise above divisive interests. Heller's (2001: 142) point that 'non-governmental organisations (NGOs) associated with or generally sympathetic to the LDF have seen their influence and role increase substantially' while NGOs associated 'with the opposition have been less active', probably reflects the political configurations existing at that time. Now that the positions of state-level political parties have been reversed, the support to be expected for the NGOs has probably also changed. In other words, the contributions from NGOs and local level associations are likely to be affected by their political leanings and should not be expected to be consistently available for the basic purposes of decentralisation in the long run.

In fact, even the KSSP's participation in PPC activities might be limited by more or less the same factor. The KSSP is not only categorised as part of the broad left but also as part of the CPI-M.[11] As long as the KSSP is believed to be close to the CPI-M, its activities in support of the PPC may also be understood in terms of partisan political activity. In that sense their activities may also not have had full acceptance beyond the broad coalition/party divide. In other words, all these organisations which were newly given shape, or were already existing and willing to support the PPC locally, did not command acceptance and trust beyond the party divide. Rather, such a position had to be built up by way of difficult, alternative, non-clientelistic practices on the ground level. This was attempted by many PPC activists but was not always very successful (as Törnquist explains in his chapter in this book).

One important development in the course of the implementation of the PPC was that of Neighbourhood Groups called *Ayalkoottams*. These were organised below the constitutionally stipulated Village or Ward Assembly (called *Grama Sabhas*). They were intended to be actively involved in the selection of 'beneficiaries', cultural activities, and projects like education, health and drinking water; to be prepared to activate social auditing and monitoring; to mobilise participation in the *Grama Sabhas*; and most importantly to create village level unity by directly settling border and family disputes and other issues (Isaac 1999: xiv–xv). Indeed, many cases of such responsibilities having been undertaken by Neighbourhood Groups were reported (SPB 1999: I–II). Yet, a disturbing aspect of their actual functioning is also reported by an evaluative study of two panchayats (Nair 2000: 42–3). This study found that they were not free from the danger of becoming instrumental in further politicisation of the system, as almost all the meetings that the author of the evaluation study attended were 'held in the local offices of the ruling party or its front organisations giving a political colour to the functioning of the system'.

The intention here is not to argue that there should be no political aims attached to such programmes. In fact, organisational structures like Neighbourhood Groups may contribute more to the objectives of the PPC if they are well informed about the political objectives of democratic decentralisation. If, however, the organisational structures at the grass-root level are divided according to clientelistic party affiliations they are not likely to generate the positive synergies that one may expect from them.

Mobilisation of the marginalised?

In addition to the vision of the PPC organisers that the campaign would function as a transformative social programme on the basis of what were assumed to be deep-rooted associational networks, the other main objective of the PPC was that these practices in turn would unleash a process of inclusive decision making in which groups that had thus far been excluded or marginalised would be helped to participate significantly.

As the earlier historical review of the developments in Kerala has shown, the undivided CPI came to power in the first state elections of 1957 on the basis of espousing the demands of the lesser peasantry and landless labourers (constituted predominantly by backward castes and castes considered to be the lowest) and those of the poorer sections of different communities. The new CPI-led government, then, took immediate steps towards comprehensive land reforms followed by other redistributive measures. It also tried to lessen regional disparity between the south and north of Kerala (Leiten 1982; Sathyamoorthy

1985). In spite of the communists' ambitions, however, their policies do not seem to have benefited those sections of the population which lacked any significant land holdings, or were not part of mainstream economic activities[12] (see Tharakan 1998 161; Kurien 2000).

In a recent survey, for instance, it was found that though Kerala's achievements in the areas of reducing child mortality and poverty and increasing literacy compare favourably with other states of India, the differentials in terms of access to toilets and access to electricity by Scheduled Castes (SC) and Scheduled Tribes (ST) are much worse than in many other Indian states. The survey also shows that the proportion of main workers outside the primary sector, thought to have higher wages and better living conditions, was very low in the case of STs (Narayana 2003: 30–1). The same study, using data generated by the census of the poor conducted by the Rural Development Department of the Government of Kerala in 1999, shows that the inability of SCs and STs to diversify their occupations results in greater poverty in terms of consumption, asset holding and housing characteristics.

The same survey also confirms that an historically evolved pattern of deprivation still persists. In the light of this, the efforts taken by the PPC (see Isaac with Franke 2000: 269–74, 331–3) are laudable but there is no evidence to show that its limited successes led to any significant gains for the traditionally deprived sections. The ability of these sections to raise issues and negotiate on the basis of them might have been given additional support by the PPC. But we should note, for example, the complaint raised by C. K. Janu, the leader of the important organisation of the tribals, *Gothra Maha Sabha*, that the decentralised Tribal Sub Plan funds under the PPC did not result in any more benefits for the Tribals than in the earlier centralised departmental phase. (This was used subsequently as a justification for centralising such funds once again by the government that came to power in 2001.) If there were any successes in this sector, they certainly were not at all outstanding.

Gurukkal (2001) has presented the ground reality of Kerala in terms of a coalition of conflicting interests. Higher social development of Kerala has generated the coexistence of diverse groups, but mainly those belonging to a broad middle class. These groups are increasingly resorting to politics of caste, community and ethnic identities cutting across class differences and political affiliations. This leads to the denial of 'development benefits' to the Tribals, Scheduled Castes, traditional fisherfolk and other marginalised sections. Majumdar (2002: 17) has pointed out that:

in a traditionally, hierarchical society like ours, characterised by entrenched inequalities, legislation and formal rules do not necessarily mean that citizens are able to take full advantage of the legitimate space for engagement in decision-making.

In this context, there may be reason seriously to consider Gurukkal's argument that political empowerment of the poor and facilitation of institutional development has not led to the expected structural changes in Kerala because decentralised planning under 'capitalist democracy' cannot generate structural changes.

The belief that participation by itself will ensure social change on the basis of people's own perception of reality was challenged quite early (Rahnema 1990: 199–226). In this context, it is necessary to look specifically into who participated in the deliberations of the PPC as well as why and how they did so. One such study has been conducted in two panchayats of the Thrissur district (Muraleedharan 2001). The findings included the following: fifty percent of those surveyed, mainly males, participated in the Ward level deliberations because they were interested in solving local problems with regard to water, roads, electricity and sanitation. Forty four percent of those attending participated for personal benefits. While most of the participants were aware of local problems, they were passive participants; active and decisive participants comprised only a small fraction. The participants came mainly from low-income families, but the unemployed, who formed the largest component of the sample as a whole, were the least well-represented among the participants. Political affiliation was a factor in persuading people to participate.

Going through these findings one is struck by their mixed nature. In other words, they do not indicate any evidence showing high quality deliberations or focussed participation, such as might have worked to create meaningful changes at the local level. Rather, the empirical results support the argument that there is quite limited space for social change

The PPC, therefore, does not seem to have been able to mobilise at all effectively the marginalised sections of the Kerala population, for whom the Kerala Model of Development itself had failed to provide significant socio-political or economic benefits.

Conclusion

In Patrick Heller's (2001) cross-country comparison, the PT-led popular budgeting in Port Alegre is found to be similar to the CPI-M-led PPC in Kerala; while the ANC-led decentralisation in South Africa seems to have diverged in the direction of a neo-liberal orthodox model. The CPI-M and PT, according to Heller, seem to have taken advantage of their social movement character to build participatory planning campaigns. Meanwhile the ANC, which was always 'more of a political organisation than a social movement' working under the fear of the danger of the democratic transition being sabotaged by apartheid hard-liners, seems to have fallen into the trap of centralising tendencies in the absence of 'viable opposition' (Heller 2001: 156–7). One wonders, however, whether this comparison is entirely correct. If the ANC is now operating from a hegemonic position, the undivided CPI and sub-sequently the CPI-M have also been in hegemonic positions in Kerala politics. Like the ANC fearing apartheid sabotage, the CPI-M is constantly challenged by the UDF – an equally powerful rival coalition. In such circumstances, it is well within the realm of possibility that the CPI-M (like the ANC) may have wished to renegotiate its relationship with social movements and 'autonomous' associations. To begin with, the undivided CPI and the CPI-M emerged from a movement-like background (Desai 2003: 170–96). Similarly the ANC was also born from the most broad-based mass democratic movement since the Congress Party in India (Heller 2001: 155). The CPI-M assumed a hegemonic position by incorporating 'autonomous' associations into its ideological framework. Just like the ANC, the CPI-M would therefore have found it difficult to mobilise the people further under any movement-like slogans. (This is subject to further analysis in the chapter by Törnquist.)

Referring to the earlier period of struggle for land reform in Kerala, Isaac and Franke conclude that 'a historic opportunity was missed for effectively linking decentralisation and agrarian reforms' (2000: 39). There is much truth in this statement. The previously missed opportunity may then have led the CPI-M and the LDF to hold onto their rank and file and to attempt to expand their political influence by adopting various participatory programmes, which were then countered by the UDF. Meanwhile the PT in Brazil, which was an alliance of progressive elements of different organisations, continued instead to maintain relations with grass-root social movements and developed decentralised internal struc-tures (Heller 2001). No such developments can be traced in the case of the CPI-M, except for its particular relationship with the KSSP.

Apparently drawing strength from its social movement character, the PT has devised its participatory budget programme with the 'central institutional feature of utilising neighbourhood-based deliberation' (Baiocchi 2003: 46). This has obviously worked out well and has been appreciated by the people of the region, who have elected the PT for three consecutive terms to the municipal administration in Porto Alegre, and 'largely as a result of the successes in Porto Alegre' to similar advances elsewhere, including a term in the Rio Grande do Sul state administration.

An equivalent degree of success in Kerala would have been if the first Kerala Communist ministry's success in piloting the Agrarian Reform had led to the party being elected to power for subsequent terms. In reality, however, Kerala's experience was different. The Communists have been voted in and out of power numerous times since the first State Assembly elections in 1957. Isaac and Heller (2003: 109) may be right that there were other reasons than PPC-related problems behind the most recent failure in the 2001 state elections. But the PPC was thought of and implemented as a campaign based on the expectation that a top-down programme would be internalised by the people of Kerala, who would then turn it into a bottom-up programme. If that had happened or if it had been about to happen, there should have been some evidence from public political behaviour – but such evidence has not been found.

This does not mean that PPC was a complete failure. New institutions have taken root at the village level, where the dynamics of decentralisation are still in operation – albeit in an incomplete form. The 58 'success stories' reported by the PPC (Puthiavila and Kunhikannan n.d.) still exist, though with very uneven levels of sustainability. The relatively successful women's self help groups (SHG's) have become a factor in local public life (Manjula 2000, Seema and Mukherjee 2000). The models of community participation in school education (Tharakan 2003: 31–53) that are available in Kerala villages are a continuation of long chain of such experiments starting with the campaign for total literacy. In this context one may recall the possibility that the Neighbourhood Groups and the SHGs can form a platform from which the PPC might still achieve the character of a movement which is pro-subaltern or pro-marginalised sections (Gurukkal 2001).

It is a major question whether such successful 'remnants' from earlier campaigns can be integrated together. Given previous experiences, there is an element of doubt even with regard to the ability of KSSP to provide effective support in such massive efforts. In 1991, the attempt by the KSSP and others to follow up the established success of the massive literacy campaign suffered greatly as government support diminished with the electoral setbacks of the LDF (Tharakan 1990, 2004: 48–92).[13] In addition, a new study of ten *panchayats* in Palakkad District has found that the PPC is also vulnerable to fractious politics (Sharma 2003: 3832–50). The *panchayats* are still functioning within centralised political systems that continue to create hurdles in the course of implementation of the best of plans.

The present UDF government has changed the name of the programme, though it continues to exhibit the fundamental features of democratic decentralisation. It is true that some actions such as re-centralisation of tribal sub plan funds, new regulatory authorities outside the structure of the old PPC over municipal areas, and allocation of funds through Members of Legislative Assembly for local development that can bypass panchayats, and demobilisation of trained resource persons have contradicted the new government's commitment to the decentralisation programme. Naturally the much reduced concern with 'real' political guidance for decentralisation comes with greater emphasis upon technocratic and administrative aspects of the earlier campaign. This, however, should not be a source of controversy because a successful campaign for democratic decentralisation must also emphasise technocratic and administrative aspects. It should be appreciated, moreover, that major features such as financial devolution have been adhered to even after the change of government, even if the new government may be more dependent on international funding, including from the World Bank.

The main lesson that can be drawn from the PPC experience, therefore, is that the widely held expectation that development will be driven by social movements and civil society organisations has not proven valid. The belief that the unique advantage of Kerala in terms of a party with a long history of popular mobilisation and various relations between left-oriented parties and social movements would give shape to the campaign, generate favourable synergies for its eventual success and also include previously marginalised sections of the populations was not rooted in an accurate reading of the history of the evolution of modern Kerala. The evolution of modern Kerala society and politics resulted in a process of party-politicisation of associational life, which subjected it to the clientelistic principle of winning support by way of partisan favours. There is every indication that this will persist as a major hurdle in the course of the People's Planning Campaign.

Notes

1. For details of the concerned Constitutional provisions, see Oommen (1995a: 1–10, 1995b: 1–5, 1998: 1–5).

2. For the national context of state-local fiscal relations see Konrad Adenauer Foundation (1998), for a study of SFC Reports, see Oommen (1998) and for specific details of Kerala case see Isaac with Franke (2000, 297–315).
3. The term 'local' is used to denote village or below, 'sub-regional' for village to district, 'regional' for state, and 'national' for all India. The constitutional Amendments provided for Village, Block and District Panchayats for rural areas, and Metropolitan Areas (not applicable for Kerala), City corporations and Municipal corporations.
4. It should be remembered that the 1989 introduction of participatory budgeting by the P.T was preceded in 1985 by the call of the Union of Neighbourhood Associations of Porto Alegre for a participatory structure involving the municipal budget. Participatory budgeting has now improved and increased the number of active neighbourhood associations and civil society organisations (Baiocchi 2003: 47, 58).
5. For detailed discussion, see Tharakan (1998).
6. Kurien (2000) has called them 'outliers' to the 'central tendency'.
7. Evidently, however, various contenders thought that this orientation might detract from the basic principle of 'class-struggle'. The emphasis on 'technical' and administrative details of plan formulation and implementation in various publications from the KSPB (SPB 1997, 1998, n.d.) strengthened this suspicion. Scepticism was also expressed about the nature of the relationship between decentralised decision-making and planning, since the latter is usually associated with centralised command economies. There were persistent misgivings as to whether decentralised planning would degenerate into the 'anarchy of the market', a perennial fear for all who preferred a planned economy. From an entirely different perspective, a similar question was also raised as to whether it was not a major contradiction that a party like the CPI-M, which is still organising internal party affairs in accordance with the principles of 'democratic centralism', should also be concerned with organising society according to principles of democratic decentralisation (Narayanan 1997). A related point of criticism was that the CPI-M would have curbed local initiatives through partisan distribution of various benefits and the working of the so-called Expert Committees. A number of arguments have been marshalled against these criticisms.(In a tightly argued seminar presentation Prabhat Patnaik (2004) argues against the doubts regarding detraction of class-struggle and degeneration into 'anarchy of the market'. Besides Isaac (1997), Isaac with Franke (2000), Heller (2001) and Isaac and Heller (2003) all argue against such skepticism.) But so far debate has not risen much above the level of a publicised controversy. There seems to be a need, therefore, first to identify some of the basic factors involved that can be studied from a concerned academic point of view.
8. Desai (2003: 170–96) argues that the CPI emerged out of something akin to a social movement.
9. Once they found that their ability to mobilise all sections of people declined even within the castes and communities that they represented under socio-religious reform objectives, the organisational inheritors of the earlier movements tried to espouse caste-chauvinist demands. (For details see Chandramohan (1981, 1987); Isaac and Tharakan (1986); Jeffrey (1992: 96–117).) Such posturing became more and more rigid as years went by, and these organisations started working more as political pressure groups – exerting significant power and

influence in democratic elections. In other words, the heritage of the social reform movements is also by now well entrenched within the party-political framework of engagement.

10. Rather, the findings support the argument that the concept of 'social capital' is 'mystifying' (Harriss 2002; Stirrat 2003: 3–22).

11. At times, however, there has been some distancing between the KSSP and the CPI-M. For instance, the Silent Valley Hydro Electric Project was opposed by the KSSP while it was supported by the leading confederation of Marxist leaning trade unions under the leadership of Centre of Indian Trade Union (CITU). In late 2003 there seems once again to be serious distancing between the two organisations.

12. For a long term review of their persistent deprivation, see Tharakan (1997).

13. In fact, the current situation is even bleaker because of the now apparent lack of trust between the KSSP and the main opposition party.

6
Social Movements, Socio-economic Rights and Substantial Democratisation in South Africa

Kristian Stokke and Sophie Oldfield

I have always said; the struggle is not over yet. I can tell you, we are free politically because black people were not supposed to take top political positions, but economically it is a struggle.... Now we think we are free and yet we are in a struggle with our own children... who are now telling us that you are going to pay or out you are. It is a bitter struggle to me and it is very difficult. I knew my enemy and it was the then [apartheid] government.... But now we are talking about our own children who were in the struggle and who is giving hell to us (VM, Western Cape Anti-Eviction Campaign activist, June 2002).

In spite of the fact that leaders of the anti-apartheid social movements have entered into political power and defined the relations between state and civil society in collaborative terms, South Africa's democratic transition has not put an end to adversarial popular struggles (Ballard *et al.* 2003). One decade into democratic rule, the South African state faces severe challenges in including and transforming a racially and socially fractured and polarised society. In fact, post-apartheid South Africa has been marked by an increase in social inequality, particularly in the context of neo-liberal macroeconomic policies (Daniel *et al.* 2003). Material deprivation, combined with increasing use of force against popular protests, have produced and radicalised a range of new social movements that politicise socio-economic rights and demand access to land, health care, housing and public services (Desai 2003). Contestation over the meaning of democratisation, and the relationship between economic liberalisation and the pursuit of social justice lie at the heart of these struggles.

This chapter focuses on the politics of a post-apartheid social movement, the Western Cape Anti-Eviction Campaign. We specifically examine how community organisations with the Campaign mobilise against state-driven privatisation and cost recovery initiatives to gain access to water, electricity and housing in Cape Town. The chapter analyses the Campaign's political strategies and capacity to fight for basic services and social justice by focusing on (a) the nature of and sources of political capacities organised through and around neighbourhood issues, (b) the ways such capacities scale up into a social movement such as the Western Cape Anti-Eviction Campaign, and (c) the implications of the mobilisation for substantial democratisation more generally in South Africa. Through this specific empirical focus, the chapter examines the clash between policies for economic liberalisation and struggles for socio-economic justice and their relationship to substantial democratisation, a democracy that should allow diverse actors both the possibility and the capacity to make use of democratic rights and institutions to promote their instrumental and democratic aims (Törnquist 1999, 2002b).

Substantial democratisation and social movements

South African democratisation has in many ways been emblematic of 'third wave' transitions to liberal democracy that form part of a burgeoning academic literature on democratisation (see Chapter 1 in this book by Harriss, Stokke and Törnquist). Grugel (2002) points out that many of these transitions and the associated academic discourse have had a narrow focus on the minimalist institutional requirements of liberal democracy, most notably the repeated conduct of free and fair elections. Beetham (1999) describes this as a tendency to elevate a means to an end, to mistake institutional instruments with their democratic purpose. Instead, he proposes that democracy should be defined in terms of its underlying principles and only secondarily in terms of the institutions that uphold them. The core democratic principles of popular control and political equality over collectively binding decisions certainly require functional institutions, but these may take different forms in different contexts. A system of decision-making is democratic to the extent that it embodies these principles, and institutions are democratic to the extent that they help realise them. In consequence democratisation will always be an unfinished process and the challenge is to undertake contextual and comparative analyses of the dynamics of democratisation.

The parallel political and academic discourse on human rights and rights-based democratisation is marked by a tendency to reduce human rights to civil and political rights, leaving out the considerably more complicated relationship between democracy and socio-economic rights (Beetham 1999). Both clusters of rights are closely linked to democracy, albeit in different ways. Civil and political rights, on the one hand, are an integral part of democracy: 'Democracy without them would be a contradiction in terms, since the absence of freedoms of speech, of association, of assembly, of movement, or of guaranteed security of the person and due process would make elections a façade and render any popular control over government impossible' (Beetham 1999: 114). Socio-economic rights, on the other hand, stand in a relation of mutual dependency with democracy: 'The widespread absence of such rights compromises civil and political equality, the quality of public life and the long-term viability of democratic institutions themselves; democracy, on the other hand, constitutes a necessary if not sufficient condition for the protection of economic and social rights' (Beetham 1999: 114). The common view that civil and political rights constitute a necessary and sufficient condition for the realisation of socio-economic rights implies that liberal democracy will automatically lead to development. Beetham's position, on the contrary, means that it is necessary to examine the ways in which socio-economic rights are politicised, institutionalised and realised through the struggles of diverse actors within the political spaces of the liberal democratic state (Millstein *et al.* 2003).

In this chapter we address the relationship between democratisation and socio-economic justice through an analysis of social movement activism. Understanding processes of substantial democracy requires analyses not only of institutions and rights, but also citizens and social movement agency to make use of these as means towards instrumental and democratic ends (Törnquist 1999, 2002b). Following Törnquist's analysis, we focus on how different actors understand their political opportunities, where in the political terrain they position themselves, which issues and interest they politicise, and how people are mobilised into movements and politics. What remain under-examined however by both Beetham and Törnquist are the sources of political capacity for different groups of citizens to engage in political practice, conceptualisation necessary to analyse the differentiation of power or capacity to participate, protest, and organise for socio-economic and political change (Stokke 2002). The following section considers this issue.

Sources of political capacity for social movements

Studies of social movements have focused on why and how collective actions emerge, but have paid much less attention to movement politics and the political outcomes of collective action. In consequence, analyses have depicted much about the structural grievances and internal organisation of movements but less about the relational and contextual aspects that are central to understanding local political dynamics. To address this issue the following section reads the literature on social movements relative to Bourdieu's conceptualisation of power (see Chapter 1 in this book by Harriss, Stokke and Törnquist). Bourdieu's (1991, 1998) basic argument is that social practices and the power to act are constituted by the actors' dispositions for practice (habitus), the different forms of capital (e.g. economic, social, cultural, symbolic capital) they possess and the fields (e.g. the political field) within which practices take place (Stokke 2002). This conception of social practice identifies principal sources of power in terms of *positions* (defined by the volume and composition of capital possessed by the occupants of different positions) and *forces* (defined by relations of domination, subordination or equivalence between different positions) within a field. Within the theme of collective action, these general concepts of power relate to more specific notions of political opportunity structures (relations within the political field), mobilisation structures (social capital), cultural framing (symbolic capital) and collective identity (habitus).

A primary source of capacity lies in a movement's relations with key actors and institutions in the political field. Tarrow (1994) observes that there are complex and dynamic political opportunity structures that social movements utilise to achieve their goals. It is common to highlight the importance of formal rights and institutions within the political system, for instance the presence of constitutional rights and institutions upholding these rights, as evident in the Bill of Rights in the South African Constitution (1996). While rights and institutions might provide a formal framework for participation, political channels and relationships appear decisive for actual access to and transformation of rights and institutions (McEwan 2000). Movement theorists also emphasise that social movements exist within a political context of collaboration and competition in society, reflecting both formal and informal associations between and within organs of civil society (Della Porta and Diani 1999).

Another source of political capacity is found in a movement's ability to mobilise individuals and groups in society. Social movement theorists use the notion of mobilising structures to conceptualise social networks and institutions that serve as a social infrastructure for collective mobilisation and to explain organisational forms within a movement (Della Porta and Diani 1999). Mobilising structures can be formal or informal in character and exist within or outside social movements. The least organised and most commonly overlooked structures include networks of friends, neighbours and colleagues in everyday life. Informal mobilising structures also include networks of activists as well as memory communities. Such social infrastructures can facilitate communication and solidarity prior to and during collective mobilisation.

A movement's ability to participate in the struggle over meaning regarding rights, issues, actors and policies constitutes an additional capacity. Social movements 'draw on the cultural stock for images of what is an injustice, for what is a violation of what ought to be' (Zald 1996: 266). Cultural framing of injustice and political goals, of rights and responsibilities are contested and changeable. This means that there is an active and competitive process of strategic framing that occurs in a variety of arenas, within movements as well as between movement activists and authorities for symbolic capital, i.e. to be recognised as legitimate representatives of certain interests and groups.

Finally, collective action is also based on self-reflexive identities among the actors (habitus). Individual participation in collective action is not based on an objective reality but rather perceptions and interpretations of it, and, social movements themselves play an active role in constructing and communicating collective identities (Melucci 1996). Previous experiences with oppositional politics facilitate and frame new mobilisation, not the least through pre-existing cultural repertoires of how to protest and organise. This means that the classificatory principles and organising principles of action in the habitus constitute a main source of capacity for collective action (Stokke 2002).

Drawing on Bourdieu general conceptualisation of power and more intermediate level notions from social movement theory, these conceptual avenues provide a basis for analysing movement politics. More specific pointers are provided by Törnquist's (1999, 2002b) identification of three key issues for the study of movement politics. These address: (a) where in the political terrain the actors choose to work; (b) what issues and interests they promote and politicise; and (c) how people are mobilised into political movements and the political sphere. The following discussion of social movement political capacity in Cape Town considers these questions and their relation to community organisation and movement capacities in the post-apartheid context.

Liberal democracy and economic liberalisation in South Africa

South Africa's democratic transition in the early 1990s produced a radical constitutional reform that granted extensive formal rights for all citizens and numerous institutional reforms to ensure their actual implementation. These changes at the national scale have been followed by local elections, extensive local government reforms and political discourses endorsing local governance and popular participation (Atkinson and Reitzes 1998; Cameron 1999; Parnell *et al.* 2002). Democratic elections have placed the tripartite alliance from the anti-apartheid struggle – the African National Congress (ANC), the Congress of South African Trade Unions (COSATU) and the South African Communist Party (SACP) – in a hegemonic political position at the national level. These transformations mean that historically well-organised political and civic associations have been placed in a situation with radically transformed and widened local, regional and national political spaces (Neocosmos 1998, Smit 2001). This combination of a vibrant civil society and a conducive political environment should, it seems, provide an ideal case for substantial democratisation, i.e. a situation where ordinary citizens have both the possibility and the capacity to make use of democratic rights, institutions and discourses to address their instrumental and democratic aims (Törnquist 2002b). Unfortunately, in practice, the post-apartheid political and socio-economic conditions have proven to be more complex and contradictory (Bond 2000a; Daniel *et al.* 2003; Desai 2003).

One major obstacle for political participation in South Africa remains the persistent and increasing problems of poverty and inequality. While the immediate post-1994 period was characterised by a remarkable political liberalisation, the ensuing post-apartheid period has been marked by a transition in macro-economic policy with important bearings on the realisation of socio-economic rights. In the early post-apartheid period, the state-led Reconstruction and Development Programme (RDP) was designed, concomitant with other restructuring processes, to rectify socio-economic differentiation and discrimination. The macro-economic context on which the RDP built was, however, constrained and circumscribed by the structural imperatives of the domestic and global economy. Thus, state-led transformation battled with and, eventually, gave way to the neo-liberal government policy for Growth, Employment and Redistribution (GEAR) (Adelzadeh 1996; Marais 2001). Current macro-economic policies, while designed to attract private investments and thereby enhance economic competitiveness in the long run, have perpetuated and deepened unemployment, poverty and inequality in the short run (Adelzadeh 1996; Nattrass and Seekings 2001; Nattrass 2003).

Although South African citizens have been granted extensive *de jure* socio-economic rights, the translation of these rights into *de facto* socio-economic empowerment has proven to be extremely complicated. While the constitution, for example, guarantees a right to adequate shelter for all citizens, it remains a daunting task to translate this into actual houses for marginalised groups. In this situation, new civil society organisations have emerged around issues of housing provisioning (e.g. the South African Homeless People's Federation) and state evictions and disconnections of services (e.g. Western Cape Anti-Eviction Campaign and Soweto Electricity Crisis Committee) (Oldfield and Stokke 2002; Millstein *et al.* 2003; Ngwane 2003). Effective political participation for new social movements, have turned out to be complicated in practice. Civic associations and trade unions, which were instrumental in the struggle against apartheid, have been curtailed through co-optation of civic leaders, declining popular support and the depoliticising effect of the neo-liberal and technocratic approach to development (Adler and Steinberg 2000; Adler and Webster 2000; Edigheji 2003).[1] Moreover the specificities of these struggles are bound up in broader politics about the role of civil society relative to the state and market (Greenstein 2003), paralleling global development debates discussed by Harriss, Stokke, and Törnquist's in the introductory chapter in this book.

In popular and elite discourses on civil society in South Africa, a distinction is commonly made between two idealised types of civil society organisations – community based organisation (CBOs) and non-governmental organisations (NGOs) – each with a distinctive relationship with the state (Habib 2003). Whereas CBOs are seen as adversarial collective actors that challenge state implementation of neo-liberalism, NGOs are seen as service-delivery mechanisms in sub-contracting partnerships with the state. This discourse constructs a binary opposition between adversarial politics and collaboration in governance, which conflates the diversity in actually existing civil society and frames civil society organisations in monolithic and simplified ways (Habib and Kotzé 2003). CBOs and NGOs choose, in reality, creative combinations of strategies of engagement and disengagement with the state. The South African Homeless People's Federation (SAHPF), for example, maintains productive political relations with state actors at national and provincial scales in order to mobilise resources for housing development that benefit local communities, but they also influence the formulation of national housing policy by providing alternative discourses and practical experiences with local people-driven housing processes (Millstein *et al.* 2003). These strategies of working as a civil organisation in collaboration with the state and adversarial struggle, stand in a relationship of mutual dependency:

The prime source of the SAHPF's political capacity has been their ability to mobilise local communities and achieve results through an alternative housing development model. These achievements and their own housing discourse have been crucial for successful political negotiations with state actors at different scales.... Thus the SAHPF's ability to function as a civil/political movement has granted them a certain capacity to participate in the complicated process of turning de jure rights to adequate shelter into de facto rights for the urban poor as citizens of a democratic South Africa (Millstein *et al.* 2003: 467).

Another of the more well known new movements, the Treatment Action Campaign (TAC), has also adopted a 'strategic positioning at the interface between community level concerns and formal institutional channels' (Jones 2004: 7). The TAC has grounded advocacy for HIV/AIDS treatment and health care within a human rights-based strategy. It has especially made skilful use of South Africa's system of extensive constitutional rights, and the currently favourable legal culture with judges who are sensitive to socio-economic rights and the courts maintaining autonomy and legitimacy *vis-à-vis* the executive (Greenstein 2003; Jones 2004). The prevalence of such combined political strategies means that there is a 'need to transcend the false divide that has emerged between opposition and engagement in South Africa' (Habib and Kotzé 2003: 266).

This brief discussion points to important challenges of substantial democratisation in the context of economic liberalisation. Although South Africa has made progress towards formal democratisation at both the national, provincial and municipal levels, the 'everyday' experiences of South Africans and the diverse movements that represent them are mired in the complex ways in which the unequal legacies of the apartheid past are reinvented in the post-apartheid present (Reitzes 1998). In the variety of daily struggles occurring around the country, community organisations and social movements draw on extensive, yet differentiated, political capacity to utilise and transform democratic rights and institutions, particularly against the privatisation of basic household services.

Social movements and anti-privatisation politics

One of the most visible expressions of the tension between substantial democratisation and neo-liberalism is the contemporary shift from statist service delivery to a domination of private sector actors and principles: 'In the latter model, the state acts as a service 'ensurer' rather than a service 'provider'... and municipal services are 'run more like a business', with financial cost recovery becoming the most important measure of performance' (McDonald and Smith 2002: 1). Set against the apartheid legacy of racially uneven service delivery and subsidies, the South African state has made repeated promises (especially through the RDP) about the delivery of basic services to the urban and rural poor (Bond 2000a). Although many South Africans do not have access to piped water and remain without electricity, there have certainly been important achievements with major expansion of service infrastructure since 1994. However, this impressive record is now being undermined by an increasingly aggressive cost recovery on public services by local governments who are largely dependent on locally generated revenue (Jaglin 2002; Wooldridge 2002). Due to a limited ability to pay, a large and growing number of low-income families have experienced service cut-offs and evictions from their homes. This situation is more likely to be intensified than alleviated in the near future. Indeed, it has been observed that: 'Privatisation, for the very poor, threatens to become the new apartheid, an instrument of exclusion, not just from a better life, but even the very basics' (Rostron 2002).

The process of privatisation and cost recovery in municipal services is controversial and contested. Various anti-eviction and anti-disconnection organisations have emerged around community issues of housing and services. National and local labour unions have also challenged privatisation of public enterprises and associated restructuring of work. Anti-Privatisation Forums and community-based organisations have emerged and are seeking to coordinate joint struggles against state-initiated privatisation processes (Ngwane 2003). This has led one commentator to observe that: 'Privatisation may yet provoke the most explosive political threat, post-1994 grassroots movements, ironically reminiscent of the anti-apartheid 'civics', organising to defend the same people against the ravages of a profit-driven democracy' (Rostron 2002).

In Cape Town confrontations over payment for services have intensified. The City has instituted harsh cost-recovery policies in an attempt to recover arrears on rates and service bills.[2] City policies have charged, for instance, that:

> Action will be taken against those who do not pay – the Council will not hesitate to cut off services and take legal action where necessary. Residents who do not pay will be without electricity or water and

will have to pay the additional costs of reconnection fees, lawyers' fees and legal costs. They could ultimately have their houses sold (if they are ratepayers) or be evicted (if they are tenants in a Council house) (City of Cape Town, in Xali 2002, 110).

Although the implementation of this policy has been piecemeal and has fluctuated with changing political party control of the municipality, disconnections of water and electricity, repossessions of furniture in lieu of rental payment, evictions, and arrests for protesting such actions have become commonplace. In response, residents live without water and electricity (even homes); many illegally reconnect themselves to services, and organise in their neighbourhoods and across the city (Smith and Hanson 2003). The Western Cape Anti-Eviction Campaign marks one response to these service delivery policies (Oldfield and Stokke 2002; Desai 2003; Desai and Pithouse 2003).

Public service delivery was a key issue in the anti-apartheid struggle and has been crucial to post-apartheid attempts to ensure actual socio-economic rights. The current tendencies towards privatisation of public services calls into question the state's parallel commitments to social justice and substantial democratisation. Thus, privatisation and cost recovery on services are not simple question of issue-based politics, but a more general test of the substance of democracy in the new South Africa. Critics of neo-liberalism argue that these tendencies demonstrate the turn to the right in South African governance and that this has come at the cost of socio-economic redistribution and justice (Bond 2000a; McDonald and Pape 2002). They claim that policies of cost-recovery in service delivery jeopardise the post-apartheid project by disenfranchising and further alienating black communities and citizens already disadvantaged by the ravages of the apartheid system. Poor households and communities face an affordability crisis due to high unemployment levels and the real difficulties in eking out livelihoods in the post-apartheid period. Ironically, in the same way that community issues of housing and public services were contentious issues behind civic struggles against apartheid (Seekings 2000), similar issues are rallying points for new social movements striving for justice in the context of South Africa's new liberal democracy. This constitutes an immediate material basis for new social movements such as the Soweto Electricity Crisis Committee and the Western Cape Anti-Eviction Campaign (Oldfield and Stokke 2002; Ngwane 2003); the latter group is investigated in the following discussion.

Political capacity and the Western Cape Anti-Eviction Campaign

The Western Cape Anti-Eviction Campaign (WCAEC)[3] was officially formed in February 2001 to fight against evictions, water and electricity disconnections, and poor health services. A diversity of issues lie behind the emergence of the Campaign, although the initial impetus was Cape Town City Council-led evictions of families from two areas of state-owned flats in former coloured group areas. In both instances, communities confronted the City Council, the police and army who had been brought in to assist officials with the eviction process (Leitch 2003). Violence between police and residents ensued and activists were arrested in the process. In February 2001 the Campaign was publicly launched in Tafelsig in Mitchells Plain, including a call to any groups facing similar issues to join the struggle. The Campaign is an umbrella body now representing approximately 25–30 communities primarily within the City of Cape Town but also with representation in out-lying small towns in the Western Cape. In practice, the capacity of the Campaign is a reflection of the various organisations under its wing as well as the ways in which community-specific struggles coalesce in the Campaign's citywide actions.

Community organisations within the Western Cape Anti-Eviction Campaign represent a wide range of contexts: from old apartheid rental housing and state-organised bank bonded properties to post-apartheid areas of state-built low-income housing and informal settlements. Not surprisingly then neighbourhood organisations organise around a variety of issues and have chosen different strategies regarding how and where to be active in the post-apartheid political terrain. Many communities seek to engage municipal and regional state institutions and political actors. However their experiences of accessibility to the state are diverse. Some CBOs have good access to, for instance, councillors (e.g. Athlone, Mfuleni and Delft) but most of the communities (e.g. Mandela Park and Tafelsig) have found it difficult to get councillors, the Provincial Minister of Housing or representatives from parastatals and banks to attend meetings and engage with the campaign in any meaningful way. This has led some organisations to a strategy of resistance through mass mobilisation and public protest (especially Tafelsig and Mandela Park) (Oldfield and Stokke 2002).

The modes of mobilisation and protest vary considerably among the organisations within the Western Cape Anti-Eviction Campaign. In some areas – many former coloured townships – activists tend to work one-on-one with residents and officials (e.g. Elsies River and Lentegeur). In other areas, it is normal to have community meetings and mass protests and residents are expected to participate in these types of activities (e.g. Mandela Park and Mfuleni). In many communities, these two modes of organising are combined (e.g. Athlone and Valhalla Park). The repertoire of protest ranges from strategies that are compatible with the rules and procedures of the formal political system (e.g. community meetings, legal demonstrations and lobbying through petitions and negotiations, as well as legal challenges in the courts) to practices that are more confrontational and unlawful (e.g. illegal water and electricity reconnections, occupations of repossessed houses, obstructions of evictions and illegal sit-ins at banks and political institutions). Many of the organisations combine diverse kinds of protests and only employ the more radical resistance strategies when negotiations and legal demonstrations fail to yield acceptable outcomes.

To understand the source and potential of the Campaign in greater detail requires analysis of the differentiated political capacity of community organisations that constitute the Campaign, as well as the overall direction and challenge that the Campaign collectively presents in the local political arena, particular to the City of Cape Town. Drawing on the experiences of two community organisations at the forefront of the Campaign, the following discussion focuses on the plurality of political strategies they combine in everyday political practice, in particular strategies of territorial control, oppositional resistance, engagement, and legal challenges.[4]

Opposition through engagement in Valhalla Park[5]

The United Civic Front of Valhalla Park provides a useful illustration of the ways in which many community activists and organisations engage with state officials and institutions in order to oppose it and its policies through overt and covert actions. As one of the more successful community organisations in the Campaign, it has won significant gains from working within and outside of state-accepted norms of behaviour.

The Valhalla Park Civic has chosen persistent and direct engagement with officials in the police and the health and housing departments who work in the Valhalla Park local area. By building up relationships with local officials over a long period of time, Civic leaders have found ways in which to make them more responsive. In the case of the police, for instance, the leaders' personal connections and participation in the Community Policing Forum have helped to improve servicing of the area. A similar relationship has developed with the local Head of the Housing

Office. Unlike officials in many poor communities in Cape Town, he has allowed unemployed residents who are unable to pay rentals to apply for indigent status to relieve them of some of the burden of their bills (WA, Valhalla Park, May 2002).

Although Civic leaders engage with officials to improve public service delivery and resolve specific immediate needs in the community, they do not depend on these types of relationships to resist evictions or to improve conditions in the neighbourhood. Activists often take direct action – for instance occupying the local housing office until a response from the city was forthcoming (W.A. May 2002) – to force the city to respond. The first community-wide protest occurred in response to the cut-off of the entire neighbourhood's electricity in the mid-1990s, despite many households paying their bills regularly. Through a series of persistent protests, the Council agreed to reconnect electricity. Two activists remember the event:

> People protested and we demanded, we actually demanded that they come reconnect the electricity.... After a lot of ups and downs, they decided to come in, to put the people's electricity back on. We got onto that yellow van that rides from house to house to put the electricity on. We civic members, we got onto the van and we rode with them till past midnight from street to street. We didn't let them go until everybody's light had been turned on (GR, GS, Valhalla Park, August 2003).

Since this period, residents and activists have been vigilant about Council activities in the area. If residents see a Council vehicle entering the neighbourhood, they alert the Civic leaders. Residents and activists then respond immediately to ensure that Council does not take any action without negotiating with the Civic. Their persistence and insistence that Council must consult with the Civic has paid off from their perspective as the Council rarely enters the area without consultation. It is the savvy mix of engagement and opposition that has generated a series of successes for the community. When negotiations with Council fail, the Civic finds it appropriate to take radical action.

The United Civic Front has recently won a High Court case against the City of Cape Town, and the result could impact on the City's legal obligations in providing for informal settlement services across the city. 'Homeless' Valhalla Park residents – those families on the housing waiting list living in backyard shacks or as sub-tenants in overcrowded flats – have occupied state-owned land and built an informal settlement in the neighbourhood to address their own desperate housing needs. When the Council failed to respond or provide sanitation and water services, the United Civic Front took the Cape Town City Council to the High Court to demand their constitutional right to services. In July 2003, the United Civic Front won this landmark case in which the High Court held the City responsible for providing services to the informal area (Case 8970/01, 7 July 2003, Neville Rudolph and 49 others vs. the City of Cape Town). Although the City initiated an appeal against the Case, their appeal was rejected by the Court, which was a major victory for the Civic after two hard years of campaigning with the assistance of an NGO, the Legal Resource Centre (F. B., Valhalla Park, November 2003).

Committed and continuous leadership that has been active in the area for a long time characterises community organising in this area. Leaders play multiple roles, but they are also supported by a structure of community activists operating at the street-level. A weekly meeting is held every Thursday night where street leaders and the executive committee report back to residents on progress on various issues. It is in these forums that decisions are taken on appropriate responses and strategies, in particular on when to work in the system and when to disrupt and challenge it. In general, leaders of the Civic continue to pursue goals through working with Council officials and politicians, but express little faith in the system:

> Council don't listen to us if we go through the right channels. They don't listen. They make as if they listen if you go through the right channels. They don't take notice of us. But, if we do what we do, then immediately they respond (GS, Valhalla Park, August 2003).

From experience, they have found that the Council responds only if they present a direct challenge to governance and the operation of the Council in the area. As long as the pressure from the community is maintained, relations with local state actors are critical for the identification and implementation of practical solutions to concrete local problems.

Resistance through public protest in Mandela Park

While evictions and disconnections in Tafelsig (Mitchells Plain) were the catalysts for the Campaign's formation, Mandela Park (Khayelitsha) is now the most visible arena for large-scale evictions and collective resistance. And whereas the Valhalla Park United Civic Front has successfully combined political engagement and mass mobilisation, the anti-eviction campaigns in Tafelsig and Mandela Park have gradually entered into a strategy of collective resistance and a confrontational relationship with local government, the banking sector, and the police.

The cornerstone of the Mandela Park Anti-Eviction Campaign (MPAEC) has been the weekly community meeting with large numbers of residents attending. The community meetings discuss the problems facing the community and make decisions about strategies and activities. Campaign activists also report back to the community about their communication with banks, councillors and state institutions. The Mandela Park Anti-Eviction Campaign has sought an active dialogue with the banks and the Provincial Minister of Housing, inviting them to community meetings but refusing to send delegates to meetings outside the community. The campaign has raised collective demands regarding the sub-standard quality of the houses, ownership of the land, housing subsidies and the handling of outstanding debts. These demands have not been addressed in any meaningful way by the relevant state institutions. Instead the campaign activists have been met with what they see as attempts at diffusing the issues and confusing the activists, as they are told to take their housing complaints to the developers, their economic problems to Servcon (a parastatal negotiating between banks and communities where the majority of residents fail to meet bond payments), and their land demands to politicians. All the invited banks, Servcon and the Provincial Minister of Housing have failed to meet with the campaign in the community (MN, FG, Mandela Park June 2002).

The explicit policy of the Mandela Park Anti-Eviction Campaign is to build alliances with those who support them in their struggle but not spend time on talks that can take the focus away from collective mobilisation. So far, no councillors, political parties, trade unions or NGOs have taken up this supportive role on terms that are acceptable to the community. This lack of meaningful political engagement combined with the actual practices and future threats of evictions have made the MPAEC take resort in various forms of public protest such as public demonstrations and occupations at banks and political institutions. The community has also mobilised against evictions and repossessions of property and has put evicted families back into their homes (Legassick 2004). These various actions have been met with increasingly harsh measures, including a court interdict on behalf of the banks against community leaders, arrests and lengthy periods of incarceration of activists, and increased use of police violence during evictions and repossession of property. At the time of writing, one Campaign leader is living under long-term bail conditions that prevent him from attending any public meetings, gatherings, marches, pickets of any nature or communicate with any evicted person.

Others are moving between different 'safe houses' to avoid harassment and arrests by the police at night.

In general terms, the MPAEC has experienced a criminalisation of the campaign and its leaders. Community members and activists are spending time and energy in court and trying to raise funds for bail and lawyers. While the Campaign has experienced a few unexpected victories at the local Magistrate Court, the MPAEC does not come anywhere close to possessing the material resources and legal skills required for successfully utilising the legal route of contestation that has been followed by the Treatment Action Campaign (Greenstein 2003). Despite this constant lack of funds, the Tafelsig and the Mandela Park campaigns nevertheless insist on maintaining their autonomy in regard to all non-governmental organisations:

> We don't accept money from anybody for a simple reason: we don't want them to direct us. We are on the ground, we will direct our struggle. So we don't want NGOs to rule us or to act on our behalf, because they don't have our interests at heart. They have their own interests at heart. We understand that and I always make it clear that the NGOs they get paid to be in the struggle – we don't. We are forced to be in the struggle because of our circumstances at home (AC, Tafelsig, May 2002).

With limited economic resources, organisational fragmentation in the absence of a coordinating ideological movement and no political allies, the collective resistance in Mandela Park and Tafelsig face the danger of becoming 'isolated militant particularisms, unable to function in the face of sustained repression' (Desai and Pithouse 2003: 23).

Scaling up to city and national politics

How do the diverse strategies of neighbourhood-based organisations mesh as a citywide and possibly national movement? Our analysis of this challenging question will consider the political field in which the Campaign operates at a city scale, the networks that formally and informally link Campaign community organisations together and that link the Campaign to other organisations within and beyond the city, and the symbolic capital that has been generated through Campaign organising since its launch in 2001.

The political field in which the Campaign operates is complex because of the co-existence and interdependence of local councils, a metropolitan government, and national and provincial government with often confusing divisions of labour between them. This complexity of political actors and the ensuing fragmentation of policy and implementation, provide both obstacles and opportunities for new movements like the Western Cape Anti-Eviction Campaign. At the city scale the Campaign draws on many positive and negative relationships with state officials and with local councillors and politicians in more senior positions in provincial government in particular. Although the Campaign is officially non-partisan and rejects any affiliation with political parties, in practice many Campaign activists are ex-African National Congress (ANC) cadre, some maintaining their membership despite Campaign politics and positions that are often read as explicitly anti-ANC. In the context of a national election in April 2004 and local government elections in 2005, these types of political affiliations have become increasingly politicised in neighbourhood organising and at a city scale (I. Petersen, personal communication, March 2004).

In challenging policy, the Campaign also works with a range of parastatals (the Public Protector, the City Ombudsperson, and the Human Rights Commission) and NGOs (the Legal Resource Centre and the Alternative Information and Development Centre), as well as trade unions such as the South African Municipal Workers Union (SAMWU) and other progressive coalitions in the city. These relationships constitute the multi-dimensional nature of local politics in Cape Town. They are sustained not only through formal policy and legal channels, but also through the intimate relationships that are generated through engagement in local politics. Nevertheless, the general shortage of economic and organisational resources within the Campaign means that activists often find it very difficult to acquire the knowledge and political networks required for successful manoeuvring in the local political field.

In this situation, the Campaign has sought to build a social movement from local struggles while continuing to fight the city on its cost-recovery and indigence policies. At the neighbourhood scale, these are issues that constitute daily struggles between activists and municipal officials. Mass action has drawn neighbourhood organisations together, acting as a cement of experience through which collective 'anti-eviction' identities have formed. The generation of this collective habitus has proved essential in crossing the spatial and racial divides that previously separated poor neighbourhoods. An activist who is very involved in organising at the Campaign scale, speaks to the important of collective public action:

Mass work is the most important form of struggle of the campaign. The strength of the campaign lies in its ability to engage in mass mobilisation, public meetings, marches, demonstrations and petitions. Mass mobilisation is the most effective way of stopping evictions and water cuts. Communities barricade streets, block entrances to prevent the sheriff from entering houses, local marches to clinics, council/rent offices, police stations and councillors. Mass marches take place during the Council Exco meetings of the Unicity, to the mayor of Cape Town and the MEC for housing. When water is disconnected, mass reconnections take place and private companies doing the disconnections are barred from entering the area. Evicted families are reinstated into their homes. Mass occupations of public offices take place to force officials to negotiate with communities. These methods have proven to be the most effective in resisting evictions and water cuts and forcing housing authorities to rethink their policies (Leitch 2003: 5).

Such mass actions are crucial to the building of a coherent campaign, while it also provides symbolic capital for progressive activists and organisations in Cape Town.

It would be foolish to romanticise the concrete difficulties the Campaign faces in its organising, for instance: a dire shortage of resources that even makes Campaign meetings difficult, criminalisation of activists by the police and some officials, and the diversity of ideologies on organisation structure and leadership roles encompassed within the Campaign. Yet organisations that make up the Campaign are strong on the ground, and their collective strength has increased due to common structural conditions and shared political experiences. Activism in neighbourhoods across the city and the growing number of legal challenges to policy are the micro-scale bits and pieces that collectively push and stretch – in other words, substantiate – the nature of democracy in Cape Town. The question remains however to what extent and at what scales social movement activism yields political influence and thereby contributes to the continued process of democratisation beyond the local arena.

There are attempts at scaling up the struggle from community-specific single issues to a more co-ordinated and ideological movement. This is most visible in the Cape Town and Gauteng Anti-Privatisation Forums, which brings together trade unions (especially SAMWU), community-based groups and campaigns and individual activists. The APF serves as a local meeting point and source of ideological and moral support, but also as a stepping-stone towards interactions and possible collaborations at the national scale as well as exposure to parallel struggles beyond South Africa.

There are also ongoing initiatives to draw together social movements like the WCAEC at the national level, for instance through the Social Movements Indaba that was formed in parallel to the World Summit on Sustainable Development in 2002, and reconvened for annual meetings of South African social movements in 2003 and 2004 in Johannesburg. Trevor Ngwane, at the forefront of this movement, describes the initial potential of such a political fusion as well as its fragility:

> The highlight was the [first] national meeting [in December 2001]. It was really a beautiful moment. . . . We went softly, softly to let co-ordination happen as naturally as possible, to exchange information, to see if we can support each other. . . . We didn't select one campaign as we want to see how things develop and to let things develop properly so they don't fall apart later . . . we are going to let the organisation develop by working on our unity (T. Ngwane, 16 January 2002).

Still in a formative stage, these processes attempt to bridge the diverse ideologies, tactics, cultures of protest and organisation and access to resources that threaten to splinter social movements on the national scale. These processes have, however, also brought out tensions among the new movements over the question of the needs for and content of joint political strategies with representatives from the Landless People's Movement and the Western Cape Anti-Eviction Campaign currently advocating a social movement strategy based on political autonomy and opposition. At the present juncture it seems safe to conclude that, although the new movements have a number of commonalities in their social basis and their struggle for socio-economic justice in the context of neo-liberalism, the process of building a co-ordinated alternative political movement is slow in the making. In the meantime, the new community-based struggles remain organisationally weak and politically divided. Despite this fragmented and particularistic character, the presence of new social movements nevertheless disrupts hegemony by posing a challenge at the symbolic level.

In simplified terms, contemporary South Africa is marked by an intensifying competition over the right to be the legitimate representatives of 'poor people in struggle'. On the one hand are the tripartite alliance and its civil society affiliates that were formed during the anti-apartheid struggle and has held state power throughout the last decade

(McKinley 1997). This alliance now possesses extensive institutionalised political capital.[6] On the other hand there are the new social movements that mobilise communities in a post-apartheid struggle for socio-economic justice in the context of liberal democracy and a neo-liberal post-apartheid state. The power of these movements originates in their strategic handling of the political opportunity structures and, their familiarity with community issues and ability to mobilise communities for public acts of resistance.

The clash between policies for economic liberalisation and struggles for socio-economic justice is an ongoing multi-faceted struggle. The local and national politics it generates are diverse and dynamic with everyday civil society characterised by balancing acts between political engagement and opposition. While political engagement may grant access to material resources for community development, it may also undermine the legitimacy of the movement as an independent representative of struggling people. Community mobilisation may empower the movement in dealing with state institutions, but may also lead to branding it as a disruptive force that is targeted for state repression. ANC representatives increasingly distinguish between positive (collaborating) social forces and disruptive (adversarial) 'ultra-revolutionaries'. The Western Cape Anti-Eviction Campaign is increasingly placed in the latter category in the hegemonic political discourse (Ntabazalila 2002; Makinana 2003).

The political discourses of the 'old anti-apartheid' and 'new post-apartheid' movements revolve around shared reference points, as both claim to be the legitimate representatives of poor people that struggle for social justice. This congruence creates a political space for constructive collaboration. The present period seems, however, to be marked by a growing mistrust between civil society organisations and actors from the state. On the one hand, state officials and politicians interpret activities by organisations like the Western Cape Anti-Eviction Campaign as by definition adversarial. On the other hand, activists and organisations interpret state actions as, by definition, neo-liberal and therefore counter to the interests of the poor and progressive politics. Grounded analysis of community organising, as the one presented in this chapter, shows that community politics include both collaboration with and opposition to the state, as well as diverse strategies that reflect specific historically and place-generated political capacities. The manner in which the state handles this challenge from the new social movements to access socio-economic rights and to participate autonomously in politics, will be crucial to the continual process of substantial democratisation in South Africa.

Notes

1. The political and developmental roles of civics, especially the South African National Civic Organisation (SANCO), are the subject of heated debates (Seekings 1997). Theorists on the left write the organisation off as a puppet of the ANC and the tripartite alliance, hamstrung through its subordinated engagement with the state (Xali 2002). Equally often, SANCO has been used to account for community representation and the vibrancy of community-level input to state discussions at a national level. Heller (2003) argues that SANCO continues to play an important role at the community level, but not as an adversarial social movement.

2. On 1 April 2004 the Cape Town City Council made a major concession to renters in public housing: Rental arrears accumulated until July 1997 have been written off; the City will match R1 for every R1 repayment on arrears accrued between July 1997 and June 2002; and, for the first time, families in arrears will be allowed to purchase their rental housing (Johns 2004).

3. Research on the Western Cape Anti-Eviction Campaign has included focus groups with activists in different organisation and interviews with leaders of organisations (Oldfield and Stokke 2002). The focus groups are ongoing and conducted in partnership with the Community Research Group, the research wing of the Campaign. Quotations and material drawn from these interviews and focus groups are credited to individuals, but initials are used to protect the interviewees' anonymity.

4. Although each strategy is discussed in the context of a particular neighbourhood and activist organisation, many activists and organisations use such strategies.

5. For a fuller discussion of the practices of opposition and engagement in community organising in the Campaign and the types of politics it challenges, see Oldfield (2003).

6. While Bourdieu presents a relatively weak theory of the political field and political institutions, he interestingly identifies politics as a symbolic struggle to define existing power relations as legitimate or illegitimate (Bourdieu 1991). Possession of political capital, which is a form of symbolic capital that is specific to the political field, gives 'the spokesperson' the legitimate right to speak on behalf of 'the people'. Such capital can be the personal capital of the spokesperson (based on fame and popularity). However, it can also reside as 'objectified political capital' within permanent institutions – accumulated in the course of previous struggles and institutionalised in positions and instruments for mobilisation – and be granted to individuals as political delegates.

7

More than Difficult, Short of Impossible: Party Building and Local Governance in the Philippines

Joel Rocamora

I am caught in an uncertain space between political action and academic observation. Accepting Olle Törnquist's 'concerned academic' robe does not go far enough to 'locate' me and my observations. All the contributors to this book deserve the name. I cannot be one or the other of the introduction's 'strange bedfellows' either. I need to be both. I want to give expression in this essay to being an intellectual struggling to deserve being called a political activist.

Without being defensive, I insist that analysis for political action can be at least as reliable, as 'objective', as academic analysis. The success or failure of political action can be as harsh a judge of analysis as academic tenure committees. But analysis for action is different. In the Institute for Popular Democracy, we call it analysis 'between honesty and hope'. In an academic book, it is important to warn readers that this essay is going to be different from the others. Not 'locating' me will be unfair to our readers because they will expect an entirely different 'voice'.

The Philippines is often acknowledged as one of the places with advanced experiences in civil society engagement of local governance. But unlike Brazil where peoples' participation in the budget process has had measurable material impact on the lives of the Brazilian urban poor, participatory planning at the *barangay* (the lowest) government level in the Philippines has had limited direct impact. Unlike Kerala, India and Brazil where experiments in participatory local governance were backed by powerful, established political parties, *Akbayan* (Citizens Action Party), the political party most supportive of participatory democracy is still a new and struggling progressive party.

But the Philippine experience might be of interest in countries of the South precisely because it is still a 'work in progress', one where the requisites for work on participatory democracy are not set as high as in Brazil and India. In the Philippines, both *Akbayan* and BATMAN, the main civil society coalition working on participatory local governance, are still in the throes of working out in theory and practice how best to advance participatory democracy. This open, highly dynamic, and often contentious process may be more accessible to those who want to do similar work in their countries.

Akbayan (Citizens Action Party)

Akbayan is often called a 'social movement' party because most of its original members come from labour, peasant, urban poor, women's and other social movements. But it could just as accurately be called a 'participatory local governance' party because its next batch of members come out of a decade long struggle to maximise the participatory and 'good governance' potential of decentralisation. The coming together of these two trends within the context of a deep ideological crisis of the Philippine Left provide the main outlines of the complex story of *Akbayan*.

Although formally founded at a congress in January 1998, the very process of conceiving *Akbayan* already marked it as a very different political formation. Several pre-party political formations, called 'political blocs' in the Philippines, discussed the possibility of forming a new party as early as the late 1980s. In 1992, these groups plus many NGOs, supported a presidential candidate. Although the experience left much to be desired (the candidate lost badly), the same groups supported local candidates in 1995, this time with many good results. This salutary experience formed the backdrop to renewed discussions in the first half of 1996. The very fact that these blocs came together, not as a coalition, as they and some NGOs had tried to do in 1992, but to work together to begin the process of building a new political party was unprecedented in the history of the Philippine Left. The resulting concept paper was then discussed first in a national meeting in July 1996, and subsequently in innumerable small and large meetings throughout the country. By the time of the founding congress a year and a half later, the party already had more than 3000 'stakeholders' who had attended these meetings.

Only a few months after its founding congress, in May 1998, *Akbayan* won one seat in the party list election of the House of Representatives. This was a considerable feat because the party list election for 20 percent of the House of Representatives has a national constituency and voters hardly knew about this new feature of the electoral system. Ten municipal mayors who won in these elections subsequently joined the party. After the next election, in 2001, *Akbayan* had two members in the House of Representatives. Nineteen municipal mayors and some 200 councillors and other local government officials were elected at the same time. On the eve of the May 2004 elections, 36 party members are contesting mayoral seats. *Akbayan* is nowhere near being a major national party. But it has grown steadily. It now has party units in 54 out of 84 provinces and in 237 cities and municipalities.

Akbayan was consciously set off from traditional Philippine political parties. These parties are unabashed elite 'old boys clubs'. There are non-elite individuals, mostly men, who identify with one or another party, but all of them are followers ('retainers' might be a better word) of elite individuals. These elite individuals are linked together in shifting coalitions from *barangays* all the way to the national government in Manila. Already weak in the period before martial law in 1972, traditional parties have not recovered from Marcos' deliberate destruction of all but his own party. In the post 1986 period, parties have been so weak that in national elections, coalitions of parties are the relevant campaign mechanisms (Abinales 2003).

In contrast, *Akbayan* has a mass membership of close to one hundred thousand mostly lower class people. This is the source of its self-identification as a 'progressive' party. *Akbayan's* base in labour unions and organised farmers is now firmly established. Three of the largest peasant federations in the country are affiliated with *Akbayan*. There is an ongoing drive to organise among middle class professionals and business people. There is a practical as well as a political reason for this. We cannot win elections only with the support of organised workers and peasants. Middle class people have networks and personal resources necessary in election campaigns. They also have technical skills needed in governance. Besides when *Akbayan* members get elected to office, they do not become mayors or congressmen only of the poor. They are public officials of all citizens.

To prevent disputes over membership numbers, there are no member organisations, only individuals. But members of the same group organised into party units can form caucuses within the party. Loosely affiliated mass organisations are linked through sectoral party committees of peasants, labour, youth and others. Party structures and processes are taken seriously. In practice, deeply embedded anti-democratic tendencies from both traditional and Left political practice continue to rear their ugly heads. But inner party democracy is fiercely defended and fought over. Autonomy of local party units is an established principle.

Akbayan also sets itself off from the dominant party building traditions of the Philippine Left. Unlike other progressive political parties, *Akbayan* is not a party with *one* ideology. Many progressive groups and political tendencies work together within *Akbayan*, national democrats, socialists, democratic socialists, popular democrats, and people who do not give themselves labels. We are also not linked with an underground party. We believe that you cannot have inner party democracy if you have another party dictating who are your leaders and what your policies are. We are not engaged in armed struggle. We take the open, legal struggle seriously, not merely as a tactical arena as other Left groups do.

Unlike other Left parties which take a 'smash the state' perspective, *Akbayan* is a vehicle for accumulating political power for political reform. From the time of its founding congress in January 1998, *Akbayan* has steadily drawn reformers from all walks of life into its ranks. It supports reform in Congress, in the parliament of the streets, and in the local governments led by elected *Akbayan* members. Having town executives provides opportunities to show that party members can promote participatory democracy and good government at the same time. It might even be said that the very formation of *Akbayan* is a political reform. By forming a new type of political party, *Akbayan* is contributing directly to transforming our political party system.

Democracy is at the core of *Akbayan* principles. Our idea of 'state' is one that imposes distinct limits on the state's powers over society. We are against a totalitarian state that insinuates itself into all the spaces of society including private spaces. We operate within a conscious, explicit 'state and civil society' framework. We will defend and promote the integrity and autonomy of civil society organisations as one of the central tasks of *Akbayan*. We will actively work to remove obstacles to political participation, especially restrictions on the self-organisation of the poor such as those on labour unions.

Working closely with social movements and other civil society organisations, in the legislature and in the 'parliament of the street', *Akbayan* is in the forefront of struggles for political and economic reform. Our two representatives in Congress have effectively championed electoral reform, migrant rights, fought against the pro-monopoly privatisation of water utilities and the energy sector and a variety of other issues. In the 'parliament of the streets', *Akbayan* and its affiliated organisations and NGOs work actively on a range of issues from agrarian reform, to anti-corruption campaigns, to women's issues and gay rights. It is in local government, however, that *Akbayan*, with the help of friendly NGOs is investing in long term political reform projects.

Political crisis and the struggle for political reform

Party building is happening in the midst of a deep political crisis. The 2004 national election campaign that is going on at the time of writing provides an excellent illustration. It is a campaign rife with threats of coup d'etat and 'civil war'. The leading candidates for president, incumbent President Gloria Macapagal Arroyo and movie action star Fernando Poe Jr embody the main elements of the crisis. Arroyo became president in January 2001 in the aftermath of massive demonstrations that brought down elected president Joseph Estrada. Although the Supreme Court legitimised then Vice President Arroyo's accession to the presidency as the constitutional successor, Estrada followers never accepted her legitimacy and now rally behind Poe.

Poe follows in the footsteps of his friend Estrada from movie action stardom to become the leading candidate in the presidential election campaign. He threatens to become president because politicians associated with Estrada and the late dictator Marcos see him as their only chance to get back into power. He is a high school dropout and does not have any experience in politics or public administration. Unlike Estrada he has never been elected to public office. He could become president largely because he has become a symbol of the deep frustration of the poor people of the Philippines with Philippine politics. Poe provides a perfect example of the rightwing populism that threatens once again to throw the Philippines into political crisis (Weekly 2000).

Rightwing populism is the product of two key elements in the Philippine political situation. The main 'democratic deficit' is the failure of the political system to respond to the needs of the rural and urban poor (Hutchcroft and Rocamora 2003). Sluggish economic growth going back to the early eighties, uncontrolled trade and capital account liberalisation, privatisation and deregulation have combined to produce an ever increasing number of desperately poor rural and urban inhabitants. Because the poor see that politicians spend more time lining their pockets than doing something about their poverty, they have become cynical about politics. They have also become vulnerable to the promises of political charlatans like Estrada and Poe.

The steady erosion of patron–client ties, the weakness of patronage based machines, and the absence of organisationally coherent, programme based political parties means that a larger and larger proportion of the 40 million strong national electorate, as it were, vote 'blind'. Because of the absence of social and political means to 'organise' electoral participation, voter preference is determined mainly by name recognition. The best known 'names' are those of movie and TV actors, sports personalities, and newscasters. Analysts believe that as little as 20 per cent of the national votes are in 'vote banks' controlled by local politicians.

'Professional' politicians have become increasingly aware of the linked problems of rightwing populism and the weakness of political parties. As early as May 2002, all major political parties gathered in a 'Political Summit' unanimously called for changes in the country's political system through constitutional reform. Political party leaders including the President, the Senate President and the Speaker of the House of Representatives worked together with civil society organisations to push constitutional reform. Leaders and groups who had opposed constitutional reform during the Ramos and Estrada administrations now supported it.

What prevented this consensus from coming to fruition was the attempt of members of the House of Representatives to control the constitutional reform process. They insisted on pushing reform by convening the two houses of congress into a Constituent Assembly. They manoeuvred to put in place a new parliamentary form of government with a ceremonial president, and a unicameral parliament elected in single member districts, the same ones that elect the House of Representatives. This way the House of Representatives would become the all powerful centre of government and incumbent representatives could get themselves elected over and over again.

Because organised civil society groups, key religious leaders and, most importantly the Senate President and a majority of senators opposed the obvious power grab of the House of Representatives, the call for a Constituent Assembly was stopped. These groups instead proposed the election of delegates to a Constitutional Convention at the same time as the May 2004 elections. By the time the Speaker conceded the need to shift to a Constitutional Convention mode of amending the constitution, it was too late to pass legislation in time for the May 2004 elections.

Despite the defeat of the third attempt in as many regimes to organise constitutional reform, there are grounds for cautious optimism on the 'demand side' of political reform. The disjuncture between a political system designed to fit the requirements of the Philippines of the 1930s and the Philippines in the 21st century is producing more insistent demands for political reform. The 1930s political system carried over to today was cut to fit the requirements of a colonial government (thus a powerful governor general/president) and Filipino political leaders with localised power. This was apparently adequate to the needs of a mainly rural, agricultural country with a small population. It is more and more obviously unable to fulfil the requirements of a large, highly urbanised population of 82 million, with a considerably more complex economy.

One of the main determinants of Philippine politics is local – central government relations. There is a powerful chief executive with vast fiscal and patronage powers. But because there is no coherent, stable political party system, the president is dependent on local political bosses to mobilise votes and to implement central government policy. There are therefore equally powerful (if at different stages in the political cycle) presidents and local bosses – a strange political system which is neither centralised nor decentralised. The result is a policy making process that is dominated by deal making, that makes it difficult to pass coherent bills, much less a series of inter related legislation. Having to operate under incoherent, often self-contradictory legislation makes implementation by the bureaucracy similarly difficult. Deal-making and negotiation continues into implementation and even the judicial process.

The effect of this strange system is illustrated in the fate of elected administrations. Most presidents elected since independence in 1946 did not initially have working party majorities. In a few months, however, enough members of the majority party shift to the president's party in order to get in (party) line for patronage and the pork barrel. By the middle of the president's term, the number of officials who have to be given patronage shares gets to the point at which it is impossible to make everyone happy. Towards the end of the president's term, the unhappy politicians outnumber happy ones, making it difficult for the president to get re-elected or after 1987 when the president was not allowed to run for re-election, to get his candidate elected (Choi 2001).

The failure of successive attempts at constitutional reform is particularly unfortunate because it had the potential to break one of the critical 'logjam' points in the process of political reform in the Philippines: local-central government relations. The decentralisation process opened by the passage of the Local Government Code in 1991 created the potential for deep reform in local government. But without equally deep reform at the central government level, a possibility closed off by the failure of attempts at constitutional reform, reforms in local governance could not be 'clinched' for the whole political system. Instead, central government acts as a lid on the dynamism of local politics.

Local politics in the Philippines, going back to the American colonial period, has mainly involved two key contests: one, who is best at generating funds from the central government, and therefore controlling its allocation; two, who controls illegal economic activity such as gambling, and smuggling. These contests have determined the qualifications of contestants, the nature of the contests including elections, and the characteristic activities of winners. The first contest 'shapes' class dynamics in such a way that family connections, university education, and membership in various networks such as university fraternities determine who the winners are. The second contest privileges contestants who are adept at manipulating illegality and the various uses of violence. Neither contest has been conducive to conventional conceptions of good governance. They have kept local governments somnolent and largely 'do nothing' operations.

The main reason why these have been the main contests in local politics is that through most of the past century local governments have not had any money. This, in turn, was because there was not very much taxable economic activity in most local areas. In most rural communities through most of the past century the main economic activity was subsistence agriculture. Where there was share tenancy, landlords also tended to control local politics and of course did not want to be taxed. Illegal economic activity by its very nature could not be taxed except in unconventional ways where the receipts did not go into government coffers (de Dios and Hutchcroft 2003).

The political economy of local communities has gradually changed. Now there are more funds available locally. The agro-export economy built by the Americans concentrated power in Manila where the central government controlled access to international markets. This continued into the post-war period when foreign financial resources, customs collections, and revenue sucked out of local areas added to the centre's power. Partly because there just is no more room physically for more industry in metro Manila, industrial growth has been moving outside – to the Calabarzon area, to Subic, Cebu and further afield in places like General Santos and Davao in Mindanao. This dispersal of industry feeds into internally generated growth in these and nearby places to spur much faster growth.

Central-local economic relations were reflected in, and exacerbated by the highly centralised presidential system of government. The Local Government Code itself might be seen as the translation in the political realm of economic decentralisation. But if economic growth in local areas that are not dependent on favours from central government continues, a whole chain of events in the political realm will follow. This local economic change, combined with the passage of the Local Government Code in 1991 which mandated an automatic transfer of 40 per cent of internal revenue collections and widened the taxing powers of local governments, has meant major increases in the revenue available to local governments (Kerkvliet and Mojares 1991, Lacaba 1995).

Local politicians naturally want more political control over resources generated by more rapid local economic growth. More revenue in local governments will change the nature of local political contests. If nothing else, local business people are increasingly participating to keep the tax bite on them low and to help determine the uses of taxes they do pay. With more money available, the administrative requirements of local government increases, with corresponding changes in the qualifications of those who contest these positions in elections. While this is not yet a nationwide phenomenon and there are still many authoritarian enclaves dominated by warlords, there are enough of these places to believe or at least hope that this is the wave of the future.

Because most studies on Philippine local politics do not posit analyses of how and in what direction change is occurring, it might seem to some that the analysis in this paper is more than a little optimistic. It is admittedly difficult to be politically active with unalloyed pessimism. It should also be pointed out, however, that the kind of change I have described is not generalised movement from patronage driven, clientelistic local politics to World Bank-style 'good governance'. As John Sidel points out in his chapter in this book, local politics in the Philippines cannot be forced into such a rigid framework. What is important is that change is happening. Determining the extent, pace, and direction/s of change requires a lot more research. Political action does not have that luxury.

The varieties of local situations described by Sidel are validated by the experience of *Akbayan*. There are areas such as in several towns in the Bondoc peninsula where the economic control and coercive capabilities of local elites generate temptation to engage in armed struggle among organised small farmers. There are provinces such as Negros Occidental where tight economic and political control by a major economic player, Eduardo Cojuangco, is difficult to challenge locally. In this case, change will have to await action at the national level on the source of Cojuangco's economic power, the coco levy and his control of a massive corporation, the San Miguel Corporation. There are many places, however, where changes in the political economy have disrupted elite control of local politics enough to generate openings for alternative politics. From the vantage point of *Akbayan*, the problem is not the supply of local reform politicians. The problem is *Akbayan's* capacity to identify and recruit them and to assist them after they join the party.

More than difficult, short of impossible

This then is the historical context of *Akbayan*'s party building project. It is a project hemmed in from the Right and ironically also from the Left. Thankfully, both the Right and the armed Left are in the throes of political crisis. The assertion of what might be called a Centre Left political project is at once made necessary and viable by this twin crisis. While there are dreams among some *Akbayan* leaders of 'political rupture' making seizure of power possible at the centre, the locus of accumulation of power by *Akbayan* is, of necessity, in local politics. It is in local politics where the motive forces and the facilitative conditions make accumulation possible.

With only two members in one of two houses in the legislature and no party members in the upper levels of the bureaucracy, *Akbayan*'s capacity to influence national policy is only marginally greater than civil society advocacy. In fact, *Akbayan* has almost always worked within civil society coalitions in pushing its positions on issues. Its capacity to do so, however, is limited by divisions in civil society. It is hemmed in by the open formations of the underground Communist Party of the Philippines and what are called 'rejectionist' breakaway groups that have greater mobilisational capacity and political command of Left rhetoric and on the other side, by civil society groups with better social connections with the Arroyo government.

There are three major ways by which Akbayan is accumulating power. The party list system provides a platform for *Akbayan* to publicise itself and its programmes and together with civil society groups to engage in advocacy on issues. But the three seat limit in the system means permanent minority status in the national legislature. There are ideological and organisational obstacles to accumulation of power through social movement organising. For *Akbayan*, abandoning the 'vanguard party' frame of other Philippine Left groups means assuring autonomy of social movement groups affiliated with it. There are also practical reasons for refusing the demand of some social movement leaders for·*Akbayan* to provide political and organisational leadership to social movements affiliated with it. *Akbayan* does not want the often acrimonious divisions among social movement groups to exacerbate existing divisions within the party. In addition, the party has not yet developed the capacity to service social movement needs. The political blocs with which most of the social movement groups within *Akbayan* are affiliated constitute an ideological and organisational 'filter' between the party and these movements. While this can be seen as a necessary, intermediate stage in party building, it also acts as an obstacle to tightening ideological and political unity within the party.

Six years of party building experience show that it is possible for *Akbayan* to recruit reformist local politicians. But until it accumulates enough power and resources to support these politicians, recruitment will be slow. Under the present political system, it will take a long time for *Akbayan* to accumulate enough electoral capacity to become a major national party. The party list system does not apply in local elections. The centre of gravity of the electoral system is in local politics where political clans and wealthy business people dominate in electoral contests determined largely by money and violence. National elections raise the financial requirements of electoral victory to astronomical proportions. The capacity to organise cheating in the vote count, another determinant in elections, requires bureaucratic influence especially in the Commission on Elections. Finally, the capacity to mobilise violence and threats of violence is in the hands of local and national elites with the exception of the Communist Party of the Philippines and its electoral fronts.

Because *Akbayan* is ideologically inhibited from developing most of these political 'resources', at least part of the national leadership of *Akbayan* has worked at pushing changes in the electoral system and form of government through legislative and constitutional reform. Changes in the electoral system through electronic counting machines and electronic transmission will weaken traditional politician control over the 'technology' of fraud in elections. Overseas voting will enlarge the electorate in a section of the population outside of the capacity of traditional politicians to mobilise. Even support for economic reform will work in this direction where specific reforms remove sources of corruption and weaken patronage networks.

The greatest potential for reform that will go some way to 'level the playing field' between reform and traditional politicians and parties will be a shift to a parliamentary form of government and an electoral system based on proportional representation. A parliamentary form of government and proportional representation will push parties to become organisationally and programmatically coherent, and facilitate party-mediated policy making. The creation of more effective and cohesive political parties, oriented to programmatic rather than particularistic goals, policy rather than pork, is arguably the single most important reform needed to strengthen Philippine democracy. Stronger parties can promote clearer choices to voters, and help to structure political competition toward the realisation of generalised rather than particularistic interests (Abad 1997; Abueva 2002).

Our electoral system, and the actual practice of elections have been one of the most important factors shaping political parties. The intensely personalised character of parties derives partly from the fact that individual candidates are elected in a 'first past the post' system. 'During elections, it is not so much the political parties that are the real mobilising organisations but the candidate's electoral machinery and network of relatives, friends, political associates and allies' (David 1994: 101). Because at the base of the electoral system, the municipality, the power and status of families are at stake, all means are availed of including cheating and violence to achieve victory.

We have become so used to money politics that unconsciously we believe that 'that's just the way politics is'. In fact, elections in many countries, in particular, in Europe do not require massive expenditure. There are many factors that can explain these differences in political practice, but the main factor is the electoral system. The proportional representation (PR) electoral systems used in Europe push elections away from personal contests towards party contests. In the process, this will also lessen the use of money and violence in elections, and create one of the conditions necessary for reforming our political party system.

The party list system introduced by the 1987 constitution provides an experiment in PR elections. But the system is so confused that it can hardly be seen as indicating the potential of PR systems. To start with, the 1987 constitution mixes up the contradictory requirements of PR and sectoral representation within the narrow political space of twenty percent of the seats in the House of Representatives. Congress then added to the problems by limiting the number of seats a single party can win to three. The Supreme Court made things even worse by imposing a formula for the allocation of seats that guarantees that only a few of the available seats will be allocated.

What we need is the revision and expansion of the existing party list system, or an outright shift of the whole system to PR. If voters choose between parties instead of individual candidates, it will lessen the intensity of personal and clan contests which are the main sources of violence and money politics. Parties will then be required to strengthen the organisational and programmatic requirements for electoral victory. Minimally, parties will be forced to distinguish themselves from each other enough for voters to make choices. The shift in the centre of gravity of organisational work away from individual candidates will force parties to strengthen themselves organisationally.

One formula that is being talked about is a system of elections for a unicameral parliament where half of the seats are elected in enlarged single member districts and the other half through a PR system. Single member districts are seen as a way of securing the support of district congress persons who have to approve legislation calling for elections of delegates to a Constitutional Convention. While a Constitutional Convention will allow non-politicians to get elected as delegates, more powerful district representatives will be able to get their people elected too. This will require some accommodation with them. In the party list PR system, existing restrictions on traditional parties would be removed. Such a system would be advantageous for *Akbayan* which is organised precisely for such contests. Not only would such a system be new for traditional politicians, most of them will be too busy contesting seats in single member districts to build parties that can successfully compete in PR elections. Until such changes happen, however, *Akbayan* will have to accumulate electoral power through long and painstaking work in local contests.

The changes in the electoral system that pro-reform civil society groups are proposing are specific to the Philippine situation. We are not making general propositions about a necessary connection between proportional representation and strong parties. As Olle Tornquist points out, India and Great Britain have strong parties without proportional representation. Here the differentiation that Martin Shefter makes between 'internally mobilised' parties of elites who are already within the prevailing regime and have access to patronage resources and 'externally mobilised' parties of those *outside the regime* who do not have access to patronage and instead rely on ideological appeals in their quest for a mass following might be useful (Shefter 1994). Philippine political history has clearly privileged 'internally mobilised' parties. The issue is what changes can be made in the electoral system that will go some distance in 'levelling the playing field' for new 'externally mobilised' parties such as *Akbayan*.

Local governance and party building

New protagonists and the changing nature of political contests have brought an edge of dynamism to local politics. Younger, better educated politicians are open to good governance ideas especially when these ideas can also strengthen them against political opponents and position them for higher office. But political change has also disrupted old patronage networks and weakened political parties. Without effective political parties, local politicians' links with the central government will be irregular and unpredictable. There are only a few available ways to strengthen a local politician's position, even then only in larger, vote rich municipalities.

What we tell these young, local politicians is that the existing ladder available for them to move up in their political careers will require them to throw out their ideals and become corrupt. This ladder, moreover, has become more and more rickety. *Akbayan* is a new ladder that will enable them to keep their ideals, and to sharpen them and put them into practice. *Akbayan* can provide an organisational base for elections and governance. The problem is that the brightest among these politicians then point out that our ladder only has a few rungs in it. At this point we invite them to help us build more rungs in the ladder.

One of the rungs in the ladder that civil society activists (led by the Institute for Popular Democracy [IPD] and the Institute for Politics and Governance [IPG]) have built is something mischievously called BATMAN. In late 1996, local leaders who had been drawn into discussions for building a new political party told *Akbayan* organisers that if they were serious about building a party they should figure out how to help the local leasers to win in elections at the *barangay* level, the lowest of the administrative and political structure. Seven Manila-based NGOs including IPG and IPD hurriedly put together a '*Barangay* Administration Training Manual', BATMAN, and trained over a thousand people to participate in the *barangay* elections in 1997. This was the first *barangay* election since the Local Government Code was introduced which allotted a share of internal revenue allotments to *barangay* and honoraria for elected *barangay* officials – accounting for the interest in the election. Because a large number of people who were trained won in the elections, there was a demand for continued work at the *barangay* level.

BATMAN represented a distinct phase in the development of civil society governance work in the Philippines. Although broadly understood there was civil society governance work before the passage of the Local Government Code (LGC), most of this 'people empowerment' did not target local governments as venues for such activity. At best civil society groups worked parallel to, and periodically did advocacy work, but seldom worked *within* local governments. After the passage of the LGC in 1991, civil society groups concentrated on campaigning for the implementation of provisions for civil society representation in special bodies in local government units. But BATMAN was the first network that systematically undertook local governance work (Fabros 2003).

But why *barangay*? The original BATMAN 'Consortium Program on Barangay Governance' said, simply 'The *barangay* is the lowest unit of governance in the Philippines. It is also the newest. It is here in rural villages and urban poor communities, which comprise the majority of *barangays*, that the greatest possibilities for citizen action to deepen democracy in the Philippines can be found . . . *Barangays*, both rural and urban, are the sites of most of the face-to-face communities left in the wake of urbanisation and commercialisation of Philippine society. Dominance of elite groups and the centralisation of politics and administration have, for most of the past century, meant that town centres and cities have been the locus of political life. Natural communities have largely been by- passed. . . . The absence of administrative units at the level of the *barangay* [until the Local Government Code was passed in 1991] was an expression of these political conditions.'

Empowerment of the poor is the bedrock of BATMAN governance intervention. The vision is a considerable distance from old 'seize the state' Left paradigms, but the ambition remains as lofty, that of changing the very nature of political relationships. 'These social and institutional arrangements generated a political culture anchored on exchanges of private instead of public goods as the characteristic "currency" of political relationships. Politicians provide jobs, money for a variety of consumption needs to individuals and their relatives who return the favour in terms of personal support for an individual politician and his clan. Many of the ills of Philippine politics – nepotism, corruption, violence, lack of transparency, government inefficiency can be traced to this essential element in Philippine political culture' (quoted from the Consortium Program of 1997, p. 2).

While reform initiatives at other levels of government can generate changes in specific elements of the political system including the central bureaucracy and the very form of government itself (as in a shift from a presidential to a parliamentary form), the most thoroughgoing changes towards democratic governance are possible only at the base of the political system, the *barangay*. It is here where the largest number of people can participate in political activities close enough to their day-to-day life to affect political behaviour, and over time, the political culture itself.

The creation of *barangay* government units under the 1991 Local Government Code created, for the first time in Philippine history, the possibility of lowering the centre of gravity of Philippine politics from the town and city centres where elites dominate to the level of the *barangay* where poor people live. The Local Government Code provides for a salaried *barangay* captain and *barangay* council, an allotment from internal revenue funds, limited ordinance making and taxation and borrowing powers. Quite simply, it is now possible to do things at the level of the *barangay*, enough to generate *barangay*-level politics instead of *barangay* politics being only an adjunct of municipal politics.

Progressives have not been too different from the elite in their neglect of the *barangay* as a community. The most extensive organising of rural poor communities that has been done by the national democratic movement has either been secret or focused on 'guerrilla zone preparation'. NGO intervention has unwittingly contributed to bypassing and disregarding *barangay*-level communities. While avoiding the traditional, family-centred political relationships, NGOs have concentrated on building 'peoples organisations', new social units only tangentially connected to pre-existing communities. More often than not, NGO organising and political reform initiatives have been couched in discourse posed as counter to local political culture.

Starting with seven Manila-based NGOs, BATMAN quickly expanded to 42 mostly local NGOs. The maintenance needs of the consortium were served by the Institute for Politics and Governance (IPG) which became its secretariat. Apart from training *barangay* officials, BATMAN assisted in *barangay* development planning. The Local Government Code provides for *barangay* assemblies with limited legislative powers where all *barangay* residents can participate, the only form of direct democracy available in the current political system. *Barangay* governments are obliged to formulate *barangay* development plans through the creation of a *barangay* development council with provisions for NGO and peoples organisation participation. These institutional arrangements open up the possibility of a broadly participatory political system. Over time *barangay* development planning became the signature activity of BATMAN.

After 5 years of work, what has BATMAN wrought? BATMAN-NGOs work in over 2500 *barangays*, among which 1200 have undertaken development planning. The BATMAN experience clearly had a multiplier effect. Even if 1200 *barangays* are a small minority of the country's roughly 45,000 *barangays*, the BATMAN experience is already spreading as local governance 'best practice'. This facilitated the adoption of development planning in adjoining *barangays*. In many cases, mayors from other towns and even governors, asked local BATMAN NGOs to implement BATMAN programmess in their areas.

There have been material benefits. Having *barangay* development plans facilitated access to resources from higher local government units and other sources. *Barangay* priorities also affected municipal budgets. Where there were sympathetic mayors, municipal development plans were based on identified priorities in the *barangay* development plans. New perspectives on the uses of public monies also began to develop.

New priorities emphasised livelihood projects, potable water supply, *barangay* electrification and communication systems. This last is crucial because it relates to the original BATMAN goal of facilitating the generation of 'public goods' as a way of changing the political nexus between *barangay* and town centre elites. 'Beautification projects' were either vanity projects of politicians or sources of graft from construction kickbacks. Projects with palpable impact on the livelihood of *barangay* residents can raise the stakes in citizen participation.

Because of the extent of need, whether for livelihood or public infrastructure, BATMAN efforts can hardly make a dent on the overall problem. BATMAN is relevant firstly as an experiment in building participatory democracy at the grassroots. From this vantage point, BATMAN has been a success. Whether from the perspective of *barangay* government institutions, or NGO and popular organisation viewpoints, or citizen attitudes towards governance, much has been achieved. The most clear cut change has occurred among leaders of popular organisations. 'They have evolved beyond their initial orientation as political activists who expose and oppose the wrong doings of government from outside formal state structures. They no longer merely point out what is wrong or lacking, but they have become actual participants in the change process, proposing solutions and alternatives, working for reforms from outside *and* inside government' (Santos 2004).

Elections to parties

Many BATMAN areas quickly moved from *barangay* development planning to electoral intervention. From elections, it is a short step to issues related to political parties. The concerns were practical/political: how do you link the people who get elected so they can work together to elect more people at higher political levels? Who will work to change the legal and policy frameworks that determine spaces for participatory politics? These issues were discussed as early as October 1997, at the beginning of BATMAN. 'Explored were the various possibilities that might arise from linking up the program visibly with a specific political party. In the end, the participants agreed that there is a need for a progressive national vehicle which can infuse sustainability into the governance efforts of individual *barangays*' (Conference Report 1997: 2).

Although *Akbayan* was not founded until three months after this discussion, BATMAN has been associated with *Akbayan* since its inception. It has been a complex and at times contentious relationship. BATMAN does not have a formal, organisational relationship with *Akbayan* or any other political party. After an acrimonious debate on the nature of relations between the Institute of Politics and Governance, the BATMAN secretariat, and *Akbayan*, the Institute of Politics and Governance formally asserted its independence as a civil society formation, an assertion that *Akbayan* also formally affirmed.[1]

Because BATMAN in fact works closely with *Akbayan* at both the national and local levels, however, the relationship continues to be a subject of discussion. The problem is not one of hiding *Akbayan*'s role as if BATMAN was a 'front' and as if there was an underground relationship.[2] The problem is more that the dominant Left experience, that of the national democratic movement, is one where NGOs and people's organisations are instrumentalised, their integrity compromised by hidden party control. Even non-national democratic Left groups continue to be influenced by this perspective to the point where even within *Akbayan* prior to the party's formal position on the issue, some leaders believed that the party should have veto power over BATMAN.

Since the dominant Left experience is so different, it is difficult to imagine, even more so actually to organise, a relationship where civil society groups such as BATMAN are autonomous but working close to a political party such as *Akbayan* – in a relationship that is negotiated along the way. While the current relationship is mutually beneficial, there is danger that *Akbayan* will push its agenda within BATMAN to the point of compromising BATMAN's integrity. Conversely, organisations within BATMAN can use BATMAN and its political and other resources to achieve certain goals within *Akbayan*.

Working with a party such as *Akbayan* will enable a project like BATMAN to link up its municipalities with each other, leverage resources from national line agencies, and most importantly, become oriented towards a 'progressive national political project'. For *Akbayan*, BATMAN is important for identifying reform-oriented local politicians who can be recruited into the party and can push its good governance agenda. But roles have to be clearly delineated to minimise friction. This cannot be done if differences and conflicts are swept under the rug.

Because BATMAN has been slow to develop programmes at the municipal level, *Akbayan* has stepped in and developed its own programme for assisting *Akbayan* mayors. The *Akbayan* Government Affairs Committee has slowly developed capacity for assisting *Akbayan* mayors with governance problems ranging from revenue generation to service delivery. When BATMAN finally gets around to developing its own municipal programmes, if nothing else because non-*Akbayan* reform mayors also need assistance, there will be more than enough to do. But the relationship between the party governance programme, and BATMAN's civil society programme will have to be carefully delineated to prevent conflicts and misunderstanding.

The Left and the 'radical democratic option'

In a careful evaluation of the BATMAN experience,[3] one common conclusion is that while it was necessary to establish a *barangay* base, BATMAN will have greater political impact only if it succeeds in scaling up to the municipal level (Estrella and Izatt 2004). Without organised intervention for participatory democracy at the municipal level, the potential gains from *barangay* level intervention cannot be clinched. Worse, with few exceptions, the generation of funds for *barangay* projects have had to be done through old circuits of patronage.

Scaling up to the municipal level is not only logical, it is also inevitable. This is because, as has been pointed out, 'municipal/city government have the power to affect drastically the programmes and reform initiatives at the *barangay* level. For instance, a *barangay* official, who is in opposition to the mayor or any key official in the municipal/city government, can have a very difficult time obtaining the release of his/her *barangay* Internal Revenue Allotment. Municipal/city governments, headed by the mayor, have the power to determine resource availability, budget allocations, the provision of support services, the kinds of development programs. With the political will, they can implement reforms in government, such as promote participatory planning, combat corruption and improve revenue collection. Our reform gains in the *barangays*, complemented with initiatives at the municipal/city level, would expand the scope for reforms and have greater impact on alleviating poverty and achieving genuine political reforms' (in Santos 2004).

If scaling up is the main organisational challenge for BATMAN, locating its politics within a broader Left frame is its main theoretical challenge. Interrogating 'official' governance and democratisation discourse is only a requisite beginning. Even more important is finding BATMAN's place in the ongoing reorientation of the Philippine Left. It is not as if the process has not been started. What needs to be done is to systematise theoretical work, to undertake an organised process of summation of often un-systematised theoretical unities from practice, and open debate on contentious issues. Relating to ongoing international debates on similar issues can also help to sharpen issues and accelerate the process.

Locating – as it were, 'scaling up' – BATMAN discourse within a 'Left-Right' frame is particularly important because of the convergence of what has been called 'revisionist neo-liberalism' and certain strands of 'post-Marxism'. According to Mohan and Stokke (2000: 249), these two intellectual streams converge in the 'belief that states or markets cannot be *solely* responsible for ensuring social equality' and economic well-being, and recognise thus the need to consider *the local* as the site of empowerment and hence as a locus of knowledge generation and development intervention' But, Mohan and Stokke also point out that these two different strands still present important differences in emphasis. Neoliberalism focuses on institutional reforms and social development through community participation and empowerment, but within the established social order, i.e. without sacrificing the power and privileges of the powerful. On the contrary, post-Marxism supports a more radical view of empowerment, mainly based on social conscientisation and mobilisation (building collective identities) to challenge hegemonic interests within the state and the market. In this line, 'empowerment of marginalised groups requires a structural transformation of economic and political relations towards a radically democratised society' (Mohan and Stokke 2000: 249).

Most BATMAN activists would probably say 'What's the big deal? It's clear we stand on what you call the 'post-Marxist' side whether we call ourselves Marxist or not.' True enough. But without consciousness of the distinction, the danger of co-optation or the related pitfall of opportunism – of being used while taking money from neo-liberal local governance projects – is great. At the same time, it will be difficult to identify areas of convergence with reformers who may operate within a neo-liberal frame but who work on projects such as anti-corruption which is a common concern. Finally, without discourse maps for navigating the white waters of local governance discourse, we cannot maximise the empowerment potential of local governance projects such as BATMAN.

Because of the ideological hegemony of Maoist armed struggle through most of the 1970s and 1980s, Left theorising on open, unarmed strategies has been slow and painful. While Maoist ideological hegemony was broken with the massive splits within the Communist Party of the Philippines (CPP) in the first half of the 1990s, Maoists continue to intimidate other Left groups ideologically. Often unconsciously, other Left groups still measure their 'revolutionary' credentials against unexamined standards set by the CPP. This has not necessarily been a problem for BATMAN. But because it works closely with political parties such as *Akbayan*, and self-consciously ideological political blocs, BATMAN's theoretical formation has been affected. One approach that has been influential within BATMAN is what might be called theoretical pluralism:

Participation can be likened to a multiple-lane highway where different vehicles traverse different lanes. Slow-moving vehicles look at participation from the vantage point of building empowered sustainable communities and promoting alternative governance models. Vehicles using the fast lane are those that view participation from the vantage point of political society – movements that try to seize 'moments of state ruptures' through heightened political participation that directly challenges the legitimacy of elite rule and the status quo. Both vehicles, however, do not compete but complement each other in the sense that the multiple-lane highway goes to one direction...By weaving these struggles together, it will somehow hasten the work of each individual form and build on the strengths of each other while minimising possible setbacks brought about by the rigidity of using only one form of struggle(Villarin 2004).

This approach is a reflection of the ideological heterogeneity of BATMAN and the Philippine Left as a whole. It has been useful for enabling ideologically diverse groups to form coalitions and to coexist in new multi-tendency parties such as *Akbayan*. But at some point, theoretical contradictions between the propositions that underlie the different 'lanes' have to be grappled with.

Elaborating on the concept, Villarin calls 'moments of state ruptures' occasions when '...political and even social movements that try to seize "moments of state ruptures" through heightened political participation that directly challenges the legitimacy of elite rule and the status quo'. This orientation is understandable given the ideological history of the Philippine Left. It is an intermediate step between Maoist 'protracted peoples war' and varieties of 'national liberation movements' frameworks and what might be called a 'radical democratic option'. It prevents a radical break with the past and enables groups who subscribe to it to think of themselves as 'revolutionary'. In other words, it is an approach, I would insist, that is different from the underlying assumptions of BATMAN which I would characterise as closer to a 'radical democratic option'.

One problem is that a 'state ruptures' orientation is akin to the Maoist and national liberation movement framework in its focus on 'seizing the [central] state'. This is in direct contradiction to the 'local governance' frame of BATMAN. This is not just a matter of division of tasks or different 'lanes' of vehicles going in the same direction. Working towards 'state ruptures' outside of an armed struggle strategy means vulnerability to coup attempts and other ways of forcing a radical break in the distribution of power at the national level. For BATMAN the problem is that a 'state ruptures' frame is hesitant about, if not averse to, political reform and the slow, painstaking accumulation of power through a combination of electoral work and mass struggles. Saying both approaches can coexist hides the judgment underlying the assignment of the 'slow lane' to 'building empowered sustainable communities and promoting alternative governance models'.

This issue needs to be explored and debated intensively because it has many ramifications. The Latin American experience clearly shows that a strategy of slow accumulation of power in local politics has been more productive than old national liberation strategies or its later non-armed version 'transition through rupture'. Lula's ascent to the presidency in Brazil was built on his Workers Party's accumulation of power and experience in local politics. In Mexico, on the other hand, the Party of the Democratic Revolution (PRD) which is oriented towards 'transition through rupture' is moving further and further away from achieving national power.

Cross-cutting divergences between old Left discourse and new Left ideas, between anti-state NGO discourse and newer ideas pushing civil society intervention in political party formation, have not been carefully debated in the Philippine progressive movement. People have tended to be reticent about discussing these issues. But precisely because of this reticence, suspicions about BATMAN being a 'front' of *Akbayan* continue to circulate. In the end what may be required is not that discourse settles into a single, stable order but that more people accept that unstable, shifting, negotiated relationships are more productive of the participatory democracy we are fighting for.

Notes

1. At a 13 July 2001 meeting between the *Akbayan* Executive Committee and the board of the Institute for Politics and Governance, the *Akbayan* Executive Committee said that: '*Akbayan* does not claim the Institute for Politics and Governance as its political institute. It has no veto powers over its internal decisions nor a claim to participate in the election of an executive director or the hiring of its staff. It is within *Akbayan*'s programme to defend the autonomy of institutions of civil society from institutions of the state and political parties who want to get into the state.... On the other hand, the history of the Institute for Politics and Governance and *Akbayan* has generated a relationship of closeness. The Institute for Politics and Governance was set up by members of political blocs that made up *Akbayan*, and individuals from the Philippine Democratic Party and the Liberal Party, to facilitate and assist in the work of progressive political groups and to help set up progressive political initiatives...*Akbayan* does not claim ownership of the Institute for Politics and Governance but reserves the right of their members who are members of

the board of the Institute to make decisions on their own from the vantage point of Akbayan's interests...'. Minutes of the Joint Meeting of the IPG Board and the Akbayan Executive Committee, 13 July 2001.

2. The standard practice in Marxist Leninist parties in the Philippines is to have an underground party controlling above ground organisations including political parties.

3. This is to be published in the course of 2004.

8
Trade Unions, Institutional Reform and Democracy: Nigerian Experiences with South African and Ugandan Comparisons[1]

Björn Beckman

Introduction

This paper is about the capacity of trade unions to intervene in a context of political and economic reform, in the interests of their own members, and in support of wider popular interests in society. It focuses on the formation of a union-based labour regime as a key area of institutional reform, creating the conditions for such democratic intervention. I begin by recalling the case against trade unions – why they are seen as an obstacle to reform, and why it is expected, anyway, that they will increasingly be marginalised in the context of globalisation. In developing the case for seeing unions as important institutions of popular representation I propose a different reading of global tendencies, suggesting that unions are in fact on the rise. Turning to Africa, where it has been assumed that this is least likely to happen, I refer to great variations in union performance, including exceptional achievements in South Africa and repression and marginalisation in Uganda. These two contrasting experiences are briefly summarized. The main empirical illustrations, however, are from Nigeria, where I have studied the national union centre, the Nigeria Labour Congress, and, in particular, the textile workers union.

The case against the unions

The *deregulation of labour markets* is for some liberalisers a critical institutional reform which they claim will achieve many things. The rights and freedoms of markets and individuals stand opposed to the collectivist, state regulated labour regimes that have entrenched themselves in both rich and poor countries. Apart from theoretical and ideological arguments there seem to be strong pragmatic reasons in favour of deregulation where regulation has already struck roots and for resisting regulation where it has not. Existing labour market regulations, including laws protecting union rights, make major national firms as well as potential foreign investors look elsewhere and discourage small local entrepreneurs on whom poor people depend for employment and income. The logic of development seems therefore to be firmly on the side of the liberalisers and the deregulators. Even fainthearted governments, the assumed captives of entrenched, recalcitrant union interests, find that in practice labour markets liberalise themselves even within the framework of existing pro-union regulation, as noted with satisfaction by Ulf Jakobsson (2000), a prominent Swedish economist. Such regulation is bypassed or diluted through the 'spontaneous liberalisation of the labour market', which, in his view, helps to explain the unexpected capacity of the Swedish economy to raise employment levels from the rock bottom levels of the early 1990s.

Liberalisers have more reasons for disliking unions. They want to shift resources from the public sector to more productive uses in the private sector which supposedly is in the interest of everyone but in particular of the poor who will benefit from economic efficiency and growth. The poor are also expected to benefit from a shift in spending within the public sector itself, from low priority to high priority areas, targeting those where markets are the least capable of offering effective solutions – public health, for instance, and education for groups with special disadvantages – as distinct from generalised subsidies. Public sector unions are seen as a particular obstacle to such public sector reforms, with their assumed vested interests in existing employment patterns and pay packages. But unions generally are expected to be opposed to the reforms, because of representing wage earners and the assumed beneficiaries of current patterns of state welfare spending.

There is an even more basic, political reason why liberalisers dislike unions. They are seen as part of a political coalition that has encouraged excessive public sector expansion and macro-economic imbalances. From this perspective, the deregulation of labour markets is seen as a way of breaking statist political coalitions that stand in the way of the wider reform project and thus of the enhanced welfare of the poor.

What are the unions, anyway? Unions are often criticised for not even being the friends of many workers, and not only by liberalisers. The latter find ammunition for their critique from within the labour movement itself. In advanced industrial societies, declining membership and low levels of participation reinforce a picture of bureaucratised organisations with weak democratic structures that fail to respond to the needs of new employees who do not fit the social categories on the basis of which unions were formed in the first place. In many instances, not the least in post-colonial societies, unions have been incorporated into statist political structures, undercutting their claims to represent the workers, turning union leaders into just another set of political rent seekers, a privileged and often corrupt 'labour aristocracy'. Moreover, the limited size of the formal wage sector in much of the world tends to make unions unlikely vehicles, in the eyes of many, for improving the material conditions of the mass of the population who are small agricultural producers, crafts people, small traders or engaged in other, often multiple livelihood strategies outside the formal labour market. Are not the lucky few who find themselves in wage employment a sort of 'labour aristocracy' compared to the rest of the population? Do unions not serve to reinforce the privileged access of a minority to a state backed formal economy and to subsidised public services – the benefits of which are outside the reach of the majority?

Looking at global trends, moreover, shouldn't unions be regarded as a spent force, the more or less atrophied remnants of a decaying social order? Triumphalist liberalisers like to think so but there are also voices of alarm on the union side which seem to confirm that a radical shift is taking place globally, a shift which may make trade unions become a thing of the past. In a study sponsored by Dutch trade union federations Thomas (1995: 3) claims that 'while for more than a century the trade union movement has been an important actor in defending the interests of workers and in struggling for independence and democracy, it now faces in large parts of the world almost total elimination as a significant social institution'. Thomas suggests that Asia, Africa and Latin America have been particularly affected, although it is a world-wide trend. In East Asia 'unprecedented rapid industrialisation has been achieved along with the oppression of labour organisation', while African unions face overwhelming problems in the absence of industrialisation.

A pro-union case

In this chapter I take a different view of the likely future role of unions in the world economy and of the relationship between trade unions, institutional reform, and democratisation. I disagree with both the liberal triumphalists and the union pessimists that unions are on their way out and argue, on the contrary, that this is a misreading. I refer to the structural and political features that are likely to strengthen the role of unions as the global working class grows in numbers, skills, organisational experience, and political competence. Despite their limitations in terms of internal structure, leadership and effective reach, unions constitute one of the few institutions capable of representing the interests of large popular strata. What they do is important not only for what happens to the welfare of their own members but for other segments of society that lack effective organisations of their own. Politically, they are instrumental in disseminating notions of individual and collective rights, and the need for representation and bargaining, to other groups in society. In some societies, the working class itself is a large and growing force, but also elsewhere, as in much of Africa, where the size of the immediate constituency is small, unions can play a leading role in wider alliances in civil society in defence of such rights and interests. In this respect, unions draw support from the activation of international regulatory agencies and conventions and from a growing network of organisations and alliances, including global civil rights movements and consumer protection groups. These make it increasingly difficult for managements or for governments to maintain or impose labour regimes that do not recognise workers' rights to collective organisation and bargaining.

Do unions obstruct necessary reforms? Unions are keenly conscious of the need to respond to the changes in the world economy, technological developments, shifts in global production and markets, the trans-nationalisation of enterprises, the accelerated mobility of financial flows, and changes in state policies and regulatory capacities. In addition, unions have to respond to local crises and conjunctures, that are often aggravated by failures of governments to manage the resources and institutions at their disposal. Some unions may indeed have vested interests in defunct social orders which have been undermined by such changes. The scope for resistance is often limited and temporary. Typically, therefore, unions develop a combination of strategies, seeking both to protect earlier gains and to accommodate change.

Unions realise that the 'new order' is not simply given but rather is the outcome of policy choices that reflect a changing balance of forces in society, in which the intervention of international creditors often plays an important role. Unions therefore seek to influence the policy process and for that purpose they forge alliances with other groups in society, and internationally. Often vulnerable if isolated, unions frame their strategies so as to enhance wider popular support in order to stand a better chance of surviving suppression by governments and employers.

Public sector unions, for instance, appeal to the wider popular stake in the provision and quality of public services, while manufacturing unions seek to mobilise support for maintaining and expanding national industrial capacity, propagating the need to defend and reconstitute an ailing national development project.

Unionists are not convinced that market forces on their own will resolve the problems of mass unemployment. On the contrary, they normally believe that it is the duty of the state to take an active part in supporting economic development and expanding employment. Nor do they necessarily change their mind because of the past failures of their own states in this respect. They draw support from historical and contemporary evidence from elsewhere which demonstrates that efficient state intervention pays off. The challenge as they see it is therefore to have the state intervene more efficiently, with less waste and corruption and greater accountability. If nothing else, they believe that the state can achieve a great deal through developing the social and economic infrastructure of the society, especially in the field of education and manpower development. They are outraged by the non-functioning of public services and they have no doubts about all the scandalous misappropriations that are behind it all. They give voice to an outrage widely shared outside union ranks.

There is amongst unionists an awareness of their privilege, and of an obligation – in view of their organisational experience – to voice popular concerns and confront the state on behalf of the people. Are they justified in this? In most societies they face developments where economic and political elites benefit glaringly from their control over private property and public institutions. Domestic and international experts may be convinced that the 'bitter pill' they offer is in the interests of everybody in the long run, and especially of the poor. Experts, however, do not operate in a power vacuum. Implementation will take place in the context of the balance of forces in society. This is where unions think that they have more legitimacy than either the power elites or their advisers to represent popular interests.

None of this suggests that unions necessarily have the right solutions. It is to argue, however, that unions often represent strategically located groups in society that are intensely concerned about development strategy, not only having regard for their own members, but for people in general and especially ordinary, poor people. What they have above all is organisation, a commodity generally in short supply but which is particularly needed when societies are undergoing major transformation. In countries where unions are repressed or controlled, this potential for organisation needs to be tapped so as to create the possibility of a transition to a more democratic social order. The potential is inherent in the organisation of wage work itself, and wage workers, even when they are few in number, are usually pioneers in establishing forms of popular organisation based on constitutionally regulated forms of representation, bargaining, and conflict resolution. They serve as role models for other groups and they bring these ideas with them when joining political parties or in dealing with the state.

The formation of a union-based labour regime

Unions may obstruct reforms. The solution, however, is for unions to be recognised, not just because they are 'stake holders' but because of their capacity for developing institutions for the regulation of conflicts of interest relating not only to individual work places but more generally to relations of domination, inequality, representation, and integration in society at large. The most urgent institutional reforms in this context are therefore those that promote and protect workers' rights to organise and bargain collectively, the institutionalisation of a *union-based labour regime*. Governments and employers need to be compelled to recognise the rights of workers to form unions, that working conditions should be agreed upon through collective bargaining and that there are agreed procedures for resolving conflicts, including the right to strike. The extent and application of these rights are contested everywhere. Certain basic standards have broad international acceptance and have been codified in ILO conventions. International human rights conventions and national constitutions also refer to such labour rights. European trade unions struggle to have a full specification of labour rights included in the treaties of the European Union.

The purpose of this chapter is to explore the implications of such institutionalisation (or its absence) – that is, the establishment, extension, and consolidation of a union-based labour regime – for wider institutional developments in society and for democratisation. I suggest that a widely accepted and well-consolidated union-based labour regime, enhances union bargaining power and encourages union participation in the politics of reform. This in turn improves the chances that an element of popular participation and accountability is asserted in the reform process.

These propositions are expanded and explored empirically below, drawing in particular on own work (much of it jointly authored with Gunilla Andrae) on Nigerian trade unions but also on comparative work on trade unions and economic liberalisation. South Africa and Uganda are used as contrasting examples, the former as a case of major union engagement with the reform process and in institution building, the latter as one where unions have been destroyed and marginalised. The Nigerian experience shows evidence of both achievements and failures. The chapter discusses the recent experience of the reconstituted Nigeria Labour Congress and, in particular, reflects on the remarkable 'success story' of the Nigerian textile workers union.

First, however, the chapter outlines an alternative reading of the global scenario where unions, far from being a social institution on the way out, as suggested above, are seen as a rising force.

The resilience of unions[2]

The rise of the new working class

The most immediate reason for the resilience of trade unions as significant players in the world economy is the rapid expansion in recent decades, especially in Asia, of production and services based on wage work. The number of wage workers in the world economy has grown at an unprecedented rate (World Bank 1995; ILO 1997). Much of this growth takes place in manufacturing work places with production processes of a conventional type, such as have encouraged the growth historically of collective forms of workers' organisations. While such work places have been on the decline in the advanced industrial economies this is not representative of the wider global economy. Attempts to prevent the emergence of trade unions or to maintain state and company control have been short-lived in the most dynamic economies. The successive upgrading of industrial structure, as in South Korea, have produced a skilled, well-organised and assertive working class. Authoritarian labour regimes continue to survive in other expanding industrial economies like China but the evidence of growing work place unrest and activism suggests that such countries have difficulties in insulating themselves from domestic as well as global pressures. The collapse of the authoritarian order in Indonesia, for instance, has led to the flourishing of new labour organisations.

Much of the increase in wage work has taken place within rapidly expanding public sectors, both facilitating and feeding on the rise in commodity production and trade. The progress of unionisation within the public services, although slow compared to manufacturing, keeps expanding globally. More categories of workers are freeing themselves from restrictions imposed by states on unionisation in essential services.

Unions, social pacts, and the politics of reform

The movement towards disengagement from authoritarian labour regimes often runs alongside new forms of engagement with state and politics, involving new social pacts as part of the economic reform process. Formal wage workers are important in the politics of economic reform, beyond their numbers. Part of the reason is their special link to crisis-ridden national development projects. Rapid industrialisation and the expansion of public services were always high on the national agenda of post-colonial states, making the emerging working class an index of progress and modernity. Crises and globalisation invariably lead to cuts in employment, wages, and the public services. This may undermine the market and work place bargaining power of labour. Simultaneously, however, the political bargaining power exerted by labour has in many instances been enhanced as a result of the impact of intensified social conflict caused by the cuts and of the weakening of state institutions.

The new concern of policy makers and international finance institutions with dialogue and social pacts is indicative of an awareness that organised labour needs to be accommodated in the reform process. The movement towards such social pacts often occurs in a political conjuncture of crisis and instability. A feature of this context seems to be that the balance of forces that has sustained existing relations of power is upset, threatening the existing political order. Social pacts may be an attempt to bolster or reconstruct a faltering political order by broadening its social base and infusing it with fresh legitimacy drawn from popular connections. For trade unions this may provide an opening for influencing the substance of the reforms while simultaneously seeking acceptance for labour rights. The politics of pacts reinforces an element of recognition, a *locus standi*, an entitlement to be heard. From the perspective of organised labour, such recognition has not come lightly where it exists at all, and it continues to be contested. By opting for strategies based on dialogue and social pacts governments and employers impose constraints on their own freedom to pursue alternative strategies based on repressing, marginalising and ignoring unions as stake-holders.

Schmitter and Grote (1997) have documented the revival of what they call 'macro-corporatist concertation' in the historic heartland of union power in Western Europe. The revival is partly prompted, they suggest, by the specific 'imperative' of meeting the convergence criteria for European monetary unification but also by the same global tendencies that we argue have opened up the space for policy bargaining by unions in the third world. The revival seems to contradict prevailing expectations that the accelerated liberalisation of the world economy will speed up the dismantling of corporatist labour regimes. The authors report on a series of economic and social pacts in Ireland, Finland, Spain, Portugal, Belgium, Italy, the Netherlands, Austria and Switzerland in the late 1980s and 1990s involving governments, employers and workers, some based in formal corporatist institutions, others being negotiated on an *ad hoc* basis. The European evidence points to the need to see dialogue and social pacts as global phenomena that are linked to problems of creating legitimacy and acceptance of policies of economic reform.

Labour rights as an international agenda

Despite the evidence of union decline in parts of the world, the overall picture suggests a more open and contested arena, with scope for fresh unionisation and greater union autonomy. The reassertion of labour rights has in recent years received fresh support at the international level. It represents a confluence of forces, involving a range of civil society actors and their international allies, as well as international regulatory agencies. The international labour movement has been reactivated since the end of the cold war. The International Confederation of Free Trade Unions (ICFTU) and the International Trade Secretariats (ITS) have increased their membership and intensified their activities globally. In the past, cold war trade union rivalry created a stalemate where many substantial third world unions decided to keep out while others were reduced to the status of clients. Although clientelism and dependence on foreign funding continue, emerging major third world trade unions, like the South Korean, South African, and Brazilian ones, insist on being important players in their own right and offer alternative sources of leadership within these international organisations. National, union-sponsored trade union support agencies, like the German Friedrich Ebert Stiftung, have expanded their programmes with government support. The regional offices of the International Labour Organization (ILO) have been strengthened and they intervene actively in support for local union rights. Governments are challenged and shamed internationally for not respecting key ILO conventions, long treated as paper declarations of no substance.

Consumers' organisations and human rights NGOs in the advanced industrial countries engage in support of labour rights and against abusive labour conditions, including child labour, excessive working hours and wage discrimination, but also in support for wrongfully dismissed, detained and victimised labour activists and union leaders. The 'Decent Work Paradigm' promoted by the Director-General of the ILO can be seen as a response to such new public concern. Major transnationals, like Nike, are threatened with consumer boycotts and damaging publicity when abuses are exposed in subcontracting factories. Companies are under pressure to accept Codes of Conduct that include the recognition of trade union rights. The inclusion of Social Clauses with a labour rights component in international trade agreements has become a major issue in the World Trade Organization, as demonstrated by the debacle at Seattle in late 1999, where the heavy involvement of trade unions, including the leadership of the ICFTU, made it difficult to dismiss the protesters as irresponsible youngsters (O'Brien *et al.* 2000).

The African experience

The comparative context

The position of unions varies between countries and regions (Beckman *et al.* 2000). In industrialising East and Southeast Asia wage labour has been on the rise, numerically as well as politically. In South Korea, a reformist government is on a collision course with increasingly autonomous and assertive unions, having failed to agree on a 'social contract'. Long-repressed Indonesian unions agitate and multiply, although undercut by economic collapse and threatened by militarist backlash. In Malaysia, where the state has retained control over a weak and ethnically manipulated labour movement, a new, increasingly skilled and 'mixed' industrial working class is emerging. Vietnamese unions, while still an integral part of socialist one-party structures, respond hesitatingly to new, antagonistic work-place relations in the wake of privatisation and foreign investment. Unions in other parts of Asia such as Pakistan, however, have suffered from the decay in the formal wage sector, being fragmented and repressed by a militarist, elitist, and unproductive political order.

This is also true for much of Africa where the working class was small in the first place and where it has been further reduced by at least two decades of public sector decline and industrial closures. In many instances trade unions barely survive within a stagnant post-colonial order and they may look unlikely candidates for a role as agents for democratic reform, often being unable even to defend a bare minimum of purchasing power for their own members. In Africa, too, the standing of unions in society varies dramatically (Beckman and Sachikonye 2000). In South Africa unions have acquired a unique position not only by virtue of the size of the wage economy but because of their leading role in the struggle against apartheid. Open confrontation with a decaying one-party state has also greatly enhanced the status and influence of the Zimbabwean unions. In Uganda, in contrast, unions barely survive, having been subdued by an assertive and adjusting one-party state. Unions in Ghana and Nigeria have been able to sustain a tenuous defence of labour rights and union autonomy despite repeated military interventions and impositions. The challenges are similar as unions face globalisation, economic crises, and policy liberalisation and as their members are hit by falling wages, retrenchment, closures, casualisation, and other forms of restructuring of the labour process. Conflicts intensify and existing modes of regulating labour are challenged, both from above and from below.

The variation in response depends on a range of factors, including the differential impact of globalisation, crises and adjustment as it affects the development of production and wage work, the formation of the working class, its size and composition. The scope for union intervention varies with the nature of the state and state-society relations as these have been influenced by specific political histories. All of this affects the way labour relations are regulated, the organisational experience of the workers, the internal politics of the labour movement and its wider alliances, and how unions identify options and constraints. The discussion below on the scope and limitations of union intervention draws primarily on the Nigerian case. It begins, however, with two polar cases, those of South Africa and Uganda, which may illustrate the wider range of union experiences in Africa within which the Nigerian one can be assessed.

South African exceptionalism?

The place of unions in post-apartheid South Africa reflects their central political role in the process of national liberation. The apartheid economy was based on a uniquely repressive racial labour regime that facilitated extreme income differentials and extreme forms of labour exploitation, especially in agriculture and mining. Import-substituting industrialisation created a new, increasingly skilled and experienced black working class and a basis for independent organisations that challenged authoritarian work place relations. Employers felt obliged to make concessions in order to ensure labour peace. Wages and working conditions were improved and labour laws were partly adjusted to accommodate the new realities on the ground. The new labour movement became an important base for the anti-apartheid struggle (Maree 1987; Baskin 1991). The transition to democracy brought a formal alliance between the leading national trade union centre, COSATU, and the ANC with a joint programme for Reconstruction and Development (RDP) (Adler and Webster 1995).

The early post-apartheid years saw attempts to build new institutions for union participation and national dialogue on the basis of an implicit social pact (Patel 1993; Barchiesi 1997), including the National Economic Development and Labour Council (NEDLAC) where the representatives of state, business, labour, and community groups met to deliberate. Divisions over policy were apparent at an early stage but unions were assumed to be well-placed to make their voices heard and they have used NEDLAC for major policy initiatives (Baskin 1994, 1996). A central feature of apartheid was the systematic discrimination in access to public services. RDP was expected to rectify this through the rapid expansion of welfare for the majority. Implementation has been seriously constrained by world market adjustment. The alliance between COSATU and the ANC has come under growing pressure as government policies shifted in a liberal direction in response to the crisis of the apartheid economy, capital flight, fiscal imbalances, and the pressure of international creditors (Satgar and Jardin 1999; Webster and Adler 2000).

The shift in policy was evident in the Growth, Employment and Redistribution (GEAR) strategy launched by the government in 1996 (Barchiesi 1997). Unions were caught between conflicting pressures and aspirations in the effort to combine support for the post-apartheid political order while fending off what they saw as excessive concessions by the government to neo-liberal adjustment thinking. The system of policy dialogue came under criticism for being ineffectual as a means of influence. By mid-1999, the growing tensions between the ANC government and the unions were highlighted by a national strike by the public sector unions, protesting government wage impositions (Barchiesi 1999). A one day general strike in May 2000 served similarly to demonstrate union concern about what was seen as government failure to address the continued and worsening problem of mass unemployment.[3]

The position of trade unions and labour rights in South African society are far from consolidated and remain contested. From the perspective of this paper, however, what needs to be emphasised is the continued vitality of the South African trade union movement and its relevance for the way in which problems of reform are addressed. The achievements may be summarised as follows:

1. The rights to organise and bargain collectively have been established through a process of broad-based workers' struggles and have been codified in an elaborate body of labour legislation. This has been achieved in a consultative process in which unions themselves have played a dominant role. The collective experience of those struggles

is likely to contribute an important element of 'path dependence', similar to that of historically successful labour movements elsewhere. A union-based labour regime is entrenched not just constitutionally and legally but through an extensive, cumulative political effort.

2. Unions have developed in response to a highly repressive labour regime which has contributed to a sensitivity within the labour movement to questions of internal representation and accountability. South African unions stand a good chance, therefore, of continuing to be responsive to members. Their internal structures for challenging and changing leadership may be deficient in the eyes of some critics but they are still quite advanced when compared to the situation in unions elsewhere.

3. Participation in broad social alliances during the struggles against apartheid have made unions sensitive to the issues and demands raised by other popular groups and conscious of alliance building as a means of influencing the state.

4. The leading role of unions in the struggle for national liberation has created a sense of 'ownership' in regard to the post-apartheid political order and to a sense of responsibility for ensuring that unions do not take a narrow view of workers' interests but rather engage in national policy and development issues. Unions have taken a lead in the development of tri- and multipartite institutions and are likely to insist that they are taken seriously.

South African unions face enormous problems at all levels, some relating to common problems such as mass unemployment, others to the crises of specific industries or the internal organisational problems of the unions themselves. Yet, in terms of the achievements so far, this, if any, is a success story. The point of recalling success stories is that others may learn. Is not the South African experience too exceptional to be useful in that respect? There is a cult of South African exceptionalism both within and outside the country, fuelled by the uniqueness of apartheid and a history of isolation. The basic ingredients of the union story, however, are familiar from union stories everywhere, the struggle for rights and recognition, the protection of members and leaders, the pursuit of alliances and political influence, the response to changes in markets and policies. There is thus much to learn.

Pride in past achievements has contributed to a confidence, assertiveness, and articulation that may be unique but is likely to be conducive to the diffusion of experiences. A proud COSATU has hosted a number of important international labour meetings, including the World Congress of the ICFTU in Durban, April 2000, and the conference of Sigtur, the Southern Initiative of Trade Union Rights in October 1999 (SALB 23: 6, 1999). One of the early measures of the new leadership of the Nigerian labour movement, emerging after the collapse of the Abacha dictatorship was to invite COSATU for a joint workshop which was held in Abuja in January 2000. Links have also been established at the industrial union level as in the case of the textile workers' unions.

The disarray of Ugandan trade unions

In contrast, trade unions in Uganda occupy a marginal and repressed position in the social order. Freedom of association and the rights of workers to form and join unions and engage in collective bargaining, although formally entrenched in the Constitution, are not respected in practice (Andrae 2000). The government, including its Ministry of Labour, does little to protect the workers' constitutional rights, despite elaborate labour legislation. Public sector unions are largely ignored by the government. An internationally sponsored structural adjustment programme has been implemented since the late 1980s, including major restructuring in the public sector, mass retrenchments, and privatisation, as well as the return of industries and other business to former Asian owners without consulting the unions. When the Chairman General of the National Organisation of Trade Unions (NOTU) appealed to the government in his May Day Address 1997 that employers should be made to respect the law of the land the response from President Museveni was: 'Do not disturb my investors!' (Andrae 2000). There is little or no sustained contestation of government positions by unions which rather appear as supplicants, pleading for government protection and funding. Financially, they are highly dependent on international agencies.

Mamdani (1994: 522) links the ineffectiveness of legal protection to the lack of union autonomy, and the way they depend on official registration which can easily be withdrawn by the government. He traces the origin of this regime to the colonial government of the 1940s and its attempt to control the rising nationalist movement, including its labour component. Post-colonial legislation has been based on this precedent, even if the extent of control and repression has varied. Barya (1991) suggests that unions have been constrained not only by the legal framework and direct repression but also by their own political isolation and failure to take on a wider political role.

There are of course obvious structural and historical reasons for the weakness of Ugandan unions, linked to the small size of the wage sector and the violent destabilisation of the society by civil war and dictatorship.

Colonialism obstructed the growth of a local business class, manufacturing, and wage employment despite the fact that Uganda had developed an advantageous base in a small-holder, cash crop economy with cotton as the main export (Brett 1973). With Independence export earnings were channelled into industrialisation and the expansion of public services. The new working class was unionised, at first under the influence of Cold War trade union competition, later under increasingly authoritarian national control (Barya 1991). Essential services regulation constrained unionisation in the public sector. An economic crisis which originated in the over-taxation of world-market dependent cash crop producers and the inefficiency of an over-extended public sector was further aggravated by dictatorship and civil war. The textile industry, Uganda's most substantial manufacturing asset with its links to domestic cotton production, has suffered from dislocation and decline. Employment had fallen from some 20,000 workers in the early 1970s to less than 5,000 in the late 1990s (Andrae 2000).

Military and political stabilisation, economic reforms, and foreign funding prepared the way for economic recovery in the 1990s. This has benefited much of the population, even though some more than others (Brett 1998). Unions have had no or little say in this process. Some of the measures, including mass retrenchments in the public sector, have directly hit at their constituency, as has trade liberalisation. Politically, unions have been severely restricted and isolated.

What have been the implications of this failure to institutionalise a union-based labour regime? In concluding his analysis of reforms and poverty in Uganda, Brett (1998: 337) notes that 'levels of participation, accountability and state capacity are still unacceptably low' and that the next generation of political leaders 'could easily return to the corrupt and predatory practices of the past, reversing recent gains'. He suggests that sustainable development will depend on people's ability to create 'the organisational systems that operate in civil society to improve people's capacity to mobilise and influence politics'. Citizens, he says, 'need to be much better informed about their political rights and responsibilities' (Brett 1998: 331). This is where the institutionalisation of a union-based labour regime seems relevant, and essential for substantial democratisation. The suppression of union rights and the failure to recognise their organisational potential is indicative of the persisting authoritarianism in Uganda's new political order which is obstructive of autonomous organisations capable of giving a voice to popular interests and aspirations. The case for 'pluralism and the right of association' in the Ugandan context has been effectively argued by

Mamdani (1994). Unions are particularly important in that they often have ethnically mixed constituencies and therefore have a particular stake in national integration.

The Nigeria Labour Congress: Failures and achievements

There are some obvious similarities between Nigeria and Uganda. Both have a background in a relatively prosperous, export-oriented and small-holder based cash crop economy. Both have experienced highly disruptive civil wars and periods of dictatorship and economic decline. Both inherited similar types of labour market institutions and regulations from the late colonial period where unions are recognised , albeit within a framework of state registration and control. Nigerian unions, like Nigerian society as a whole, have been greatly damaged by two decades of incompetent military dictatorship. However, unlike in Uganda, unions continue to be significant players in national politics, with a history of independent organisation, shop-floor militancy, and political intervention. Attempts by governments to co-opt and suppress the labour movement have only had limited success. By African standards Nigeria, with a population of some 100 million, has a large working class, much of it based in a public service sector that was financed initially from exports of cash crops and later greatly boosted by petroleum earnings (Forrest 1993). Commodity income, commerce, and public spending have created a modest base for a manufacturing industry, despite periods of mismanagement and decay. The official membership of the Nigeria Labour Congress, based on compulsorily deducted union fees, was well over two million.

Elsewhere post-colonial labour pacts emerged as part of the transition to national independence where labour movements tended to be incorporated by and subordinated to increasingly repressive national political structures, as in Uganda in the late 1960s. The Nigerian case is different. Although involved in an early phase of the struggle for independence, unions retained their political autonomy *vis-à-vis* competitive but essentially regionally based party politics (Cohen 1974). A renewed impetus towards incorporation into an agenda of national development came with the rise of the military as a dominant political force, as a result of the collapse of the first republic, the subsequent civil war (the Biafra War), and the shift from fragmented, regionalised agricultural exports to a centrally controlled petroleum economy.

A corporatist pact was imposed by the military government of General Obasanjo in the late 1970s, the period of the oil boom. The purpose was no doubt to ensure a higher level of state control 'in the interest of national development', especially in view of the strong inflationary pressures caused by the expansion of the petroleum economy. A Nigeria Labour Congress (NLC) was established by military decree as the sole national labour centre and a multitude of company unions and federations were amalgamated into national industrial unions funded by the compulsory payment of fees by employers on behalf of union members. Although the intervention was at first seen as an hostile act, union leaders sought accommodation, realising that the new unitary structure could be put to good use. The state had banned some old labour leaders from holding office but it could not prevent the election of a new set of radical office holders. They confronted the state over minimum wage policy and fought a running battle for much of the 1980s over the government's structural adjustment policies (Hashim 1994).

Oil revenue fell sharply in the early 1980s and heavy foreign borrowing brought pressures from creditors and the IMF for far-reaching economic reforms. Confrontation was particularly acute over the domestic price of petroleum products which the international finance institutions insisted should reflect world market prices. The NLC spearheaded popular resistance, causing fresh intervention by the Babangida military government in 1988, suppressing the leadership. Popular support and effective grass root organising then obliged the government to renegotiate a pact with the labour leaders (Beckman 1995).

The continued decline of the economy, retrenchments, and the sharp erosion of real wages, however, had undercut the position of the industrial unions, especially those in the public services which had provided the backbone (and funding) of the NLC. While sections of the leadership fought with some success to raise the government minimum wage, attention at the centre shifted towards bargaining with the state over political access and state subsidies for the NLC itself. Labour as a political bloc joined the Social Democratic Party, one ('a little bit to the left') of the two parties that the Babangida regime designed for its highly manipulative and fraudulent 'transition to civilian rule'. The labour movement half-heartedly resisted when the military suppressed the results of the 1993 presidential elections. The new military government of General Abacha dissolved the NLC and imposed a 'Sole Administrator' in 1994. The leadership had become too compromised to lead and, unlike in 1988, cadres were unable to put up much effective resistance. Their loyalties had been divided on regional grounds as part of their entanglement with Babangida's transition politics. A period of political pacting and involvement with the state had thus ended in a collapse.

With the NLC decapitated, the focus of state-union relations shifted to the level of individual industrial unions. An increasingly repressive military government sought to enforce its own agenda by bribing and co-opting pliant labour leaders, issuing new decrees which undercut the autonomy of the unions. The labour movement became divided between those who submitted and those who sought to resist. Even the latter felt obliged to make concessions in order to fend off state repression. The government used stick-wielding thugs to break up meetings and labour leaders were detained without trial. The fate of the Ogoni activists who were arraigned before a sham tribunal and hanged in 1995 underscored the length to which the regime was prepared to go in repressing dissent (Andrae and Beckman 1998).

By the time that Abacha died in 1998, military rule was profoundly discredited and a swift transition to civilian rule was brought about. Obasanjo, a general and former head of state with liberal credentials and with good international connections, was elected president in 1999. The ban on the NLC was lifted and a new labour leadership was elected. The new NLC president, Adams Oshiomhole, was drawn from the textile workers' union that had played an important role in organising resistance to efforts by the Abacha government to take control over the labour movement (Andrae and Beckman 1998). Unions had kept a distance from the forces both at home and abroad that had sought to overthrow the Abacha dictatorship, and they had little direct influence on the politics of the transition. Their defence of union rights, however, helped to sustain some level of organisational autonomy and integrity within civil society.

The prolonged crisis has exacerbated sectional grievances and undermined popular commitment to the national project. The reconstruction of the labour movement itself was high on the agenda of the new leadership. Simultaneously, it saw new avenues for influencing the direction of public policy. In the past, the weak and erratic response of the state to the problems of economic crises and reform had paralysed economy and society. The state in Nigeria is deeply discredited and needs to cultivate the few lines of popular political legitimation that may be open to it.

Nigerian petrol prices and the minimum wage

The capacity of the new NLC to intervene in policy and muster broad popular support was demonstrated in the June 2000 general strike protesting against a 50 per cent increase in local petrol prices. The government signed an agreement on resumed lending with the World Bank in late

May. A few days later the price increase was announced. An adjustment to world market prices had been a longstanding demand by the IFIs. The decision, however, was not preceded by any consultations either at the parliamentary or civil society level. The NLC threatened a general strike and refused to accept a compromise offer. NLC insisted that they had not been consulted and that therefore no serious discussions about possible future increases could be entertained until the government had first restored the original price. The strike action met with wide national support and was joined by market women and other popular groups, causing a virtual paralysis of economic life in major cities and the transport system generally. Students boycotted schools and engaged in demonstrations and agitation. Other civil society groups joined the protests and even parliamentarians representing the ruling party dissociated themselves from the government position. Some State Governors, too, expressed understanding for labour's intransigence. After a five-day strike a compromise was reached allowing for a 12.5 per cent increase. The Head of State apologised to the nation, admitting that the first, drastic increase had been a mistake. An official statement signed by both parties said that a joint committee comprising various interests groups and the federal government would be formed 'to review all aspects of products supply and distribution sector of the Nigerian economy and make recommendations' (Nigerian daily press reports, mostly *Vanguard*, http://www.vanguardngr.com).[4]

The success of the June 2000 general strike may tell us as much about the weakness of the state as of the strength of the unions. It served, however, to reactivate a public image of the labour movement as a force in enhancing people's capacity to mobilise and influence the state. It added weight to union and popular participation in the reform process generally. The new government has initiated an extensive reform programme in consultation with the IFIs and lively debates take place within the labour movement. On electricity, for instance, the NLC president has come out in support of privatisation while the General Secretary of the National Union of Electricity Employees is against, although participating in the Power Sector Reform Implementation Committee alongside the local World Bank representative (NLC-CRD Seminar, Lagos, February 2000; Interview with P. Kiri-Kalio[5]).

Other protracted struggles concern the implementation of a national minimum wage. Government wage awards have played a leading role in wage setting since the late colonial period, reinforced by the dominance of the public service employees and their unions in the wage economy. The awards have served as a benchmark for much of the formal private sector. A general strike in the early 1980s by the newly formed NLC forced a doubling of the minimum wage. By the end of the decade persistent pressures from the NLC obliged the government to accept another major revision after a decade of rapid erosion. High rates of inflation and repeated devaluations continued to cut workers' real income. In some successful, commodity producing sectors, such as textiles, unions were able to obtain compensation from employers but the dominant public sector unions were paralysed by the erratic, irresponsible and corrupt management of public finances. As the Abacha regime collapsed in 1998, the new leaders agreed to major wage increases which, on second thoughts, they decided to revise downwards, causing a conflict with the new NLC leadership. By mid-2000 the new wage levels remained to be implemented fully. Local agitation and strike action had been boosted by support from NLC.

In the context of massive misappropriations of national resources by political and military elites, fighting the impoverishment inflicted on workers in the public services is an obvious priority for the Nigerian unions. In arguing their case they also emphasise the need to revamp the debased public services themselves and raise the quality of the services offered. A sustainable living wage for public sector workers can only be achieved as a part of such a wider strategy of reform and the capacity of Nigerian unions to play a constructive role in that context remains to be tested.[6] Apart from some areas where privatisation is contemplated, little had been achieved on this front (at the time of writing of this chapter).

The Nigerian Textile Workers' Union

The formation of a union-based labour regime in the Nigerian textile industry

The basis of union capacity to intervene in the reform process and defend popular interests needs to be traced to the balance of forces in the organisation of work itself. This will be illustrated here by drawing on the conclusions from a study of the development of the Nigerian textile industry during two decades, from the late 1970s to the late 1990s (Andrae and Beckman 1998). Nigeria's textile workers are organised in the National Union of Textile, Garment and Tailoring Workers of Nigeria (NUTGTWN) which was established in 1977 as a result of the re-organisation initiated by the state, amalgamating previous rival industrial and house unions. It allowed for the compulsory deductions of union dues ('check-offs') by management once a majority of workers had joined the union, providing a strong financial basis for hiring staff, renting offices, paying for transport, and organising meetings. In most companies, union branches had a tradition of competitive branch politics with regular elections, usually with high participation. The 1976–78 reforms facilitated industry-wide collective agreements, generalising conditions of service from the better organised firms to the unionised part of the industry as a whole. The industry faced a major crisis in the early 1980s due to over-expansion, stagnating markets, and smuggled imports. It was aggravated by the foreign exchange crisis which followed on the decline in petroleum sales. The union negotiated higher redundancy payments to discourage lay-offs and induce companies to hold on to excess workers while waiting for better times. Both closures and retrenchments were subjected to collective bargaining at the plant level. The scope for making companies show restraint was enhanced by the latent threat of a violent breakdown if the aggrieved workers felt badly treated.

Real wages declined fast as consumer prices rose while government imposed a wage-freeze. The union circumvented it by negotiating allowances, bonuses and incentives. The employers were in most cases obliged to accept whatever the local balance of forces seemed to suggest as reasonable. A modest consolidation of the textile industry, at a reduced level of output, provided openings for a union wage offensive as the wage freeze was lifted, but the scope for making sustainable gains was limited in a context of extreme macro-economic instability and decaying public institutions. The system of orderly, periodic collective bargaining was disrupted and new proposals for fresh negotiations had to be drafted as soon as an agreement had been signed. Yet, the textile union was notably successful in the new type of bargaining game. The recovery in employment was sustained despite the decline in local markets thanks to exports, largely unofficial ones, to the West Africa region. By the late 1990s the textile union had some 75,000 members despite decades of restructuring and national decline. An average textile worker had recovered roughly half of his 1981 wage in real terms while most public sector employees had been able to keep less than one-quarter of theirs'. The balance within the labour movement had shifted in favour of commercial and commodity producing unions.

The role of the union in industrial restructuring

We see a remarkable capacity of both industry and union to restructure and adapt to new market constraints in a volatile and disruptive policy environment. In particular, we note the ability of the workers to sustain a continued and deepening process of unionisation – a union-centred labour regime – founded in the militant self-organisation of the workers, and providing an autonomous political basis for union bargaining power. It related in particular to the upper echelons of the industry, the large, integrated textile mills which dominated in terms of output and formal employment and which controlled the textile employers' association. The achievements at that level, however, tended to be diffused further down the scale, to smaller, single-process firms which were more hostile to the union. The diffusion was promoted by industry-wide collective bargaining in combination with active union enforcement. We see a paradoxical expansion and vitality at all levels of the organisation at a time marked by overall economic decline as well as by labour's diminishing share in the cost structure of the industry. Production was re-organised, with more machines being managed by fewer workers, and labour controls were stepped up. The process provided for the emergence of a better organised and more qualified work force. The upgrading of competence and work discipline went hand in hand with the generalisation of collective bargaining. The union assisted managements in disciplining labour, but achieved at the same time an extension of workers' rights in the work place. The union's ability to supervise and challenge managerial practices of labour control was enhanced. The generalisation of collective bargaining at national and company levels accelerated the modernisation of the industry. Confronted with a powerful union, weak companies were obliged either to restructure in line with 'industry standards' or fold up.

Our evidence suggests that the union had a genuine base in the self-organisation of the workers. This was reflected in its mode of responding to workers' grievances and in what it achieved in these respects. It also manifested itself in the political process at the branch level, and the scope this offered for influence and control from below. We saw evidence of accountability rooted in the militancy of the cadres at the shop-floor and their preparedness to challenge and defy union officials when feeling short-changed. It constrained co-optation by state and management while simultaneously providing the union with a basis for confronting the latter and exacting genuine concessions on behalf of the workers. The union had to be accommodated, it could not simply be repressed. The prevailing conditions of crisis and shifting policies reinforced the imperatives of accommodation as the firms faced dislocations and shortages and the need to restructure production. Rather than risk provoking 'spontaneous', unpredictable, and potentially violent forms of labour resistance, the employers sought to enlist the co-operation of the union.

Our study pays particular attention to the wider societal determinants of this paradoxical development of a union-based labour regime in a context where union bargaining power might have been expected to have declined. This development can, we think, be ascribed to the constructive role of unions in the organisation of industrial production. Workers were weakly socialised into the role expectations associated with factory work, less accustomed to the indignities of authoritarian factory regimes, and prone to defy what they perceived as unacceptable working conditions and offensive managerial practices. In particular, they were prone to withdraw their labour if offended, either temporarily in some form of industrial action, or by leaving the factory. Union leaders spoke of the mentality of 'damning the consequences'. The insertion of the industry into a surrounding culture of independent production made the moulding of workers to fit the requirements of factory work more difficult.

The militant self-organisation of the workers was conditioned by the way their industry was situated simultaneously as islands of wage work in a sea of independent producers, and, within the wage economy, as the junior partner to the dominant public service sector. The strength of the union lay in its ability to give organisational cohesion to the forces on the ground. The acceptance of its leadership by the workers, at least for most of the time, was assisted by their understanding that unions were natural participants in the organisation of the work place, also in striking contrast to other early industrialising regions of the world. It was based on expectations derived from already established patterns in the public services as further generalised by the 'corporatist pact' of 1978.

Far from being a hindrance to industrial restructuring, the union played an active part in the upgrading of the industry. The unconsolidated nature of the industrial working class reinforced the centrality of union mediation in the labour regime, making the union itself a crucial agency of consolidation. The process had two sides. On the one hand, it involved the formation and qualification of labour in terms of the requirements of the production process. New workers were educated about proper behaviour by union cadres. Managers appealed to the union for help when they themselves failed to control unruly workers. On the other hand, the union was an instrument of the development of a collective identity, expectations of rights, and the promotion of collective interests. The two sides went together; rights and duties. In both respects, it involved asserting leadership, enforcing discipline, and providing cohesion in a work force that was readily provoked into outbursts of independent, militant industrial action.

The centrality of the union was reinforced by the extreme strains on industrial relations imposed by the successive crises of the early 1980s and the subsequent changes in economic policy. The combined vulnerability of both labour and capital in this situation enhanced the dependence of both parties on the union as a mediator. To the workers it offered a defence in a situation where their bargaining position was extremely weak. To the managers, the union provided an unofficial ally in the difficult process of adjusting the industry and its work force to the drastic changes in markets and production conditions.

Disciplining state and capital: The wider role of unions

The experience of the Nigerian textile union points to the paradoxical development of a union-based labour regime in the midst of profound national, economic and political crisis. The persistence of union power can be explained in terms of the interaction between national state regulation (a corporatist pact), the dynamics of working class formation (workers' self-organisation), and union mediation. The experience suggests that trade unions may play an important role in overcoming some of the institutional deficiencies that go with the unconsolidated nature of capitalist relations of production. They promote the formation of an industrial working class capable of entering into long-term contractual relations with both state and capital. In doing so, they contribute to the formation of capital itself as an agent capable of enrolling labour in productive work.

The textile union also became engaged in struggle over state policy, its direction and implementation. It sought to restrain the state from intervening in support for the despotism of some employers and to enlist its support in the effort to extend constitutional work place relations and defend work place legality. It obliged the state to develop its own capacity to regulate labour relations, an important precondition for capitalist production in this conjuncture. This could be seen, for instance, in the involvement of the union with the police, the courts and the local representatives of the Ministry of Labour. These were used at an early point by employers to victimise labour activists and union organisers but came under increasing pressure from unions, their lawyers and political allies, to respect the law of the land. In disciplining the state from below, the unions contributed to the process of state formation. Unions added to the forces in civil society that made democratic demands on the state, claiming civic rights for themselves and their members, including rights to organise and bargain collectively.

State institutions and laws depend on acceptance and enforcement from below by the social groups which are affected. The textile union pressurized the agents of the state into upholding the constitutional legality of the emerging union-based labour regime. But the process also worked the other way. By giving legal recognition to the social forces on the ground the state contributed to the strengthening of the unions as social institutions. The democratic content of the latter was enhanced through the struggles for the rights of organisation. The state was under pressure to be more responsive, especially to those institutions that had grounded claims to represent their members and a capacity to lead them in defiance of authoritarianism.

Comparisons, implications and conclusions

Defending a union-based labour regime

A major difference between Nigerian and South African unions relates to legal underpinnings of institutional autonomy. In South Africa unions have played a leading role in initiating and negotiating the basic labour laws that regulate union rights. This is not the case in Nigeria where unions operate within a legal framework that is the result of state intervention and imposition. Although they have been partly successful in defending their autonomy even within a state-stipulated order, the Nigerian unions are vulnerable to further, hostile state intervention, as demonstrated in 1988 and 1994 when the government dissolved elected executives and imposed state administrators. Still, there is a difference with Uganda where unions are too weak to compel state and employers to uphold the recognition of unions prescribed by the Constitution. In this respect Nigerian unions have been strong enough to defend the formal rights conceded by the state under the imposed corporatist pact, even if they have been unable to prevent the state from using the pact also as a platform for intervention. Their capacity to defend themselves against such interventions depends on the ability of workers to come out in support of their organisations and leaders, even when risking their employment. Their willingness to take such risks, however, also depends on the union's past record of protecting their members against victimisation. It is a mutually reinforcing process that can work both ways and generate either positive or negative path dependence.

The experience of the Nigerian textile workers' union seems to suggest that the ground work has to be laid at the level of the individual workplace. Its success in this respect created a basis for its ability to play a leading role in the defence of union rights against state suppression during the Abacha dictatorship. This again gave it a central role in the reconstruction of the NLC after the demise of Abacha, and a basis for intervening, credibly, on a popular democratic platform in the process of economic and political reform as in the battle over petrol prices.

Defending wages and working conditions

The differences in the consolidation of a union-based labour regime are reflected in differences in the capacity of the unions to engage in defence of wages and working conditions. South African unions may not feel that they have been able to achieve what they have set out to achieve in this respect. Yet, the level of recognition has ensured genuine collective bargaining for most categories of workers. The intervention by the South African government in 1999 to restrict public sector wage increases was widely rejected by the labour movement as undue inter-ference in collective bargaining. In contrast, the suppression of unions in Uganda has allowed private employers to fix wages and working con-ditions at will, shifting to forms of casual labour with a minimum of obligations relating to social security. In Nigeria the picture is more mixed. While based on a common legal framework, the labour regime has developed very differently in different sectors of the economy. In textiles we find that a union-based labour regime is well advanced and has been effectively used in protecting the interests of the workers. Elsewhere, as in much of the public sector, the experience of collective bargaining is weak. Wage levels were the outcome of national negotiations over the minimum wage. Unions which were once well-established have found themselves helpless in the face of decaying management, especially after the state's take over of the NLC in 1994. The restoration of the NLC in 1999 has reactivated central negotiations on the minimum wage but also bargaining based on individual unions as in the case of the teachers.

In much of Africa it is clear that the massive destruction of workers' real income in the past has not been part of a productive 'race to the bottom', making low-cost African labour more competitive and attractive in the global investment plans. The decline in the ability of African workers to feed themselves and their families is not primarily part of some global adjustment of labour costs but of the destruction of the productive base itself. Raising the productivity of labour in the context of modern industry and public service provision requires the upgrading of labour and its skills in participating and performing effectively in an industrial and administrative environment. To achieve this the work force needs to be stable, secure, well-trained and responsible. A living wage is part of it. The experience of the Nigerian textile industry suggests that trade unions can play a vital role in the process of industrial restructuring, facilitating the upgrading of the competence and organisation of the labour force, raising both wages and productivity.

Defending popular access to the reform process

My general argument suggests that the consolidation of union-based labour regimes allows unions to play an active role in the reform process and in democratisation, defending popular policy options and access to public services. This has clearly been the case in post-apartheid South Africa where unions have been active at all levels, both in developing the general reform programme and in reforms at the local and community level. The Municipal Workers Union (SAMWU), for instance, has been involved in local bodies seeking to reform municipal structures which are based on the administrative and financial segregation that was inherited from the apartheid order. Unions in health and education are engaged in sectoral reforms. There is a widespread resentment within the unions that the scope for such popular participation has diminished as the post-apartheid order has consolidated itself, generating its own political and administrative cadres. While such a shift may be inevitable, unions continue to appear as active stake-holders in the reform process. In Uganda such participation seems out of reach for the time being. The decentralization of control over public services, however, may generate some modest scope for activating local unions in monitoring the use of public funds at the local level, contributing to the expansion of the public space (Sjögren 2000). This again may be a precondition for the development of autonomous popular organisations capable of intervening in the reform process.

In the Nigerian context some unions that are directly affected by public sector reforms, as in the case of privatisation of electric power supply, have been included on public committees. This reflects a government effort to secure acceptance for reforms that in the past could be expected to meet with strong union resistance. It remains to be seen if unions will have an effective input in the process or merely serve as hostages. The effective suppression or neutralisation of the national leadership during much of the 1990s have led to a discontinuation of earlier attempts by the NLC to make itself relevant in the context of reform.[7] During much of the 1980s, the NLC produced its own policy platforms, like the 'Workers' Charter of Demands' of 1980 (Beckman

1995). Occasionally, the NLC backed the demands and strike actions of unions and associations in public institutions such as hospitals and universities, with specific reference to the need to rescue these institutions from decline, in the general interest of the workers and their children. Unlike in South Africa, there have been few attempts by unions to engage more directly with the state over public services and welfare policies, or to participate in developing institutions for such dialogue. Occasionally, unionists have been admitted into government policy bodies on an individual basis, as in the controversial 'Vision 2010 Committee' set up by Abacha. In attempting to influence government policy, unions have had the option of resisting or of engaging in dialogue. In the past there has been more of the former than the latter. The successful general strike over petrol prices in June 2000 was of course a show of resistance but it is likely to oblige the government to involve unions and other organisations in more serious dialogue over its reform programme. It creates new scope for political bargaining where unions are likely to press their own demands in alliance with other civil society groups.

How 'popular' are such demands likely to be? Will unions speak for the marginalised sections of the population? Not necessarily, but both the South African and the Nigerian experience suggests that unions are likely to voice broad popular demands, partly out of concern with their own political base and the need to engage in alliances in order to avoid isolation and enhance their impact, partly out of a perception of their own role as the guardians of popular concerns in a context dominated by self-seeking elites.

Institutional capacity building from below

There is an awareness amongst economic reformers of all shades of the need to develop institutional capacity to sustain reforms. It is not enough to 'get your policies right', you must ensure that they are institutionally grounded, sustained and reproduced. There is also a realisation that the political problem lies as much with the institutions of civil society as with those of the state and that the two are, in fact, intimately connected. The problem with the liberals' vision is that they have difficulties in identifying the social carriers of their programme, except in terms of right-thinking technocrats who are supported by international finance institutions and insulated from local political pressure that threatens to derail the reforms. Most existing organised interests, and trade unions in particular, tend to be dismissed as vested interests of an old, discredited social order.

In this chapter I have argued, on the other hand, that a union-based labour regime is a central civil society institution capable of contributing to capacity building in support of sustainable reforms as well as of democratic processes. The experience of the Nigerian textile workers union obtains its wider significance in the context of wider processes of institution building at the level of society, of capacity building from below. I showed how the institutions for regulating conflicting interests in the industry interacted with and reinforced a process of capacity building at the level of the state. The constitutionalisation of labour relations at the level of industry placed pressures on the institutions of the state, the police, the courts, and the labour ministry officials, to abide by the rules and respect the contractual relations between workers and employers.

Rueschmeyer, *et al.* (1992) have emphasised the role of large work places in socialising workers into new collective identities, providing the basis for organised intervention in politics – and, in the European and Latin American experiences, to their putting pressure upon the middle classes to commit to democracy. Drawing on the study of Nigerian unions I want to add the role of collective bargaining with employers as a basis for establishing a culture of rights. Collective bargaining is as much about procedures and rights as about actual material entitlements. Central to procedure is a notion of union rights, rights to organise, rights to be represented, and not least, the negative right not to be victimised for engaging in union activity. In this respect, union rights are both a variety and a prefiguring of political rights in general. Unions have a primary interest in upholding these rights and they therefore have vested interest in alliances with other groups that have similar needs. This is what tends to give trade unions such an important role in democratic movements.

Notes

1. This chapter was first presented to a conference on 'New Institutional Theory, Institutional Reform and Poverty Reduction', Development Studies Institute (DESTIN), London School of Economics and Political Science, 7–8 September, 2000; and another version appears in *Transformation – Critical Perspectives on Southern Africa*, 48, 2002. It originates in work done with Gunilla Andrae on the Nigerian textile workers' union, with the close co-operation of the union itself, as documented in Andrae and Beckman (1998).
2. The argument of this section draws heavily on a recent report for the United Nations Research Institute for Social Development concerned with the extent to which organized interests, like labour, have been able to provide an alternative source of popular democratic impact on institutional reform. (Beckman *et al.* 2000)

3. Profound misgivings in the South African union movement over privatisation and other aspects of government policy have not as yet caused the alliance with the ANC to be abandoned.
4. Another increase in petrol prices in January 2002 led to a similar standstill, despite the use of police and the courts to intimidate the unionists.
5. Interview with P. Kiri-Kalio, General Secretary, National Union of Electricity Employees, Yaba, Lagos, 24 February 2000.
6. The NLC decided in 2001 to support the idea of a labour party, in which unions are expected to play a key role, primarily as the leaders of a broad coalition of civil society groups. Unions hope for a political platform on which to challenge prevailing policies and politics.
7. But see note 5 above.

9
The Political Deficit of Substantial Democratisation

Olle Törnquist

There is wide agreement that the essence of democracy is 'popular control of public affairs based on political equality'. In addition democracy is characterised by the qualities of participation, authorisation, representation, accountability, transparency, responsiveness and solidarity (Beetham 1999). The challenging question is what instruments and actors can promote these aims.[1] This chapter is about problems of substantial democratisation. What kind of democracy is that? Definitions matter. Substantial democratisation is when important actors with popular constituents find that the best way of affecting matters of common concern in a society is to fight for and develop significant pro-democratic rights and institutions that citizens have both the possibility and the capacity to make use of.

This is in sharp contrast to the argument by many concerned scholars that democracy will be only formalistic unless its substance also includes (a rarely specified degree of) social and economic equality in the society at large. Such wide definitions are rejected here. This is because they are deterministic, closing our eyes to the possible importance of political democracy *in the promotion of* social and economic equality. In this respect, we rather agree with mainstream political studies that it is analytically most fruitful to limit the core instruments of democracy to human rights and basic judicial, administrative, political and civil–society institutions.[2]

There is also a need to qualify, however, the standard assumption that it is only these rights and institutions as such that are intrinsic to a substantial democracy. Aside from performing well, they must also be spread beyond the metropolis and cover vital issues of public concern. Otherwise democracy would indeed be a formality by only covering a limited territory (excluding, for instance, indirectly ruled 'tribal' areas), only including a narrowly defined public sphere (excluding, for instance, gender issues), and being 'choiceless' (because of excluding, for instance, public control of fundamental economic regulation). Finally and just as important, the instruments of democracy do not work by themselves. People in general must possess sufficient powers and other capacities to access and make use of the tools. This is not to say that substantial democracy presupposes social and economic equality – only that people must be resourceful enough to be present in vital parts of the political system, politicise their basic interests and mobilise broad support, so that they stand a fair chance of using the rights to freedom of speech and organisation as well as the free and fair electoral institutions. Otherwise, democratisation and democracy will not be substantial enough to constitute a meaningful way for people to try to solve common problems and build a better life.[3]

What are the problems of fighting for and promoting substantial democracy? The focus of this chapter will be on three sets of obstacles and solutions. The *first* set is that the standard theories of democratisation take it for granted that 're-accommodation between authoritarian and democratic elites' is more feasible and favourable for democracy than popular mass action. There are good reasons for questioning this assumption and for avoiding it as a premise for further work. The *second* dilemma is that no alternative theory and strategy has grown out of the more promising popular efforts at democratisation like those of Porto Alegre and Kerala. As indicated in the introduction to this book, the usual explanations for why these impressive showcases were possible are insufficient. In this chapter, we shall analyse why the experiments in Kerala were not only possible but also destabilised, and why similar efforts in the Philippines and Indonesia have been less successful. The root of the problem seems to lie in the *political deficit* in new forms of popular democratisation, especially with regard to the weakness of the links between civic and political action. The *third* challenge is the need to develop an analytical tool to 'test' the general validity of such case study-based results and provide more conclusive arguments in discussions on effective politics of democratisation. This is tried out in the case of Indonesia.

Elitist vs popular democratisation

The currently dominant school of thought about democratisation in developing countries grew out of earlier empirical generalisations about the positive role of liberal modernisation and the middle classes. While this positive role had been held back in countries such as those of Latin America, the new school of thought added the 'intuitive assumption' (Whitehead 2002: 63), that it was both possible and necessary in this context to proceed directly by way of peacefully negotiated transitions towards democracy in the way that happened in Spain in the 1970s.[4] The first argument for this assumption is that alternative democratisation by left-oriented mass based actions is unrealistic and undermines the immediate importance of democracy. Such politics is presumed to come with demands for radical socio-economic change that would be stubbornly resisted and blocked by the dominant forces. Radical change would then call for the employment of quite drastic means, including violence and riots, interventionist states and Machiavellian parties, which would weaken democracy.[5] The second argument, then, is that the prospects for democratisation are more optimistic by way of the internationally supported negotiation of pacts between moderates among the authoritarian and democratic elites as well as by the crafting of the fundamental institutions related to human rights, rule of law, 'free and fair' elections, 'good governance' and civil society. The underlying belief is that the incumbents will be prepared to accept and adhere to the most fundamental rights and institutions in exchange for protection of their assets and businesses.

While positively stressing the importance of politics against structural determinism, these mainstream perspectives not only refute the view that extensive modernisation and radically altered power relations are a precondition for democracy but also the more modest requirements of substantial democratisation. Is that convincing? Should substantial democratisation be ruled out at the onset? There are three major reasons for questioning the dominant assumptions: their dubious historical perspective, the poor outcome of their own projects, and the fact that popular efforts have often proved more genuine and promising.

First, the poor reading of history. While radical structural modernisation has often been associated with turbulent upheavals, quite a few of these have also been recognised as having been fundamental to democratisation, including the French revolution and the anti-colonial liberation struggles. A trustworthy analysis may not start, therefore, by excluding the possibility that such radical transformations might be essential for democratisation in certain contexts. Besides, several leftist mass organisations have managed to combine demands for structural change and peaceful political democratisation, including in Scandinavia. It is true that many post-colonial states turned authoritarian, 'patrimonial', and predatory, but it is not clear whether this was mainly because of the states as such, or because of the actors and forces that hijacked them in the midst of the cold war and in the context of poorly reformed agrarian and other power relations. Further, of course, Marxist theories and mass based organisations have sometimes been associated with this authoritarianism. Their democratic deficit is undisputable. Yet, the same goes for the conservative architects of the Asian developmental state and the liberal middle class politicians who are in favour of Samuel Huntington's thesis (1965, 1968) that there is a need for top-down 'politics of order', if necessary with the active support of the army, before ordinary people may be allowed to participate. Moreover, the common commitment to democracy on the part of radical labour organisations and sometimes even by significant communist parties points to the importance of contexts and of specific analyses and strategies rather than there being something inevitably destructive in Marxism and radical mass organisation (cf. Törnquist 1989 and 1991a; Rueschemeyer *et al.* 1992, see also Beckman's chapter in this book).[6]

Contemporary history lashes back as well. The end of the cold war removed some of the devastating tendency to subordinate vital issues such as democratisation to the struggle against an externally imposed main enemy, as well as the possibility for various rulers to substitute foreign backing for popular support.[7] It is true that global neo-liberalism has undermined much of the previous attempts at promoting democracy through citizens' education, basic social and economic independence, popular mass organisations, and programmatic political parties, but it has also helped to do away with a good deal of harsh statist repression, thus creating more liberal public spaces. Similarly, the worldwide expansion of capital not only promotes transnational business but may also pave the way for a more unified left-oriented struggle over democracy, including, as pointed to in Beckman's chapter, among labour. This is partly because economic expansion undermines *both* the old Communist argument that since capitalism has been impeded by imperialism there must be enlightened political shortcuts to progress, *and* the Social Democratic thesis that since modernisation is delayed, but remains a precondition for democracy, there may have to be middle-class coups and technocratic engineering to pave the way for modern development. At any rate, for the last two decades or so, those sections of the Left that have been engaged in the re-thinking of old orthodoxies, and new generations of activists, have made use of the wider space both to fight neo-liberalism, and to substitute self-management and networking groups and movements for the old top-down driven efforts by party and state. One may well problematise the democratic character of these new spaces and reactions (as has been done in several of the preceding chapters and as will be done in this one as well), but it would be premature to negate their potential and vitality by holding on to outdated assumptions.

The second case against the dominant democratisation project is based on its own poor results. Liberties and rights have often been expanded but many observers question their substance for ordinary people and mention the high number of 'illiberal' (electoral) democracies' (Bell *et al.* 1995). 'Semi-authoritarian' regimes seem to come back (Ottaway 2003). There are strong indications that democratic advance requires that the old forces should be defeated before they are accommodated (McFaul 2002). Actually existing civil society does not match up to normative expectations. Much of the social capital that is supposed to 'make democracy work' flourishes instead within ethnic and religious communities. Delegation of authority through 'free and fair' elections is rarely supplemented by representation of basic interests and ideas. The limited capacity of people to make use of various means of democracy is often accompanied by a similarly limited capacity of politicians and institutions to take independent decisions and implement them. These are the conditions of so-called 'choiceless democracies' (Mkandawire 1999; Abrahamsen 2000). Scholars and practitioners trying to 'consolidate' democracy give priority to the timing and crafting of best possible institutions but lack convincing answers as to what interests, powers, and actors are able to enforce and implement their recommendations (cf. World Bank 1997; UNDP 2002). Others focus on how the old oligarchies manage to adjust their old interests and practices to new and supposedly democratic institutions rather than being disciplined and transformed by them. On reflection, O'Donnell (1994, 1996, 2002) argues that institutional changes have proved insufficient. New or restored democracies are often characterised by popular delegation of power to populist and clientelist leaders within formalised institutions, including 'free and fair' elections. These delegative practices come close to what scholars on Africa (and Asia) have labelled neo-patrimonialism (cf. Clapham 1985; Chabal and Daloz 1999). The basic dynamics of such undisputable tendencies, however, are mainly explained in terms of long-term cultural patterns within the elite, such as the Latin American *caudillo* leader who is deemed capable of almost magically taking into account all contradictory interests that back him. This thesis obscures the processes through which such practices are upheld and reinvented; processes which are more fruitfully analysed in the literature on the legacy of indirect rule (Mamdani 1996 and see Nordholt in this book), the links between state and society (Migdal *et al.* 1994) and on the *ménage á trois* between primitive accumulation, liberal elections and bossism (see Chapter 3 by Sidel in this book). In Indonesia, for example, the standard recommendation to exchange protection of private property and business for political democracy and the rule of law is not misplaced for special cultural reasons but because of the simple fact that business remains in critical need of partisan intervention by politicians, bureaucrats, judges and officers who themselves are engaged in primitive accumulation of capital (see Törnquist 2003b).

The third development that speaks against the 'transition' theories is that even if popular efforts at democratisation have rarely been decisive they have certainly proven increasingly important and genuine. The list could be extended and include examples from local peasant, labour, women's and environmental groups, to activists against neo-liberal globalisation. Previous chapters in this book (by Stokke and Oldfield, and Sidel) have drawn attention to the consistent popular efforts of democratisation in spite of the ANC's semi-authoritarian tendencies and the subordination of the Philippines middle class to elitist democracy. Other chapters (by Schönleitner and Tharakan) have analysed the currently available showcases – which happen to be leftist participatory practices in Brazil and attempts to renew the widely acclaimed Kerala model of human development by way of democratic decentralisation and a People's Planning Campaign.[8] Even poorly organised pro-democrats made a difference in the 1986 velvet revolution against Marcos in the Philippines as well as in the 1998 dismantling of one of the most effective and longest serving dictatorial regimes, that of Soeharto in Indonesia. By now, moreover, the core of these 'old' activists is among the few who consistently try to deepen the 'actually existing' elite democracies.

The political deficit

While the basic assumptions of the dominant school of thought, therefore, have not proven solid enough – but rather have obscured analyses and support for some of the most promising tendencies and efforts at democratisation – this does not mean that the hopeful popular experiments are sufficiently strong and well organised as to constitute a full-scale alternative. In view of the poor outcome of the standard 'transition' projects, it is true that popular efforts seem to be necessary for *substantial* democratisation, but there is comparatively little interest in and knowledge of the politics of fighting for and implementing such changes. This is the *political deficit* of the new forms of popular democratisation. As discussed in the introduction and in several chapters of this book, there is a strange convergence between institutions like the World Bank and the 'radical polycentrists' within NGOs and new social movements in their ideas about overcoming the drawbacks of standard democratic politics of elections, parties and mass based interest organisations by way of citizen participation as users, consumers and members of civil society associations, and through the nourishing of communitarianism based on customary law.[9] One of the major assumptions is that people may thus come to trust each other (or enjoy 'social capital'), put an end to struggles amongst themselves over their different interests, resist state interventionism, and so promote 'good governance' and economic development. Alternatively, in the view of radical students of 'post-industrial capitalism' and globalisation like Michael Hardt and Toni Negri (2000), power has been so localised that there is no decisive central unit left to fight, and the dominant producers are regulating social relations themselves, so that strong parties and representative democracy are unnecessary. In short: a depoliticised and unconstitutional form of democracy that negates conflicts over ideas, interests and power relations.

The more balanced left-oriented thinkers and campaigners behind the significant cases of popular democratisation in Brazil and Kerala, on the other hand, realise, as was also noted in the Introduction to this book, the need to link new polycentric activities in civil society with local government and political activism and to generate common agendas. They promote, therefore, wider and more institutionalised public spaces than the Habermasian coffee shop discussions and media debates, where people who are active in various citizen organisations and self-managed activities can meet, deliberate, and communicate directly with the politicians and local administrators as well as take basic decisions with regard to local government priorities. The major dilemma, however, is that much of the political deficit still applies. Little is said and done about how such links and public spaces emerge, endure and further develop. The argument of this chapter is that the popular experiments have called for *political* intervention, and that their further development is not only a matter of institutional design by committed intellectuals but also of peoples' capacity to develop new forms of interest organisation and political work, including the combining of direct and representative governance in order to withstand various clientelistic practices, whether rightist or leftist.

The political foundations

In Porto Alegre, the formative neighbourhood committees, for instance, largely stand out as the products of long political struggle against and attempts to survive dictatorship and lack of proper public services, rather than as a result of citizens' passionate desire to spend hours in meetings and 'participatory' activities in order to get access to basic services such a clean water. The importance of the winning of the mayoral elections by the *Partido dos Trabalhadores*, (PT) – which is a history in itself about the importance of 'old' forms of trade union activities and political organisations in addition to 'new' movements – is hard to exaggerate. The capacity then to use the executive powers of the mayor and his staff to facilitate and institutionalise the public spaces and specific principles and practices of participatory budgeting, was partly driven from the top down, and partly depended on the politics of decentralisation in Brazil as a whole. Further, is it possible to reconcile the ideal principles of democracy with the fact that PT and the mayor and his staff seem to have bypassed the majority of the anti-PT city councillors by way of centralisation, in order to introduce the practices of not always constitutionally regulated and accountable direct democracy? It is true that the councillors were products of clientelism, but they were also elected, partly by middle class voters who may not always appreciate (or be appreciated within) participatory processes. As pointed out in the chapter by Schönleitner in this book, 'deliberative participation is embedded in rather than autonomous from local power dynamics, which it is meant to transform'.

Moving on to the popular experiments in Kerala,[10] history did not exactly start in 1996 with the launching of the celebrated People's Planning Campaign.[11] The usual argument is that the campaign depended upon a strong and democratic civil society. But how did that society come about? It did not emerge on its own but was shaped within the context of state and radical politics. One of its roots is in the late 19th century socio-religious reform movements against caste oppression, which demanded equal rights and favourable policies from the relatively autonomous princely states in south and central Kerala. Another pillar is the class based socialist and communist movement with its deepest roots in north Kerala, where the onslaught of indirect colonial rule was most directly felt. Within the framework of the nationalist struggle against the British and for a unified Kerala the class based movements then merged with subaltern civic organisations in southern and central parts of Kerala. These joint forces succeeded in mainstreaming ideas of politically negotiated and balanced development based on political and social equality, social security, labour rights and land reform. Then much of the reform thus fought for was implemented through strong unions, political movements and a comparatively well developed state and executive government.

Does this mean that the Left Democratic Front and its leading party the Communist Party of India-Marxist (CPI-M) was the propelling force behind the launching of the People's Campaign in 1996? In fact, this is only part of the story. It was essential that the CPI-M approved of the Campaign, but it is also important to recall the background. After the land reform, by the late 1970s and 1980s, the established Left stagnated. The initiation of the People's Campaign rested instead with those who opted for reforming the Left, not by abandoning it (as several NGOs, intellectuals and ultra radicals did) but by increasing their bargaining power through the shaping of a wider public space outside conventional politics and through the generation of dynamic democratic activities within that sphere. The People's Science Movement, KSSP,[12] was their main organisational vehicle. During the late 1980s and early 1990s, until the Left was voted out of power in 1991, the reformists began to gain the initiative in the public discourse on how to rescue the Kerala model, as well as to prove themselves capable of implementing practical solutions outside the seminar rooms. The background was the struggle to protect the Silent Valley rainforest against reckless developmentalism. By the end of the 1980s, four new campaigns followed suit. One was for full literacy, thus addressing wider and immediate popular concerns and reaching out to many of the underprivileged groups that had not been included in the mainstream Kerala reforms. Second was the promotion of group farming, which not very successfully aimed at stimulating production among the many atomised beneficiaries of the land reform, and generating more jobs and better pay for the agricultural workers. Third was resource mapping with popular participation that aimed at sustainable development through the promotion of 'land literacy'. Fourth was the continuous lobbying of politicians to implement democratic decentralisation.

Was the launching of the People's Campaign in 1996, therefore, merely the concerted revival of these earlier efforts, once the Left was back in power? No, because the first generation of campaigns had come up against serious political problems that now had to be addressed in order to move ahead. The Left had not followed up the literacy campaign among the strategically important subordinate groups. Dubious non-productive interests among farmers,[13] who used to vote for the Left, as well as centralist policies of the Left's own state ministers, undermined group farming. The lack of a broad social base (similar to that for land reform) was a major drawback of the participatory resource mapping. Hardly any politician gave priority to decentralisation. The reformists themselves proved politically much too weak to make a difference in these matters. Their campaigns did not even generate new votes. For those reasons, the campaigns petered out after 1991 when the Left Democratic Front could no longer provide government support.

During the intermediate period of non-leftist government rule, between 1991 and 1996, the reformists tried to make up for several of these problems. Left-oriented politicians in opposition were made to commit themselves publicly to decentralisation. Various issues and proposals were aggregated into fresh agendas in huge conferences with scholars and experienced activists – who thus gained the upper hand in the public discourse. Models were tried out on how to include various groups and interests on the ground, and for generating broader agendas by combining local governments and a series of participatory councils on different levels. The lack of a social movement for the alternatives and commitment among most of the established Left was not subjected to scholarly studies and public debate but was compensated for in three ways. First because of enjoying the leadership of the leftist patriarch E. M. S Namboodiripad, with his long term commitment in favour of decentralisation, thus making it impossible for the established Left, and especially the CPI-M, openly to oppose the new initiatives.[14] Second, (and again with the backing of EMS) by favouring de-(party)politicisation of efforts at promoting popular oriented development, and the forming of a broad front that would include sympathetic non-leftist politicians as well as KSSP activists.[15] Third, by gaining top-level political support for the shock therapy of massive disbursal of funds to local governments in order to generate popular expectations and engagement (rather than starting by designing proper legal institutions – a process that, history suggests, would most probably have turned into a battlefield for the established elite and its clients).

Before the 1996 elections, therefore, the reformists not only had some ideas and strategies on how to move ahead, but their models also stood out as the only fresh alternative policy. Yet, this was still not enough to launch the People's Campaign. First, the established part of the Left had to win the elections, something that the reformists would have been unable to do. Then it was essential that politically well-placed reformist leaders were also the best qualified scholars-cum-professionals to direct the State Planning Board, through which they were able to reach out widely and stand up against centralist ministers, party apparatuses and local bosses. Only thereafter was the Peoples' Campaign a viable proposition.

The politics of mixed results

Thereafter, what were the major factors behind the implementation and outcome of the Campaign? Much of the discussion of it has focussed on institutional design and management, but there are questions about context as well. Where were the roughly one fifth of the *panchayats* that did well? Some point to the strength of civil society, others add the role of social capital, but the successes were clustered neither in the south, where civil society is most deeply rooted, nor in the north, where there may be more social capital within communities. Neither does there seem to be a clear correlation between successful outcomes and the local dominance of Left Front- or Congress led coalitions (Heller and Chaudhuri 2002). The 'good cases' seem rather to be associated with fruitful co-operation between civic activists, usually related to the KSSP, and positive, dynamic politicians in command of local government.

So when and how did that co-operation come about? And why was it so relatively difficult to achieve? Knowledge is limited. Very few have studied the experience closely and talked about it seriously in public. This political deficit, as we shall see, boils down to four major problems of (a) combining different activities in the political system; (b) replacing party-politicised clientelism with more fruitful re-politicisation rather than de-politicisation of ideas and socio-economic issues; (c) preventing powerful actors from conquering potentially progressive institutions such as those related to decentralisation, by combining the practices of direct and representative governance; and (d) of studying and deliberating publicly the politics of democratisation. Moreover, how specific was this for Kerala? While analysing the Kerala experience, we may also compare it briefly with a series of similar efforts over time in two quite different contexts. On the one hand, Asia's Latin America, the Philippines – where democratic middle-class and NGO-led uprisings made Maoist revolutionaries irrelevant. On the other hand Indonesia – where three decades of anti-leftist mass repression and quick modernisation with middle-class consent collapsed in 1998 and thus generated some space for democratic aspirations in the ruins of 'liberal despotism'.[16]

First, the combining of different activities in the political system. The Kerala reformists were good at combining actions at local and central levels but failed to generate a viable alternative to neo-liberalism by overcoming the dualism between, on the one hand, their own new efforts at participatory development 'between state and market', and, on the other, the traditional and still dominant leftist preoccupation with state, service and industry. This conflict did not resemble the controversy between the two main organised factions of the dominant leftist party, the CPI-M. It is true that the trade union, civil service and industry related faction has been particularly negative in its attitude towards the ideas of popular development, deeming it communitarian and 'greenish', while the at times ideologically more principled, conservative, rural worker-oriented group, with one of its roots in the *Ezhava* caste community, occasionally (until recently) came closer to some of the reformists' positions.[17] In the main, however, the reformists have not received committed backing from any faction but have rather aimed at distancing themselves from party infighting, trying to present instead an alternative development perspective in co-operation with civil society activists, primarily from non-party arenas within an extended public space. Yet, this did not enable the reformists to overcome the division between their own participatory development projects at the local community level and the old leftist organised interests, particularly with regard to the public sector and 'modern' service and industry. Rather, a *modus vivendi* evolved, according to which both sides agreed to fight neo-liberalism and reactionary communalism and then to work according to an informal division of labour. The 'etatists', to begin with, have monopolised the commanding heights of mainstream politics and government, including finance and industry, in such a way that they have had to compromise with various party groups and organised interests among labour as well as business. They have consequently been unable to present a viable agenda for the revitalisation of the economy or for rescuing government and the public sphere as major arenas for democratic decisions on public affairs.[18] Meanwhile the reformists, on their part, have largely been confined to their popular participation campaigns at the local level, in addition to seminars and the expert-oriented State Planning Board, trying, then, to mobilise popular engagement behind alternatives from below. Their impressive experiments, however, have not proved sufficiently forceful as to have enabled potentially interested community development activists to make decisive inroads into mainstream politics and government, create linkages with dynamic sectors of the economy, and develop a comprehensive non-'etatist' alternative to neo-liberalism.

Their Philippine and Indonesian counterparts, by contrast, rarely managed to relate central and local actions and never came anywhere near to a dualistic *modus vivendi* between their renewal-oriented efforts and previous leftist priorities. The legendary founding father of the Philippine New People's Army, Bernabe 'Dante' Buscayno, for instance, was marginalised when he sought to keep both old Maoists and new civil society activists at bay and to start anew with peasants' co-operatives. The Horacio 'Boy' Morales – Isagani Serrano – Edicio de la Torre faction of the reformist 'Popular Democrats' slipped twice. First they failed to convince the dominant Maoist Left to supplement traditional guerrilla struggles and mass-movements with self-management in civil society. Second, they rallied masses behind the alternative populist patron and President Joseph Estrada but failed to affect people positively and became instead prisoners of Estrada's abusive governance. The most interesting combination between new civic action and 'old' interest based struggles has rather come about when many activists finally distanced themselves from both the old Left and populist shortcuts in favour of building a new Citizen Action Party/*Akbayan*. This is a joint venture of dissident 'popular democrats', former Maoists, radical socialists, related NGOs and popular organisations, and a new generation of younger leftists. *Akbayan's* comprehensive organisation, however, has mainly been related to central level institutions (including party-list elections) and it remains to be seen whether its new engagement in local government (which is further explored in Joel Rocamora's chapter in this book) will facilitate the aggregation of priorities at that level as well (see also Stokke and Oldfield's chapter on the South African experience.).

Efforts in Indonesia at combining different activities at various levels have been even less successful, suffering still from the suppression since the 1960s of all mass based progressive organisations. Civic associations are not even moderated via general NGO-consortiums (as in the Philippines), but only by loose and temporary networks, and through popular and/or resourceful leaders. After the fall of Soeharto, the first priority of popular oriented groups was to escape form old repressive organisations rather than to favour better co-ordination. We shall return to this in the final section of the chapter.

The second element of the political deficit is the general de-politicisation rather than re-politicisation of socio-economic conflicts. The Kerala reformists bravely argued that one of the major problems in the state was party-politicisation of most aspects of government and society. As discussed in more detail in Tharakan's contribution to this book, narrow and clientelistic party-politics had come to dominate even at the village and hamlet level, within co-operatives, public administration, and, for instance, education. Their alternative model was the extension and institutionalisation of local public spaces within which people themselves would be able to deliberate and negotiate welfare and development priorities and control implementation of various measures. According to the same argument, the less rigid class differences following land reform would not prevent people from participating as reasonably independent and equal citizens.

While practising this, however, the reformists had to handle resistance not only from conservative groups but also from the organised interests and the political parties of the Left, at the central as well as local level. Favourable statements by a few veterans like EMS were not enough (especially after he passed away in 1998). The reformist argument that there would still be ample space for politics in the form of competition among various parties on how to facilitate the best possible welfare for all people, was deemed to be naïve by party activists who had to sustain organisations and win elections under the present conditions. The reformists, therefore, had to compromise with the mainstream Left in order to win some space and support to propel their own alternative project – which, they hoped, would then gain enough popular backing to convince the leftist establishment of altering its way of working.

In addition, the reformists might have spoken out about the character of the current form of party-dominated clientelistic politicisation and combined their project work with the mobilisation of popular support behind demands for change. But the reformists gave priority to general de-politicisation rather than to alternative, non-clientelistic re-politicisation of socio-economic conflicts. The latter would have called for hard debates in the public sphere on whether the problem was really politicisation as such, or rather that the Left had embraced the politics of clientelism by catering to close sympathisers instead of broad interests of wide sections of the population, especially, as pointed out in Tharakan's chapter in this book, after the land reform struggle. In that context, after land reform, the reformists would also have had to discuss publicly whether the interests of these party-sympathisers carried a potential for transforming Kerala in a progressive direction, or, as also indicated in Tharakan's chapter, if one should rather include marginalised sectors of the population, and emphasise gender equality and production oriented policies, at the expense of people who made use of various monopolistic practices – regardless of whether they used to vote Left Front or not.

The Kerala activists' policy of institutionalising public spaces in relation to the existing local governments proved quite successful in tackling the fragmentation of single issue- and special interest related activities that continue to be endemic in the Philippines and especially Indonesia.

The Kerala failure, however, in re-politicising more productive and sometimes new conflicts in order to enforce such a new agenda seems to be universal. The Philippine 'popular democrats' whose civic projects were refuted by the Maoists got lost in trendy greenish civil society-cum-social capital perspectives and then tried to compensate their political futility by taking what proved to be devastating populist shortcuts behind President Joseph Estrada. Dissenting commander Dante, on his part, banked instead on idealised peasant interests in increasing production but was let down by contradictory interests within peasant households. And when he finally realised the need to rally people around a common political agenda, time was short and local elections were lost even in his old stronghold. *Akbayan*, by contrast, has developed slowly from its disappointing pre-party attempts in the early 1990s at generating an electoral agenda by summing up the demands of various cause-oriented groups, to more comprehensive perspectives based on alliances with broader popular movements, in addition to NGOs and other groups. *Akbayan's* problems, however, (as also discussed in Rocamora's chapter in this book) continue to include the questions of what and how issues and interests should be politicised and given priority. The idea of a social movement based party is fine but the crucial question – as also discussed in the chapter by Stokke and Oldfield in the context of South Africa – is how to link the two, without devastating party dominance or movement fragmentation.

In Indonesia, finally, most activists still argue against any politicisation of conflicts within civil society in order to uphold or build broad unity against the state, including the abusive politicians, bureaucrats and the military, and their business associates. Those who question the basis for such a unity, and who argue instead in favour of entering into politics, usually lack a clear social constituency, as well as strategies for promoting comprehensive movements, and so tend to end up within elitist shortcuts.

The third component of the political deficit is the unresolved challenge of combining direct democracy and self-management with representative democracy and professional administration in order to prevent powerful actors from conquering potentially progressive institutions such as those related to decentralisation and popular participation. During the first part of the Kerala Campaign, nothing drastic happened. The 'etatists' held on to the heights of state and government while the reformists pushed for decentralisation, discussed and trained cadres at the Planning Board, and then initiated popular participation in the *panchayats*. After about a year the Planning Board began to implement the decision to devolve one third of the investment budget to projects to which people had given priority at the local level. At this point dominant groups became worried and tried to take advantage of the new local funds and powers. The Campaign was soon exposed, in consequence, to intense criticism for delays, irregularities, partisan priorities, and 'decentralisation of corruption'. While most central level politicians and administrators were dragging their feet, the committed reformists themselves were not powerful enough to defend the principles of the Campaign. The reformists relied instead on their cadres and on generating local enthusiasm and pressure. Locally, however, politicians and administrators were not always prepared to follow the principles that had been laid down by the Planning Board and enthusiastic Campaign experts and set in motion through various committees and popular forums.

The resistance was not limited to those who claimed that the entire experiment was a leftist conspiracy but spread also to left oriented parties (and related administrators) which were lacking a critical mass of strategically localised activists who could make a difference in the participatory practices. One of these parties was that of the minority communists (CPI). Their major argument was that the primacy of decentralisation, democratically elected representatives and accountable public administrators had to be respected as against various Campaign experts and various *ad hoc* committees which, the CPI claimed, were all appointed by the Planning Board and dominated by the CPI-M. It was quite possible to question the consistency of most of these worries, and to argue that since the CPI and others did not present any alternative way of fighting local abuses and corruption, they were putting the entire Campaign at risk. Yet the democratic and administrative principles were important in themselves. And so long as the reformists lacked good answers, all the other parties could join in the cause of bashing the Campaign and nailing the CPI-M.

By the first part of 1999, the situation was critical. Indeed, there was a serious lack of clear-cut rules and regulations and there was still no firm model for how the participatory practices would be reconciled with representative constitutional governance. There was also a lack of training of local administrators and politicians. The reformists had given priority to popular mobilisation in order to enforce changes that would be institutionalised when no more advances were possible. But now the dominant forces were already taking advantage of democratic decentralisation and the devolution of funds. They even managed to use good arguments about constitutional democracy to undermine the campaigners' ability to prevent delays, abuses and corruption.

KSSP leaders proposed a campaign for intensified popular vigilance but claimed that the Planning Board rather wanted them to give priority to the implementation of good local projects. Meanwhile, ironically, the big communist party, the CPI-M – whose major leaders had always been sceptical of the Campaign but who on principle never accepted any criticism from the CPI – negotiated a compromise with their political contenders, rescued the campaign and finally, during the second part of 1999, despite their earlier reluctance, came out in almost full support of it. The cost for the reformist campaigners, however, was very high. In reality, the party never fully accepted the principles of the Campaign, as designed by the reformists. In addition the reformists were unable to enforce the much overdue public rules and regulations; and the badly needed education of local administrators and politicians never really took off, despite some sincere efforts. Meanwhile the prioritising of the mobilisation and channelling of people' expectations and enthusiasm did not generate a social movement against those abusing decentralisation and the Campaign. The various problems of delays, irregularities, partisan priorities, and outright corruption seemed to increase and the public critique was snowballing.

The finale was tragic. In the selection of candidates for the local elections late in 2000 – in which committed and successful campaigners were widely expected to gain overwhelming support – the established leftist-party politicians gave priority to their own people instead of allowing activists with good record of accomplishment from work with the Campaign to run. Besides, many of the reformists do not seem to have been strong and/or willing enough to put up a fight. So the potentially favourite candidates could not harvest what they had sown, and the training and experience invested in them were lost. The defeat of the Left in the local elections was devastating, even in places where the campaign had really been successful. Moreover, while the reformists were thus stabbed in the back in the local elections, the established CPI-M cadres' own mismanagement of state and government also came to the fore in the 2001 Assembly elections. Their poor liquor policies, unfortunate handling of educational reforms, miserable financial management, and inability to counter both the affects of global neo-liberalism and the rise of local communal forces led to an electoral disaster for the Left.[19]

In comparative perspective, the Porto Alegre-activists have also not been able to synthesise new and old democratic practices. Hence it is tempting to conclude that their more successful participatory policies may be because the political Left around the PT had less deeply rooted stakes in party-clientelistic practices than the CPI-M – which in turn seems to experience similar problems in relation to more or less independent civic associations and social movements as the ANC in South Africa (following the analyses of Stokke and Oldfield in this book).

The renewal-oriented activists in the Philippines have also relied on decentralisation, but in the absence of land reforms (like those in Kerala), and a broad established Left to relate to (as in both Kerala and Brazil), the activists have fought an uneven battle against local bossism, elitist traditional politics (within one-man constituencies), and rigid Maoist practices. Efforts to combine direct democracy and self-management in civil society with conventional electoral and administrative practices have therefore been as difficult as they are important. Initially, even the activists themselves did not vote for their own candidates; and conventional lobbying and pressure politics often remain more feasible than alternative interest- and policy based projects with regard to elections and governance, such as those initiated through *Akbayan* (and elaborated upon in Joel Rocamora's chapter in this book).

In Indonesia, by contrast, decentralisation emerged as a major trend only after the fall of Soeharto, and then, primarily, as a framework for re-organising privileged access to resources among the members of a more broadly defined elite. This has made it less easy for the democratic groups to unite against a visible enemy. The democratic movement remains too fragmented and socially as well as politically isolated to take advantage of the new spaces. It is true that the movement was influential immediately after the fall of Soeharto, and that local plebeian aspirations flourished around the country. This was based, however, on disjointed civic action, lobbying and pressure that had been loosely brought together by networks, leading personalities and patrons (*bapaks*). As soon as institutionalised representative politics in terms of elections as well as governance were brought onto the agenda, the broad democratic movement collapsed. The often committed but socially and politically 'floating' individuals and groups took shelter, again, behind principled NGOs and a few emerging popular organisations. There is a tendency to compensate the lack of a mass constituency with access to good contacts and the ability to carry out specific civic action. These practices, however, makes best sense in relation to personality oriented one-person constituencies. Ironically, thus, many of the Indonesian groups favour the kind of one-man constituencies that already (as convincingly argued by Rocamora in his chapter) prevent the growth of consistent and comprehensive democratic alternatives in the Philippines.

Finally, the fourth dimension: the lack of a scholarly and public discourse on the politics of popular democratisation. In Kerala it remains to be established whether there have been significant self-critical discussions amongst the Left about the stabbing of the Campaign, as opposed to continuing squabbles between the different factions. In a rare moment of transparency after the elections, even reformists bound by party discipline spoke up about their frustrating experiences, at least privately and off record. This, however, is also an indication of the fourth dimension of the political deficit: the lack of a scholarly *public* discourse on the politics of democratisation. It is true that the reformists are critical of the conventional, centralised and non-transparent leftist politics and that they have stayed away from most of the politicking. It is also true that one of their major priorities has been the generation of wider public spaces. Leading reformist Dr. T. M. Thomas Isaac has written some of the best and often self-critical analyses of the campaigns. The sensitive and crucial political problems, however, remain non-issues. They still seem to be part of neither the scholarly nor the general discourse in the public space. This is not only a serious problem of transparency, integrity and democracy. It is also a political obstacle: how will it ever be possible to overcome the political deficit of substantial democratisation, if those who aim to reform the current priorities and practices of the mainstream Left (instead of abandoning and become isolated from it) are not actively studying, discussing, proposing alternatives and mobilising support for fresh perspectives within an open, and transparent, and democratic *public* space? The lack of clearly stated perspectives and public discussions may even have contributed to some of the bizarre accusations that the reformists and sympathetic foreign scholars are linking up with the participatory policies of the World Bank, the 'radical polycentrists', and even the CIA.[20]

In Indonesia, by contrast, it is rather the absence of knowledge about the historical importance and experiences of the earlier left-oriented movements that prevents a fruitful debate about how to proceed from the dominant practice under Soeharto of struggle in civil society against state and politics. A new track might imply giving primary attention to the support of people's organisations from below based on their common interests and ability to reform and make use of state and politics.

So far, it is instead in the Philippines that renewal-oriented scholars and activists have initiated critical analyses of both old leftist and new civil society activities.[21] Interestingly, however, most of the sensitive and crucial political problems only became part of the public discourse when the preparatory work for the Citizen Action Party/*Akbayan* was put on top of the agenda.

Broader alternative assessment

What is the general validity of these case study results? The first round of a broader Indonesian survey substantiates the conclusion about the political deficit of substantial democratisation. The primary aim of the survey is to generate more conclusive background information for deliberations on a renewed agenda within the democracy movement (Demos 2004). It is also, however, a pilot-study to find a way of countering the four major weaknesses that we have identified (in the course of this chapter) of both the mainstream institutionalist as well as the alternative social movement-oriented approaches to democratisation. First, therefore, the alternative framework refutes the assumption that popular mass aspirations should be ruled out at the outset in favour of elitist solutions. The new approach is based instead on two rounds of extensive interviews with 400 experienced and reflective democracy activists, in each round, in 29 provinces and on some 13 issue-areas, to be followed by a re-study. In a country with a scarcity of reliable data, these respondents are deemed the best and the most important sources of grounded information about problems and options of substantial democratisation. Second, the new framework abandons the common tendency to identify democracy with its generally accepted instruments (like the right to organise and free and fair electoral institutions) in favour of examining the extent to which such rights and institutions (a) really contribute to the *aims* of democracy, (b) are widely spread in the country and (c) include the most vital public concerns.[22] Third, one needs to consider both institutional and human capacities to promote democracy. The focus on rights and institutions in ordinary democracy-barometers is supplemented, therefore, by the inclusion of the propelling forces of democratisation that are emphasised in social movement studies. The major factors in this respect are citizens' resources and powers actually to use and develop rights and institutions by combining activities in various parts of the political system, politicising issues and interests and organising popular support. As outlined in the Introduction and as further elaborated in the chapter by Stokke and Oldfield, this political capacity building, in turn, is conditioned by the opportunity structure, various sources of power as well as views and values. Similarly, and fourth, the alternative framework also rebuts the opposite tendency among social movement theorists to negate organised politics in favour of direct democratisation and self-management in civil society. The focus is instead on the problems of combining such practices with more conventional tools of democracy like major constitutional, representative and administrative rights and institutions.

In what way do the first round conclusions from this survey support and further develop the case study results? To begin with, the pro-democracy informants qualify the popular thesis that Indonesia's democracy has already collapsed. Exaggerating the situation may pave the way for authoritarian 'solutions'. A series of freedoms, and civil society, are deemed to function reasonably well, except, of course, in Aceh and Papua. This public space is vital and must be defended. The political violence continues, however, and the judiciary, the civil- and military administration, the central and local government and especially the representative political system are in a sorry state. The worst cases include not only the fact that the rule of law is defunct as well as the violence and corruption that have so far attracted most attention, but also the poor standard of socio-economic rights and, most essentially, the lack of representation of people's ideas and interests by way of parties, mass organisations and politicians. The gap, moreover, between the 'good freedoms' and those 'bad instruments of democracy' have widened since 1999. This is particularly serious with regard to the means for improving the conditions in a democratic way through good representation.

Not only do the strategic tools for building democracy need to be improved. People in general and pro-democrats in particular must also be better equipped to alter and make use of them. The persistent critical view of state, elections and parties is well taken, but at the same time, these fields are left wide open for the dominant forces. Two thirds of the democracy movement give priority instead to direct democracy in civil society, partly supplemented by lobbying and pressure politics. A majority of groups co-operate only through loose networks and suffer from lack of organised popular constituencies. Single issues and specific interests are most frequent and there is a shortage of ideologies (as opposed to given truths) about how various interests and issues might be aggregated in order to affect priorities for political programmes and alternative governance. The 'hottest' current campaign, for instance, focuses upon corrupt politicians without offering a constructive altern-ative. Activists who try shortcuts through popular leaders or established parties tend to be short of a clear constituency and strategy, thus being easy to co-opt or marginalise. Promising seeds for broader agendas, including a green left-of-centre agenda,[23] are not rooted in the broadening of the labour movement, combined with liberal middle class concerns, that has been so important in other processes of democratisation, most recently in Brazil.

The room of manoeuvre, finally, for 'crafting of democracy' during the post-Soeharto period of transition has been radically reduced. While the 'international community' gives priority to the struggle against terrorism rather than democratisation, an extended Indonesian elite has taken over the means of democracy and makes use of them without promoting the aims of democracy. Even militia and paramilitary groups take part in this 'new game in town'. In Latin America and Southern Europe, former authoritarian rulers survived within an extended private sector by allowing others to take over a limited democracy. In Indonesia, it is not only the former rulers but also their linking of economic, military and bureaucratic power that survives – within the framework of a decentralised state and elitist democracy. Hence, suppression, the defunct rule of law, and corruption continue, and several of the major points in this respect made in the chapters by Nordholt and Sidel are thus confirmed.

Conclusions and the way ahead

What overall conclusions on the problems of substantial democratisation can we draw? To begin with, the basic assumption of the dominant school of thought that popular action is democratically less fruitful than elite-compromises must be abandoned. Sound analyses should not start by excluding the need in certain contexts for radical transformation, by negating the possibility for leftist organisations to combine structural change and peaceful political democratisation, and by neglecting the democratic potential of the new series of civil–society driven efforts. In addition, the dominant project has not lived up to its expectations. In many cases it is rather the popular efforts at democratisation that have proven significant, genuine and promising, despite the efforts at side-tracking them.

At the same time, however, these hopeful experiments suffer from the comparative lack of interest in, and knowledge of, the *politics* of fighting for and implementing such changes. Balanced left-oriented thinkers and campaigners realise the need to link new polycentric activities in civil society with government and politics and to generate common agendas, but little is said and done about how such links and public spaces emerge, endure and further develop. The case study of the People's Planning Campaign in Kerala in this respect, and the brief comparison with similar efforts in the Philippines and Indonesia, clearly indicate that the popular experiments call for *political* intervention. In addition, the further development of such efforts is not only a matter of institutional design but rests with peoples' capacity to develop new forms of interest organisations and political work. This is the *political deficit* of the new forms of popular-driven substantial democratisation. In particular, it relates – as I have argued – to the problems of (a) combining different activities in the political system, (b) replacing party-clientelism with re-politicisation rather than de-politicisation of ideas and socio-economic issues, (c) preventing powerful actors from conquering potentially progressive institutions such as those related to decentralisation, by combining the practices of direct and representative governance, and (d) of studying and deliberating publicly the politics of democratisation.

These and similar results from case studies should be controlled through broader surveys, designed to counter the fallacies of the mainstream assessments of democratisation and their tendencies to separate institutional and popular capacities for promoting democracy – thus generating more conclusive analysis to support deliberation about improved politics of democratisation. The first round of an attempt to establish such an alternative analytical framework in the context of Indonesia substantiates and expands the argument about the political deficit thesis. Experienced democracy-activist-respondents from around the country clearly indicate that while a series of vital freedoms as well as a reasonably functioning civil society have been introduced in many (though not all) parts of the country, the advancement of democracy is held back by the poor substantive rights and institutions related to justice and the rule of law. The largely defunct political representation of people's major ideas and interests through broad organisations and parties is particularly serious, as it prevents improvements in a democratic way. This has often been neglected in the public discourse, including that among international supporters but also within the democracy movement itself. Worse, the popular capacity to use and improve these strategic means of democracy is also not good. The pursuit of direct democracy in civil society, and the prominence of single issues, specific interests, loose networks, and shortcuts via popular leaders and strong 'traditional' movements, in addition to pressure and lobbying, reflect the pro-democrats' failure to develop ideologies to aggregate issues and interests and generate common programmes in tandem with the building of broad genuine organisations and representative political parties. Finally, these limitations cannot be adjusted by skilful engineering only of better institutions. An enlarged elite has put an end to the transition to substantial democracy by capturing and making use of the supposedly democratic means for its own non-democratic purposes of sustaining the old but now increasingly localised symbiosis of economic, military and political power. Substantial democratisation presupposes, thus, that the strategic tools of democracy are re-appropriated. This calls for giving absolute priority to the improvement of political representation and, particularly, the enhancement of the pro-democrats' capacity to use and improve it, to make up for the political deficit of substantial democratisation.

Notes

1. This implies that we object to the tendency to equate institutional instruments with their democratic purpose.
2. Hence, the other extreme in the form of Schumpeterian definitions that would also include 'electoral democracies' are also set aside. Rather we use instead Beetham's (1999) and Beetham *et al.* (2002) broadly accepted identification of some 80 essential rights and institutions. In an alternative assessment project that we shall return to, a few have been added and then all have been boiled down to 40, which relate to (a) law and judiciary, citizenship and human rights, (b) government, public administration, representation of citizen's ideas and interests and accountability, and (c) civil society (including instances of direct democracy and self-management) (Törnquist 2003a, 2004; Demos 2004).
3. This is, thus, despite the fact that an 'actually existing' democracy may have passed the test of Linz and Stepan (1996) of being 'the only game in town', since that game may be limited and only meaningful to an established elite.
4. The formative research projects were initiated in the 1980s, the best known of which were led by O'Donnell and Schmitter (1986), Diamond *et al.* (1988 and 1989), Huntington (1991), and Linz and Stepan (1996).
5. Even if the radicals, quite unexpectedly, had been successful on the battlefields.
6. Such communist parties have been active, for instance, in India since the early-1950s , and another was the world's third largest communist party in Indonesia after independence until 1957–59, when Sukarno and the army began to impose 'guided democracy'.
7. Even though some of this may now have been eroded in the 'war against terrorism'.
8. The Kerala 'model' gave birth to UNDP's alternative measurements and much of Amartya Sen's ideas of entitlements and public action.
9. Even old colonial classifications of various types of indigenous rule (while employing indirect rule) seem to have come to the fore again, not only in Afghanistan and Iraq (cf. Nordholt's chapter in this book.).
10. Which I have followed a bit more closely since the mid-1980s, see e.g. Törnquist (1991b, 1995, 2002a, b).
11. See especially Tharakan's chapter in this book and Törnquist (1995).
12. *Kerala Sastra Sahitya Parishad.*
13. For instance in land speculation and in getting rid of labourers rather than in developing more intensive agriculture.
14. E. M. S Namboodiripad (of the socially most prestigious Namboodiri cast) was one of the foremost and generally respected leaders in the Indian struggle for national liberation, a noted Marxist theoretician, historian and journalistic writer, one of the founding members of the Kerala communist movement, Kerala's first chief minister – thus also the head of the world's first indisputably liberally-elected communist government – and later on not

only the 'golden egg' of the Indian Communist Party-Marxist but also for many years its secretary general. E. M. S, as he was commonly known, had since long, but often in vain, argued in favour of decentralisation. At the time of the new initiatives in Kerala, E. M. S had returned to his home-state, though still being very active politically and intellectually. Namboodiripad passed away a few years later, in 1998.

15. Including those like M. P. Parameswaran who had turned green socialist Gandhians.

16. For the Philippine and Indonesian cases, see at first hand Törnquist (1990, 1993, 1997, 1998, 2002b) and Adi Prasetyo, *et al.* (2003).

17. For the time being, for instance, the latter group has closed ranks with sections of the trade union faction, as against rival and somewhat less conservative party leaders – in the process, then, rather taking the opposite position of strongly opposing the reformists: see *The Hindu* (Chennai) 15 February 2004.

18. Ironically, for instance, the 'old' organised interests and politics that constituted a basic pillar of the Kerala model have been restricted in the 'new' dynamic sectors, tourism and IT.

19. Just about the only exception was that the dynamic leader of the People's Campaign, Dr T. M Thomas Isaac, entered successfully into electoral politics.

20. See e.g. *Frontline*, 15 August 2003, pp. 40–45, and *The Hindu*, 18 July 2003 and 30 July 2003.

21. Primarily in relation to the Institute for Popular Democracy.

22. In the British audit, following the design of Beetham (1999), and in International IDEA's further developed general assessment scheme (Beetham *et al.* 2002), some 80 rights and institutions are identified as the means of human rights based democracy. To allow for additional vital questions, the alternative framework has aggregated them, considered some revisions and arrived at 1 plus 40. The first relates to the extent to which people identify themselves in political matters with the prevailing definition of the citizens, the *demos* or, for instance, ethnic or religious belonging. The following 40 relate to the standard of rights and institutions with regard to (a) law and judiciary, citizenship and human rights, (b) government and public administration, representation and accountability, and (c) civil society (including instances of direct democracy and self-management). For the details, see Demos (2004) and Törnquist (2003a, 2004).

23. Not green in terms of being Muslim-oriented but interested in 'sustainable participatory development'.

References

Abad, Florencio (1997). Should the Philippines turn parliamentary? – the challenge of democratic consolidation and institutional reform. In Soliman Santos (ed.), *Shift*. Manila: Ateneo Center for Social Policy and Public Affairs.

Abers, R. N. (2000). *Inventing Local Democracy: Grassroots Politics in Brazil*. Boulder: Lynne Rienner.

Abinales, P. (2003). 'Governing the Philippines in the early 21st century'. Unpublished paper.

Abrahamsen, Rita (2000). *Disciplining Democracy: Development Discourse and Good Governance in Africa*. London and New York: Zed Books.

Abueva, Jose (2002). Dissatisfaction with the way our democracy works. In Jose Abueva (ed.), *Towards a Federal Republic of the Philippines: A Reader*. Manila: Center for Social Policy and Governance.

Acciaioli, G. (2002). 'Re-empowering the art of the elders: the revitalisation of *adat* among the To Lindu people of South Sulawesi and throughout contemporary Indonesia'. In M. Sakai (ed.), *Beyond Jakarta: Regional Autonomy and Local Society in Indonesia*. Adelaide: Crawford House.

Adelzadeh, A. (1996). From the RDP to GEAR: the gradual embracing of neo-liberalism in economic policy. *Transformation*, 66–95.

Adi Prasetyo, Stanley, Priyono, A. E. and Törnquist, Olle *et al.* (2003). *Indonesia's Post-Soeharto Democracy Movement*. Jakarta: Demos.

Adler, G. and Steinberg, J. (eds). (2000). *From Comrades to Citizens: The South African Civics Movement and the Transition to Democracy*. London: Macmillan.

Adler, G. and Webster, E. (1995). 'Challenging transition theory: the labour movement, radical reform, and transition to democracy in South Africa'. *Politics and Society*, 23(1).

Adler, G. and Webster, E. (eds). (2000). *Trade Unions and Democratization in South Africa, 1985–1997*. Johannesburg: Witwatersrand University Press.

Alvarez, S. E., Dagnio, E. and Escobar, A. (eds) (1998). *Cultures of Politics/Politics of Cultures: Re-Visioning Latin American Social Movements*. Boulder: Westview.

Amrih Widodo (2003). Changing the cultural landscape of local politics in post-authoritarian Indonesia: the view from Blora, Central Java. In E. Aspinall and G. Fealy (eds), *Local Power and Politics in Indonesia: Decentralisation and Democratisation*. Singapore: Institute of Southeast Asian Studies.

Anderson, B. (1983). 'Old state, new society: Indonesia's New Order in comparative historical perspective'. *Journal of Asian Studies*, 42, 477–96.

Andrae, G. (2000). 'Anti-worker adjustment in the Ugandan textile industry'. In G. Williams (ed.), *Democracy, Labour and Civil Society*. London: Macmillan.

Andrae, G. and Beckman, B. (1998). *Union Power in the Nigerian Textile Industry: Labour Regime and Adjustment*. Uppsala: Nordiska Afrikainstitutet; Somerset, New Jersey: Transaction (1999) and Kano: CRD (1999).

Antlöv, H. (1994). 'Village leaders and the New Order'. In H. Antlöv and S. Cederroth (eds), *Leadership on Java: Gentle Hints, Authoritarian Rule*. Richmond, Surrey: Curzon Press.

Antlöv, H. (1995). *Exemplary Centre, Administrative Periphery: Rural Leadership and the New Order in Java*. Richmond, Surrey: Curzon Press.

Antlöv, H. (2003). 'Not enough politics?: regional autonomy and the democratic polity'. In E. Aspinall and G. Fealy (eds), *Local Power and Politics in Indonesia: Decentralisation and Democratisation*. Singapore: Institute of Southeast Asian Studies/Leiden: KITLV.

Antlöv, H. (2004). 'National elections, local issues: the 1997 and 1999 national elections in a village on Java'. In H. Antlöv and S. Cederroth (eds), *Elections in Indonesia: The New Order and beyond*. London: Routledge Curzon.

Appadurai, A. (1996). *Modernity at Large: Cultural Dimensions of Globalization*. Minneapolis: University of Minnesota Press.

Aragon, L. V. (2001). 'Communal violence in Poso, Central Sulawesi: where people eat fish and fish eat people'. *Indonesia*, 72, 45–79.

Arghiros, D. (2001). *Democracy, Development and Decentralization in Provincial Thailand*. Richmond, Surrey: Curzon.

Arretche, M. (2000). *Estado Federativo e Políticas Sociais: Determinantes da Descentralização*. Rio de Janeiro: Editora Revan.

Arrow, K. J. (1963). *Social Choice and Individual Values*. 2nd edn. New York: Wiley.

Asia Foundation (2002). *Indonesia Rapid Decentralization Appraisal, Second Report*. Jakarta: The Asia Foundation.

Aspinall, E. and Fealy, G. (eds) (2003). *Local Power and Politics in Indonesia: Decentralisation and Democratisation*. Singapore: Institute of Southeast Asian Studies/Leiden: KITLV.

Atkinson, D. and Reitzes, M. (eds). (1998). *From a Tier to a Sphere: Local Government in the New South African Constitutional Order*. Sandton: Heineman.

Avritzer, L. (2000). 'Democratization and changes in the pattern of association in Brazil'. *Journal of Interamerican Studies and World Affairs*, 43(3), 59–76.

Avritzer, L. (2002). *Democracy and the Public Space in Latin America*. Princeton: Princeton University Press.

Baiocchi, G. (2001). 'Participation, activism and politics: the Porto Alegre experiment and deliberative democratic theory'. *Politics and Society*, 29(1), 43–72.

Baiocchi, G. (2003). 'Participation, activism, and politics: the Porto Alegre experiment'. In A. Fung and E. O. Wright (eds), *Deepening Democracy, Institutional Innovations in Empowered Participatory Governance*. London and New York: Verso.

Ballard, R., Habib, A., Ngcobo, D. and Valodia, I. (2003). *Globalization, Marginalization, and Contemporary Social Movements in South Africa*. Durban: Centre for Civil Society, University of Natal Durban.

Barchiesi, F. (1997). 'Beyond the State and civil society: African transitions and the prospects for labour movements. South Africa and Nigeria compared'. Paper to SASA Congress, Umtata.

Barchiesi, F. (1999). 'The public sector strikes in South Africa'. *Monthly Review*, 51(5).

Bardhan, P. (1997). 'The State against society: the great divide in Indian social science'. In S. Bose and A. Jalal (eds), *Nationalism, Development and Democracy: State and Politics in India*. Delhi: Oxford University Press

Barya, J. J. B. (1991). 'Workers and the law in Uganda'. Kampala: Centre for Basic Research, Working Paper No. 17.

Baskin, J. (1991). *Striking Back: a History of COSATU*. London: Verso.

Baskin, J. (ed.) (1994). *Unions in Transition: COSATU at the Dawn of Democracy*. Johannesburg: National Labour and Economic Development Institute (NALEDI).

Baskin, J. (ed.) 1996). *Against the Current: Labour and Economic Policy in South Africa*. Johannesburg: Ravan Press.

Bebbington, A., Guggenheim, S. Olson, E. and Woolcock, M. (forthcoming). 'Exploring social capital debates at the World Bank'. *Journal of Development Studies*.

Beckman, B. (1995). 'The politics of labour and adjustment: the experience of the Nigeria Labour Congress'. In T. Mkandawire and A. Olukoshi (eds), *Between Liberalisation and Oppression: The Politics of Structural Adjustment in Africa*. Dakar: Codesria Books.

Beckman, B., E. O. Akwetey, and L.Lindstrom (2000). Labour unions, social pacts and democratisation. Background Paper to UNRISD *Visible Hands*. Geneva: United Nations Institute for Social Development.

Beckman, B. and Sachikonye, L. M. (eds) (2000). *Labour Regimes and Liberalisation: The Restructuring of State–Society Relations in Africa*. Harare: Zimbabwe University Press.

Beetham, D. (1999). *Democracy and Human Rights*. Oxford: Polity Press.

Beetham, D., Bracking, S., Kearton, I. and Weir, S. (2002). *International IDEA Handbook and Democracy Assessment*. The Hague, London, New York: Kluwer Law International.

Bell, Daniel A. *et al.* (1995). *Towards Illiberal Democracy in Pacific Asia*. Oxford: St. Martin's.

Benda, H. (1966). 'The pattern of administrative reforms in the closing years of Dutch rule in Indonesia'. *Journal of Asian Studies*, 25, 589–605.

Benda Beckmann, F. von and Benda Beckmann, K. von (2001). Recreating the Nagari: decentralisation in West Sumatra. Halle: MPI for Social Anthropology, Working Paper 31.

Bohman, J. (1997). Deliberative democracy and effective social freedom: capabilities, resources, and opportunities. In J. Bohman and W. Rehg (eds), *Deliberative Democracy: Essays on Reason and Politics*. Cambridge, Mass., and London: The MIT Press.

Boix, C. and Posner, D. (1998). 'Social capital: explaining its origins and effects on government performance'. *British Journal of Political Science*, 28(4), 686–95.

Bond, P. (2000a). *Cities of Gold, Townships of Coal: Essays on South Africa's New Urban Crisis*. Trenton, NJ: Africa World Press.

Bond, P. (2000b). *Elite Transition: From Apartheid to Neoliberalism in South Africa*. London: Pluto.

Bourdieu, P. (1990). *The Logic of Practice*. Stanford: Stanford University Press.

Bourdieu, P. (1991). *Language and Symbolic Power*. Cambridge: Harvard University Press.

Bourdieu, P. (1998). *Practical Reason: On the Theory of Action*. Cambridge, UK: Polity Press.

Brazil (2000). *SUS é Legal: Legislação Federal e Estadual*. Porto Alegre: Conselho Estadual de Saúde.

Brett, E. A. (1973). *Colonialism and Underdevelopment in East Africa: The Politics of Economic Change 1919–39*. London: Heinemann.

Brett, E. A. (1998). 'Responding to poverty in Uganda: structures, policies and prospects'. *Journal of International Affairs*, 52(1).

Cameron, R. (1999). *Democratisation of South African Local Government: A Tale of Three Cities*. Pretoria: J. L. van Schaik Academic.

Carvalho, A. I. de (1995). *Conselhos de Saúde no Brasil – Participação Cidadã e Controle Social*. Rio de Janeiro: FASE/IBAM.

Castells, M. (1996). *The Rise of the Network Society*. Oxford: Blackwell.

CDS/UN (1975). *Poverty, Unemployment and Development Policy: A Case Study of Selected Issues with Reference to Kerala*. New York: UN.

Chabal, Patrick and Daloz, Jean-Pascal (1999). *Africa Works: Disorder as Political Instrument*. Oxford: James Currey.

Chambers, R. (1994). *Paradigm Shifts and the Practices of Participatory Development*. Sussex: Institute of Development Studies.

Chandhoke, N. (2002). 'The limits of global civil society'. In M. Glasius, M. Kaldor and H. Anheier (eds), *Global Civil Society 2002*. Oxford: Oxford University Press.

Chandramohan, P. (1981). 'Social and political protest in Travancore: a Study of the Sree Narayana Dharma Paripalana Yogam, 1900–1938'. MPhil. dissertation, Javaharlal Nehru University, Delhi.

Chandramohan, P. (1987). 'Popular culture and socio-religious reform: Narayana Guru and the Ezhavas of Travancore'. *Studies in History, III(I)*.

Chathopadhyaya, S. *et al.* (1999). *Panchayat Resource Mapping to Panchayat Level Planning in Kerala: An Analytical Study*. Thiruvananthapuram: Centre for Earth Science Studies.

Cherian, P. J. (1999). 'Radical movements in twentieth century: A: Thiruvitamkur and Kochi'. In P. J. Cherian (ed.), *Perspectives on Kerala History, The Second Millennium: Kerala State Gazetteer*, Vol.II, Part II, 511–46. Thiruvananthapuram: Government of Kerala.

Choi, Jungog (2001). 'Philippine democracies old and new: elections, term limits, and party systems'. *Asian Survey*, 41(3), 488–501.

Chubb, J. (1982). *Patronage, Power, and Poverty in Southern Italy: A Tale of Two cities*. Cambridge: Cambridge University Press.

Clapham, Christopher (1985). *Third World Politics. An Introduction*. London and Sydney: Croom Helm.

Cohen, J. (1997). 'Procedure and substance in deliberative democracy'. In J. Bohman and W. Rehg (eds), *Deliberative Democracy: Essays on Reason and Politics*. Cambridge, MA: The MIT Press.

Cohen, R. (1974). *Labour and Politics in Nigeria, 1945–1974*. London: Heinemann.

Collier, R. B., J. Harriss, P. Houtzager and A. Lavalle (2002). 'Rights, Representation and the Poor: Comparisons Across Latin America and India'. Working Paper No 31. Development Studies Institute, London School of Economics.

Conference Report (1997). 'National Conference Toward the Development of a Consolidated Consortium Project on Barangay Governance'. 22–24 October.

Corbridge, S. (1998). 'Beneath the pavement only soil': the poverty of post-development'. *Journal of Development Studies*, 34, 138–48

Corbridge, S. and Harriss, J. (2000). *Reinventing India: Liberalization, Hindu Nationalism and Popular Democracy*. Oxford: Polity.

Cox, K. (ed.) (1997). *Spaces of Globalization: Reasserting the Power of the Local*. New York: Guilford.

Crook, R. C. and Manor, J. (1998). *Democracy and Decentralisation in South Asia and West Africa: Participation, Accountability and Performance*. Cambridge: Cambridge University Press.

Current Data on the Indonesian Military Elite: 1 July 1989-1 January 1992 (1992). *Indonesia*, 53.

Current data on the Indonesian military elite (2003). *Indonesia*, 75, 9–60.

Daniel, J., Habib, A. and Southall, R. (eds). (2003). *State of the Nation. South Africa 2003–2004*. Johannesburg: HRSC Press.

David, R. (1994). 'Political parties in the Philippines'. In Randolph David (ed.), *Reflections on Sociology and Philippine Society*. Manila: University of the Philippines Press.

Day, T. (2002). *Fluid Iron: State formation in Southeast Asia*. Honolulu: University of Hawai Press.

de Dios, E. and Hutchcroft, P. (2003). 'Philippine political economy: examining current challenges in historical perspective'. In Arsenio Balisacan and Hal Hill (eds), *The Philippine Economy: Development, Policies, and Challenges*. Quezon City: Ateneo de Manila University Press (2002) and New York: Oxford University Press.

Degung Santikarma (2001). 'The power of "Balinese culture"'. In U. Ramseyer and I. G. R. Panji Tisna (eds), *Bali. Living in Two Worlds. A Critical Self-portrait*. Basel: Museum der Kulturen.

Della Porta, D. and Diani, M. (1999). *Social Movements: An Introduction*. Oxford: Blackwell.

Demos (2004). 'Executive Report from 1st Round Study of the Problems and Options of Indonesian Democratisation (with separate data summary)' (by A. E. Priyono and Olle Törnquist *et al.*). Jakarta: www.demos.or.id

Desai, A. (2003). *We Are the Poors: Community Struggles in Post-Apartheid South Africa*. New York: Monthly Review Press.

Desai, A. and Pithouse, R. (2003). *'But We Were Thousands': Dispossession, Resistance, Repossession and Repression in Mandela Park*. Durban: Centre for Civil Society, Research Report no. 9.

Desai, M. (2003). 'From movement to party to government: why social policies in Kerala and West Bengal are so different'. In J. A. Goldstone (ed.), *State, Parties and Social Movement*. Cambridge: Cambridge University Press.

Diamond, L., Linz, J. J. and Lipset, S. M. (eds) (1988 and 1989). *Democracy in Developing Countries. Vol. 2: Africa, Vol 3: Asia, Vol. 4: Latin America*. Boulder: Lynne Rienner.

Diamond, L., Plattner, M. F., Chu, Y.-H. and Tien, H. M. (eds) (1997). *Consolidating the Third Wave Democracies: Themes and Perspectives*. Baltimore: Johns Hopkins University Press.

Dormeier-Freire, A. and Maurer, J.-L. (2002). 'Le dilemme de la decentralization en Indonesie'. *Archipel*, 64, 255–87.

Dreze. J and Sen. A. (1995). *India: Economic Development and Social Opportunity*. Delhi: OUP.

Dryzek, J. (2000). *Deliberative Democracy and Beyond: Liberals, Critics, Contestations*. Oxford: Oxford University Press.

Edigheji, O. (2003). 'State–Society relations in post-apartheid South Africa: the challenges of globalisation in co-operative governance'. In G. Mhone and O. Edigheji (eds), *Governance in the New South Africa: The Challenges of Globalisation*. Cape Town: University of Cape Town Press.

Elster, J. (Ed.) (1998). *Deliberative Democracy*. Cambridge, New York: Cambridge University Press.

Endang Turmudi (2004). 'Patronage, *Aliran* and islamic ideologies during elections in Jombang, East Java'. In H. Antlöv and S. Cederroth (eds), *Elections in Indonesia: The New Order and beyond*. London: Routledge Curzon.

Escobar, A. (1995). *Encountering Development: The Making and Unmaking of the Third World*. Princeton: Princeton University Press.

Escobar, A. and Alvarez, S. E. (eds) (1992). *The Making of Social Movements in Latin America: Identity, Strategy, and Democracy*. Boulder: Westview.

Estrella, M. and Izatt, N. (eds) (2004). *Beyond Good Governance – Participatory Democracy in the Philippines*. Manila: Institute for Popular Democracy

Fabros, A. (2003). 'Civil society engagements in local governance – the case of the Philippines'. Paper prepared for the IPD LogoLink Project, March.

Fiorina, M. P. and Skocpol, T. (1999). *Civic Engagement in American Democracy*. Washington, DC: Brookings Institution Press.

Forrest, T. (1993). *Politics and Economic Development in Nigeria*. Boulder: Westview.

Franke, R. W. and Chasin, B. H. (1994). *Kerala: Radical Reforms as Development in an Indian State*. Delhi: Promilla and Company.

Frerks, G. and Otto J.-M. (1996). *Decentralization and Development: a Review of Development Administration Literature*. Leiden: Van Vollenhoven Institute, Research Report 96/2.

Fung, A. and Wright, E. O. (eds) (2003a). *Deepening Democracy: Institutional Innovations in Empowered Participatory Governance*. London: Verso.

Fung, A. and Wright, E. O. (2003b). 'Thinking about empowered participatory governance'. In A. Fung and E. O. Wright (eds), *Deepening Democracy Institutional Innovations in Empowered Participatory Governance*. London and New York: Verso.

Gay, R. (1998). 'Rethinking clientelism: demands, discourses and practices in contemporary Brazil'. In *European Review of Latin American and Caribbean Studies*, 65, December, pp. 7–24.

George, K. K. (1993). *Limits to Kerala Model of Development: An Analysis of Fiscal Crisis and Its Implications*. Thiruvananthapuram: Centre for Development Studies.

George, P. S. (1979). *Public Distribution of Foodgrains in Kerala, Income Distribution Implication and Effectiveness*. New York: International Ford Policy Research Institute Report.

Gopalankutty, K. (1989). 'The task of transforming the Congress', Malabar 1934–40'. *Studies in History New Series*, 5(2).

Gopalankutty, K. (1999). 'Radical movements in twentieth century: B: Malabar'. In P. J. Cherian (ed.), *Perspectives on Kerala History, The Second Millennium, Kerala State Gazetteer*, Vol.II, Part II, 547–70. Thiruvananthapuram: Government of Kerala.

Government of Kerala (1989). *Group Farming for Rice Development in Kerala State*. Thiruvananthapuram: Government of Kerala.

Greenstein, R. (2003). *State, Civil Society and the Reconfiguration of Power in Post-apartheid South Africa*. Durban: Centre for Civil Society, Research Report no. 8.

Grugel, J. (2002). *Democratization: A Critical Introduction*. Basingstoke: Palgrave Macmillan.

Gurukkal, R. (2001). 'When a coalition of conflicting interest decentralises: a theoretical critique of decentralization politics in Kerala'. *Social Scientist*, 29(9–10), 340–41.

Gutmann, A. and Thompson, D. (1996). *Democracy and Disagreement*. Cambridge, MA: The Belknap Press of Harvard University Press.

Habermas, J. (1996). *Between Facts and Norms: Contributions to a Theory of Law and Democracy*. Cambridge: Polity Press.

Habib, A. (2003). 'State–civil society relations in post-apartheid South Africa'. In J. Daniel, A. Habib and R. Southall (eds), *State of the Nation. South Africa 2003–2004*. Johannesburg: HRSC Press.

Habib, A. and Kotzé, H. (2003). 'Civil society, governance and development in an era of globalisation: the South African case'. In G. Mhone and O. Edigheji (eds), *Governance in the New South Africa: The Challenges of Globalisation*. Cape Town: University of Cape Town Press.

Hadiz, V. (2003a). 'Power and politics in North Sumatra: the uncompleted *reformasi*'. In E. Aspinall and G. Fealy (eds), *Local Power and Politics in Indonesia: Decentralisation and Democratisation*. Singapore: Institute of Southeast Asian Studies/Leiden: KITLV.

Hadiz, V. (2003b). 'Decentralization and democracy in Indonesia: A Critique of Neoinstitutionalist Perspectives'. Hong Kong: City University of Hongkong, WorkingPaper Series 47.

Hansen, T. B. (1999). *The Saffron Wave: Democracy and Hindu Nationalism in Modern India*. Princeton: Princeton University Press.

Hardt, M. and Negri, T. (2000). *Empire*. Cambridge: Harvard University Press.

Harriss, J. (2002). *Depoliticizing Development: The World Bank and Social Capital*. London: Anthem.

Harriss-White, B. (2003). *India Working: Essays on Society and Economy*. Cambridge: Cambridge University Press.

Hashim, Y. (1994). *The State and Trade Unions in Africa: A Study of Macro-Corporatism*. The Hague: Institute of Social Studies.

Held, D. (1996). *Models of Democracy*. Cambridge: Polity.

Held, D. and McGrew, A. (2002). *Globalization/Anti-Globalization*. Cambridge: Polity.

Held, D., McGrew, A., Goldblatt, D. and Perraton, D. (1999). *Global Transformations: Politics, Economics and Culture*. Oxford: Polity.

Heller, P. (2001). 'Moving the State: the politics of democratic decentralization in Kerala, South Africa and Porto Alegre'. *Politics and Society*, 29(1), 131–63.

Heller, Patrick and Chaudhuri, Shubham (2002). *The Plasticity of Participation. Evidence from a Participatory Governance Experiment*. Columbia University and Brown University: mimeo.

Herring, R. (1983). *Land to the Tiller: The Political Economy of Agrarian Reform in South Asia*. New Haven: Yale University Press.

Hidayat, S. and Antlöv, H. (forthcoming). 'Decentralisation and regional autonomy in Indonesia'. In *Decentralisation and Democratisation in Developing Countries*. Washington: Woodrow Wilson Center.

Hodgson, G. (2001). *How Economics Forgot History*. London and New York: Routledge.

Hofman, B. and Kaiser, K. (2002). 'The making of the Big Bang and its aftermath: a political economy perspective'. Paper presented at the conference 'Can Decentralization Help Rebuild Indonesia?' Georgia State University, Atlanta.

Houtart, F. and Lemercinier, G. (1978). 'Socio-religious movements in Kerala: a reaction to the capitalist mode of production'. *Social Scientist*, 6(11–12), 3–34.

Houtzager, P. (2003). 'From polycentrism to the Polity'. In P. Houtzager and M. Moore (eds), *Changing Paths: International Development and the New Politics of Inclusion*. Ann Arbor: University of Michigan Press.

Houtzager, P., Gurza Lavalle, A. and Acharya, A. (2003). 'Who participates? civil society and the new democratic politics in Sao Paulo, Brazil'. Working Paper, Institute of Development Studies, University of Sussex.

Huntington, Samuel P. (1965). 'Political development and political decay'. *World Politics*, 17(3).

Huntington, Samuel P. (1968). *Political Order in Changing Societies*. New Haven: Yale University Press.

Huntington, Samuel P. (1991). *The Third Wave: Democratisation in the Late Twentieth Century*. Norman and London: University of Oklahoma Press.

Husken, F. (1994). 'Village elections in central Java: state control or local democracy?' In H. Antlöv and S. Cederroth (eds), *Leadership on Java: Gentle Hints, Authoritarian Rule*. Richmond, Surrey: Curzon Press.

Hutchcroft, P. and Rocamora, J. (2003). 'Strong demands and weak institutions: the origins and evolution of the democratic deficit in the Philippines'. Unpublished paper.

IBGE/PME (1996). *Pesquisa Mensal de Emprego – Abril 1996: Associativismo, Representação de Interesses e Intermediação Política*. Rio de Janeiro: IBGE.

IBGE/PNAD (1988). *Pesquisa Nacional por Amostra de Domicílios – Suplemento Político-Social*. Brasília: IBGE.

Ichlasul Amal (1992). *Regional and Central Government in Indonesian Politics: West Sumatra and South Sulawesi 1949–1979*. Yogyakarta: Gadjah Mada University Press.

ILO (1997). *World Labour Report 1997–1998: Industrial Relations, Democracy and Social Stability*. Geneva: International Labour Office.

Isaac, T. M. T. (1997). *Janakeeyasoothranam Sidhanthavum Prayogavum*, (Malayalam). Thiruvananthapuram: Kerala State Planning Board.

Isaac, T. M. T. (1999). 'Janakeeyasoothranavum Ayalkoottangalum: Anubhavangal – Padangal, (Malayalam)'. In T. N. Seema, *et al.* (eds), *Ayalkootta saṁghamam '99*, Part I, SPB, pp. VII–XXIII.

Isaac, T. M. T. and Ekbal, B. (1998). *Science for Social Revolution*. Thiruvananthapuram: KSSP.

Isaac, T. M. T. and Heller, P. (2003). 'Democracy and development: decentralized Planning in Kerala'. In A. Fung and E. O. Wright (eds), *Deepening Democracy Institutional Innovations in Empowered Participatory Governance*. London and New York: Verso.

Isaac, T. M. T. and Kumar, M. S. (1991). 'Kerala Election, 1991: Lessons and Non Lessons'. *Economic and Political Weekly*, 26(47).

Isaac, T. M. T. and Tharakan, P. K. M. (1986). 'Sree Narayana Movement in Travancore, 1888–1939: A Study of Social Basis and Ideological Reproduction'. Thiruvananthapuram: Centre for Development Studies, Working Paper 214.

Isaac, T. M. T with Franke, R. W. (2000). *Local Democracy and Development: People's Campaign for Decentralized Planning in Kerala*. Delhi: Leftward Books.

Isaac, T. M. T. *et al.* (1995a). *The Kallisseri Experiment*. Palakkad: Integrated Rural Technology Centre (IRTC), KSSP.

Isaac, T. M. T. *et al.* (1995b). *Local Level Planning: Learning from Kallisseri*. Thiruvananthapuram: Centre for Developmenty Studies, Kerala Research Programme on Local Level Development (KRPLLD).

Ismet Fanany (2003). 'The first year of local autonomy'. In D. Kingsbury and H. Aveling (eds), *Autonomy and Disintegration in Indonesia*. London/New York: Routledge/Curzon.

Jaglin, S. (2002). 'The right to water versus cost recovery: participation, urban water supply and the poor in sub-Saharan Africa'. *Environment and Urbanisation*, 14(1), 231–45.

Jakobsson, U. (2000). 'Arbetsmarknaden behöver reformeras (The labour market needs to be reformed)'. *Dagens Nyheter* (Stockholm), 18 July.

Jeffrey, R. (1975). 'Religious symbolisation of the transition from caste to class: the temple-entry movement in Travancore, 1860–1940'. *Social Compass*, XXVIII(2–3).

Jeffrey, R. (1981). 'The Temple Entry Movement in Travancore'. *Social Science*, Vol. 415.

Jeffrey, R. (1992). *Politics, Women and Well-being: How Kerala became a Model*. London: Macmillan.

Jessop, B. (2002). *The Future of the Capitalist State*. Cambridge: Polity.

John, M. S. and Chathakulam, J. (2003). 'Decentralised planning and growth in the productive sectors: case study of a village panchayat in Kerala'. *Review of Development and Change*, VIII(I), 1–24.

Johns, L. (2004). 'City scraps R90 m in rent arrears'. *Cape Argus*, 1 April, pp. 1.

Jones, P. (2004). 'A Test of governance': rights-based Struggles and the politics of HIV/AIDS policy in South Africa'. Oslo: Norwegian Centre for Human Rights, Research Notes 01/2004.

Kahin, A. (1999). *Rebellion to Integration: West Sumatra and the Indonesian Polity*. Amsterdam: Amsterdam University Press.

Kaldor, M. (2003). *Global Civil Society: An Answer to War*. Cambridge: Polity.

Kammen, D. (2003). '*Pilkades*: democracy, village elections, and protest in Indonesia'. In J. T. Siegel and A. R. Kahin (eds), *Southeast Asia Over Three Generations: Essays Presented to Benedict R. O'G. Anderson*. Ithaca: Cornell University Southeast Asia Program.

Kana, N. *et al.* (eds.) (2001). *Dinamika Politik Lokal di Indonesia: Perubahan, tantangan dan harapan*. Salatiga: Pustaka Percik.

Kerkvliet, Benedict J. and Mojares, Resil B. (eds) (1991). *From Marcos to Aquino: Local Perspectives on Political Transition in the Philippines*. Quezon City: Ateneo de Manila University Press.

Kingsbury, D. and Aveling, H. (eds) (2003). *Autonomy and Disintegration in Indonesia*. London/New York: Routledge/Curzon.

Klinken, G. van (2001). 'The Maluku wars of 1999: bringing society back in'. *Indonesia*, 71, 1–26.

Klinken, G. van (2002). 'Indonesia's new ethnic elites'. In H. Schulte Nordholt and Irwan Abdullah (eds), *Indonesia: In Search of Transition*. Yogyakarta: Pustaka Pelajar.

Klinken, G. van (2003). 'Ethnicity in Indonesia'. In C. Mackarras (ed.), *Ethnicity in Asia: A Comparative Introduction*. London: Routledge.

Knight, J. (1992) *Institutions and Social Conflict*. Cambridge University Press.

Knight, J. and Johnson, J. (1997). 'What sort of political equality does deliberative democracy require?' In J. Bohman and W. Rehg (eds), *Deliberative Democracy: Essays on Reason and Politics*, Cambridge, MA: The MIT Press.

Kohli, A. (1990). *Democracy and Discontent: India's Growing Crisis of Governability*. Cambridge: Cambridge University Press.

Konrad Adenauer Foundation (1998). *Local Government Finances in India*. Proceedings of the National Conference on 'Emerging Trends in Indian Local Government

Finances', held at the National Institute of Rural Development, Hyderabad, 24–25 October. Delhi: Manohar.

KSS (n.d). *Akshara Keralam, Kerala Total Literacy Programme.* Thiruvananthapuram: Kerala Saksharatha Samithi.

Kunhaman, M. (2000). 'Koottukashi Bharanamo Koottukashi Rashtreeyamo, (Malayalam)'. *Samakalika malayalam Varika*, Special Issue, 7 January, 103–6.

Kurien, J. (2000). 'The Kerala Model: its central tendency and the outlier'. In G. Parayil (ed.), *Kerala: The Development Experience*. London and New York: Zed.

Lacaba, Jose F. (ed.) (1995). *Boss: 5 Case Studies of Local Politics in the Philippines.* Metro Manila: Philippine Center for Investigative Journalism and Institute for Popular Democracy.

Laclau, E. and Mouffe, C. (1985). *Hegemony and Socialist Strategy: Towards a Radical Democratic Politics.* London: Verso.

Leeuwen, L. van (1997). *Airconditioned Lifestyles: Nieuwe rijken in Jakarta.* Amsterdam: Het Spinhuis.

Legassick, M. (2004). *Housing Battles in Post-Apartheid South Africa: The Case of Mandela Park, Khayelitsha.* Labor's Militant Voice. http://www.laborsmilitantvoice. com/feaSA.htm (8 April 2004).

Legge, J. (1961). *Central Authority and Regional Autonomy in Indonesia: A Study in Local Administration* 1950–1960. Ithaca: Cornell University Press.

Leitch, R. (2003). *Campaign Notes.* Cape Town: Community Research Group, Western Cape Anti-Eviction Campaign.

Leiten. G. K. (1982). *The First Communist Ministry in Kerala*, 1957–59. Calcutta: K P. Bagchi.

Lewis, B. (2001). 'Dana Alokasi Umum: description, empirical analysis, and recommendations for revision'. Paper presented for the Indonesian Regional Science Association Conference, Jakarta.

Liddle, R. W. (1970). *Ethnicity, Party, and National Integration: An Indonesian Case Study.* New Haven/London: Yale University Press.

Linz, J. J. and Stepan, A. (1996). *Problems of Democratic Transition and Consolidation: Southern Europe, South America, and Post-Communist Europe.* Baltimore: Johns Hopkins University Press.

Lipset, S. M. (1959). 'Some social requisites of democracy: economic development and political legitimacy'. *American Political Science Review*, 53(1), 69–105.

Lucas, A. (1999). 'The mayor who fell down the well'. *Inside Indonesia*, 59.

Lucas, A. and Warren, C. (2003). 'The State, the people, and their mediators: the struggle over agrarian law in post-New Order Indonesia', *Indonesia*, 76, 87–126.

Lukes, S. (ed.) (1974). *Power*. New York University Press: New York.

M. Syahbudin Latief (2000). *Persaingan Calon Kepala Desa di Jawa.* Yogyakarta: Penerbit Media Pressindo.

MacDougall, J. (1982). 'Patterns of military control in the Indonesian higher central bureaucracy'. *Indonesia*, 33, 89–121.

Magenda, Burhan D. (1989). 'The surviving aristocracy in Indonesia: politics in three provinces of the outer islands'. PhD thesis, Cornell University.

Magenda, Burhan D. (1994). 'Ethnicity in Indonesian politics'. In D. Bourchier and J. Legge (eds), *Democracy in Indonesia: 1950s and 1990s*. Clayton: Monash Asia Institute.

Majumdar, M. (2002). *Decentralization Reforms and Public Schools: Human Development Perspective*. Chennai: Madras Institute of Development Studies (MIDS), Working Paper 170.

Makinana, A. (2003). 'Thugs put her dream to torch', *Cape Argus*, 6 May, pp. 1.

Malley, M. (1999a). *Resource Distribution, State Coherence, and Political Centralization in Indonesia, 1950–1997*. PhD dissertation, University of Wisconsin – Madison.

Malley, M. (1999b). 'Regions: centralization and resistance'. In D. Emmerson (ed.), *Indonesia Beyond Suharto*. Armonk/London: M.E. Sharpe.

Malley, M. (2003). 'Historical patterns of centralization and decentralization'. In E. Aspinall and G. Fealy (eds), *Local Power and Politics in Indonesia: Decentralisation and Democratisation*. Singapore: Institute of Southeast Asian Studies/Leiden: KITLV.

Mamdani, M. (1994). 'Pluralism and the right of association'. In M. Mamdani and J. Oloka-Onyango (eds), *Uganda: Studies in Living Conditions, Popular Movements and Constitutionalism*. Vienna: JEP Books.

Mamdani, M. (1996). *Citizen and Subject: Contemporary Africa and the Legacy of Late Colonialism*. Princeton: Princeton University Press.

Mamdani, M. (2001). 'Beyond settler and native as political identities: overcoming the political legacy of colonialism'. *Comparative Studies in Society and History*, 43, 651–64.

Manjula, B. (2000). 'Voices from the spiral of silence: a case study of samatha self help group of Ulloor'. Paper presented at the International Conference on Democratic Decentralization, Thiruvananthapuram, 23–27 May.

Marais, H. (2001). *South Africa. Limits to Change: The Political Economy of Transition* (2nd edn). London: Zed Press.

Maree, J. (ed.) (1987). *The Independent Trade Unions 1974–1984*. Braamfontein: Raven.

Mathew, G. (1989). *Communal Road to a Secular Kerala*. New Delhi: Concept Publishing Company.

Maurer, J.-L. (1994). 'Pamong Desa or Raja Desa?: wealth, status and power of village officials'. In H. Antlöv and S. Cederroth (eds), *Leadership on Java: Gentle Hints, Authoritarian Rule*. Richmond, Surrey: Curzon Press.

McCarthy, J. F. (2002a). 'Power and interest on Sumatra's rainforest frontier: clientelist coalitions, illegal logging and conservation in the Alas Valley'. *Journal of Southeast Asian Studies*, 33(1).

McCarthy, J. F. (2002b). 'Turning in circles: district governance, illegal logging, and environmental decline in Sumatra, Indonesia'. *Society and Natural Resources*, 15(10).

McDonald, D. and Pape, J. (Eds.). (2002). *Cost Recovery and the Crisis of Service Delivery in South Africa*. Cape Town: Human Sciences Research Council Publishers.

McDonald, D. and Smith, L. (2002). 'Privatizing Cape Town: Service Delivery and Policy Reforms since 1996'. Cape Town: Municipal Services Project, Occasional Papers no. 7.

McEwan, C. (2000). 'Engendering citizenship: gendered spaces of democracy in South Africa', *Political Geography*, 19(5), 627–51.

McFaul, Michael (2002). 'The fourth wave of democracy *and* dictatorship: non-cooperative transitions in the post-communist world', *World Politics*, 54, 212–44.

McKinley, D. T. (1997). *The ANC and the Liberation Struggle: A Critical Political Biography.* London: Pluto.

McNeill, D. and Bøås, M. (2003). *Multilateral Institutions: A Critical Introduction.* London: Pluto.

McVey, R. (ed.) (2000). *Money and Power in Provincial Thailand.* Singapore: Institute of Southeast Asian Studies.

Meeker, M. E. (2002). *A Nation of Empire: The Ottoman Legacy of Turkish Modernity.* Berkeley: University of California Press.

Melucci, A. (1996). *Challenging Codes: Collective Action in the Information Age.* Cambridge, UK: Cambridge University Press.

Mietzner, M. (2003) 'Business as usual? the Indonesian armed forces and local politics in the post-Soeharto era'. In E. Aspinall and G. Fealy (eds), *Local Power and Politics in Indonesia: Decentralisation and Democratisation.* Singapore: Institute of Southeast Asian Studies/Leiden: KITLV.

Millstein, M., Oldfield, S. and Stokke, K. (2003). 'uTshani BuyaKhuluma – the grass speaks: the political space and capacity of the South African Homeless People's Federation'. *Geoforum*, 34, 457–68.

Migdal, J. S. (1988). *Strong Societies and Weak States: State–Society Relations and State Capabilities in the Third World.* Princeton: Princeton University Press.

Migdal, J. S. (2001). *State in Society: Studying How States and Societies Transform and Constitute One Another.* Cambridge: Cambridge University Press.

Migdal, J., Kohli, A. and Shue, V. (eds) (1994). *State Power and Social Forces – Domination and Transformation in the Third World.* Cambridge: Cambridge University Press.

Minako Sakai, (2003). 'Resisting the mainland'. In D. Kingsbury and H. Aveling (eds), *Autonomy and Disintegration in Indonesia.* London/New York: Routledge/Curzon.

Mkandawire, T. (1999). 'Crisis management and the making of "choiceless democracies"'. In Joseph, R. A. (ed.), *State, Conflict and Democracy in Africa,* Boulder: Lynne Rienner.

Mohan, G. and Stokke, K. (2000). 'Participatory development and empowerment: the dangers of localism'. *Third World Quarterly*, 21(2), 247–68.

Moore, B. (1966). *Social Origins of Dictatorship and Democracy.* Boston: Beacon.

Mouzelis, N. P. (1986). *Politics in the Semi-Periphery.* Basingstoke: Macmillan.

Munck, R. (2002). *Globalisation and Labour: The New 'Great Transformation'.* London: Zed Press.

Muraleedharan, K. (2001). 'Participatory planning in Kerala: addressing Some Basic questions'. Paper presented at the Workshop on Decentralisation in Kerala: Assessment. Thiruvananthapuram: Centre for Development Studies, KRPLLD, 22–24 October.

Nair, N. D. G. (2000). 'People's planning in Kerala: a case study of two village panchayats'. Thiruvananthapuram: Centre for Development Studies, KRPLLD, Discussion paper 16.

Namboodiripad, E. M. S. (1978). Note on Report of the Committee on Panchayat Raj Institutions. In *Report of the Committee on Panchayat Raj Institutions.* New Delhi: Government of India.

Namboodiripad, E. M. S. (1989). *Vikasanathinte Rashtreeyam* (Malayalam). Thiruvananthapuram: Deshabhimani Book House.

Namboodiripad, E. M. S. (1992a). 'District Council Electionu sheshamulla Kerala Rashtreeyam (Malayalam)'. *Deshabhimani*, 17 February.

Namboodiripad, E. M. S. (1992b). 'Keralathinte Sambathika Asoothranavum Rashtreeyavum'. In *Keralathinte Vikasana Prasnangal* (Malayalam). Thiruvananthapuram: Chintha.

Namboodiripad, E. M. S. (1992c). *Presidential Address, International Congress on Kerala Studies*. Thiruvananthapuram: AKG Centre for Research and Studies.

Namboodiripad, E. M. S. (1994). 'Power to the people'. *Frontline*, 6 May.

Narayana, D. (2003). 'Persistence of deprivation in Kerala, in Centre for Poverty Analysis, (CEPA), Improving Capacities for Poverty Research (IMCAP) Program. University of Colombo, Sri Lankan Association for the Advancement of Science (SLAAS)', (eds), *Poverty Issues in Sri Lanka, Towards New Empirical Evidence*. Orugodanatte.

Narayanan, M. G. S. (1997). 'The concept of decentralization: expectations, limitations and possibilities'. In N. P. Chekkutty (ed.), *The People's Plan: A Debate on Kerala's Decentralized Planning Experiment*. Kozhikode: Calicut Press Club.

Nattrass, N. (2003). 'The state of the economy: a crisis of employment'. In J. Daniel, A. Habib and R. Southall (eds), *State of the Nation. South Africa 2003–2004*. Johannesburg: HRSC Press.

Nattrass, N. and Seekings, J. (2001). 'Democracy and distribution in highly unequal economies: the case of South Africa'. *Journal of Modern African Studies*, 39(3), 470–98.

Neocosmos, M. (1998). 'From people's politics to State politics: aspects of national liberation in South Africa'. In A. Olukoshi (ed.), *The Politics of Opposition in Contemporary Africa*. Uppsala, Sweden: Nordic Africa Institute.

Ngwane, T. (2003). 'Sparks in the township', *New Left Review*, 22, 37–56.

NLC-CRD Seminar (2000). *Joint Seminar of NLC and Centre for Research and Documentation, (CRD, Kano)*. Lagos 23 February, 2000. Beckman's personal notes.

Ntabazalila, E. (2002). '"Champions of poor" target homeowners'. *Cape Times*, 8 November pp. 1.

O'Brien, R., Goetz, A. M., Scholte, J. A. and Williams, M. (2000). *Contesting Global Governance: Multilateral Economic Institutions and Global Social Movements*. Cambridge: Cambridge University Press.

O'Donnell, Guillermo (1994). 'Delegative democracy'. *Journal of Democracy*, 5(1), 55–69.

O'Donnell, Guillermo (1996). 'Illusions about consolidation', *Journal of Democracy*, 7(2), 34–51.

O'Donnell, Guillermo (2002). 'In partial defence of an evanescent "Paradigm"', *Journal of Democracy*, 13(3), 6–19.

O'Donnell, G. and Schmitter, P. C. (1986). *Transitions from Authoritarian Rule: Tentative Conclusions about Uncertain Democracies*. Baltimore: The Johns Hopkins University Press.

Ockey, J. S. (1992). 'Business leaders, gangsters, and the middle class: societal groups and civilian rule in Thailand'. PhD dissertation, Cornell University.

Oldfield, S. (2003). 'Polemical politics and the practice of community organising in Cape Town, South Africa'. Paper, Contested Urban Futures: Grassroots Activism and Neoliberalization in Europe, North America and the Global South, Center for German and European Studies and the Institute for Global Studies, University of Minnesota, 6–9 November.

Oldfield, S. and Stokke, K. (2002). *Western Cape Anti-Eviction Campaign Report*. Cape Town: Department of Environmental and Geographical Sciences, University of Cape Town.

Olowu, D. (2001). *Decentralisation Policies and Practices under Structural Adjustment and Democratisation in Africa*. United Nations Research Institute and Human Rights Programme.

Oommen, M.A. (1993). 'Development experience, development priorities and fiscal resources of Kerala'. In M. A. Oommen (ed.), *Essay on Kerala Economy*. New Delhi: Oxford and IBH.

Oommen, M. A. (1995a). 'Devolution of resources from the State to the Panchayati Raj institutions, search for a normative Approach'. New Delhi: Institute of Social Science, Occasional Paper Series 18.

Oommen, M. A. (1995b). 'Panchayat finance and issues relating to inter-governmental transfers'. In M. A. Oommen and Abhijit Datta (eds), *Panchayats and Their Finance*. New Delhi: Institute of Social Science and Concept Publishing Company.

Oommen, M.A. (1998). 'Devolution of resources to rural local bodies: a comparative study of select State Finance commission Report, Karnataka, Kerala, Punjab, Rajasthan, West Bengal'. New Delhi: Institute of Social Science, Occasional Paper Series 21.

Ottaway, Marina (2003). *Democracy Challenged: The Rise of Semi-Authoritarianism*. Washington, DC: Carnegie Endowment from International Peace.

Panikkar, K. N. (1989). *Against Lord and State, Religion and Peasant Uprising in Malabar*. Delhi: Oxford University Press.

Parnell, S., Pieterse, E., Swilling, M. and Wooldridge, D. (ed.). (2002). *Democratising Local Government: The South African Experiment*. Cape Town: UCT Press.

Pasuk, P., Sunsidh Piriyarangsan and Nualnoi Treerat (1998). *Guns, Girls, Gambling, Ganja. Thailand's Illegal Economy and Public Policy*. Chiang Mai: Silkworm Books.

Patel, E. (ed.) (1993). *Engine of Development: South Africa's National Economic Forum*. Kenwyn: Juta.

Pathiyoor, G. *et al*. (1990). *Group Approach for Locally Adapted and Sustainable Agriculture (GALASA): A Blue Print for Decentralized Agricultural Development*. Palakkad: Integrated Rural Technology Centre (IRTC), KSSP.

Patnaik, P. (2004). 'Theoretical reflections on Kerala style decentralized planning'. Note presented at the workshop on Panchayat Human Development Report, Organised by Kanjikuzhi Grama Panchayat, Kerala Health Studies and Research Centre, S. N. College, Cherthalla in collaboration with UNDP, 1–3 January, Cherthalla.

Pellizzoni, L. (2001). 'The myth of the best argument: power, deliberation and reason'. *British Journal of Sociology*, 52(1), 59–86.

Pemberton, J. (1986). 'Notes on the 1982 general election in Sol'. *Indonesia*, 41, 1–22.

Potter, D. (ed.) (1997). *Democratization*. Cambridge: Polity.

Pradnja Resosudarmo, Ida Ayu (2003). 'Shifting power to the periphery: the impact of decentralization on forests and forest people'. In E. Aspinall and G. Fealy (eds), *Local Power and Politics in Indonesia: Decentralisation and Democratisation*. Singapore: Institute of Southeast Asian Studies/Leiden: KITLV.

Puthiavila, M. K. and Kunhikannan, T. P. (eds) (n.d). *Janakeeyathayude Ponkani*. Thiruvananthapuram: SPB.

Putnam, R. (1993). *Making Democracy Work: Civic Traditions in Modern Italy*. Princeton University Press.

Rahnema, M. (1990). 'Participatory action research: the last temptation of Saint Development'. *Alternatives*, XV(2).

Raj, K. N (1984). 'Some thoughts on decentralization of development planning and implications'. Keynote Paper at the Seminar on Decentralized Planning and Implementation, Institute of Social and Economic Changes, Bangalore (ISEC), 29 November–1 December.

Raj, K. N. (1992). 'Decentralized development and local government in Kerala', *Sri Damodara Menon Memorial Lecture*. Kozhikode: Gandhi Peace Foundation.

Raj, K. N. *et al.* (1993). 'Some notes on possibilities of decentralized development in kerala'. *Seminar on Panchayati Raj*. Thiruvananthapuram: Centre for Development Studies (CDS).

Raj, K. N. and Tharakan, M. (1983). 'Agrarian reform in Kerala and its impact on the rural economy – a preliminary assessment'. In Ajit Kumar Ghose (ed.), *Agrarian Reform in Contemporary Developing Countries*. London: Croom Helm and New York: St. Martin's Press.

Ramachandran, V. (1988). *Report on the Measures To Be Taken for Democratic Decentralization at the District Levels*. Thiruvananthapuram: Government of Kerala,.

Ransome, P. (1992). *Antonio Gramsci: A New Introduction*. London: Harvester Wheatsheaf.

Raphael, J. C. (2000). *Decentralised Planning in India*. New Delhi: Anmol.

Ray, D. and Goodpaster, G. (2003). 'Indonesian decentralisation'. In D. Kingsbury and H. Aveling (eds), *Autonomy and Disintegration in Indonesia*. London/New York: Routledge/Curzon.

Reitzes, M. (1998). 'Democratic consolidation: local government and civil society'. In D. Atkinson and M. Reitzes (eds), *From a Tier to a Sphere: Local Government in the New South African Constitutional Order*. Sandton: Heinemann.

Richards, R. A. (1978). 'The Kabupaten program and administrative reform'. *Indonesia*, 25, 183–202.

Rifai Amzulian (2002). 'Regional autonomy: the implications for the legal system'. In Minako Sakai (ed.), *Beyond Jakarta. Regional and Local Society in Indonesia* (Adelaide: Crawford House).

Rohdewohld, R. (2003). 'Decentralisation and the Indonesian bureaucracy: major changes, minor impact?' In E. Aspinall and G. Fealy (eds), *Local Power and Politics in Indonesia: Decentralisation and Democratisation*. Singapore: Institute of Southeast Asian Studies/Leiden: KITLV.

Rostron, B. (2002). 'South Africa: the new apartheid?', *Mail and Guardian*, 21 February 2002.

Rouyer, A. R. (1987). 'Political capacity and the decline of fertility in Kerala'. *American Political Science Review*, 81(2), 453–70.

Rueschemeyer, D., Stephens, E. H. and Stephens, J. D. (1992). *Capitalist Development and Democracy*. Cambridge: Polity.

Ryaas Rashid, M. (2003). 'Regional autonomy and local politics in Indonesia'. In E. Aspinall and G. Fealy (eds), *Local Power and Politics in Indonesia: Decentralisation and Democratisation*. Singapore: Institute of Southeast Asian Studies/Leiden: KITLV.

Ryter, L. (1968). 'Pemuda Pancasila: the last loyalist free man of suharto's order', *Indonesia*, 66, 45–73.

Ryter, L. (2000). 'A tale of two cities'. *Inside Indonesia*, 63.

SALB (0000). *South African Labour Bulletin*. Braamfoutein: Umanyano Publications.

Santos, A. (2004). 'Combining multiple strategies for community organizing and local governance in an urbanizing community'. In Estrella, M. and Izatt, N. (eds), *Beyond Good Governance – Participatory Democracy in the Philippines*. Manila: Institute for Popular Democracy.

Satgar, V. and Jardin, C. (1999). 'COSATU and the tripartite alliance', *South African Labour Bulletin*, 23(3).

Sathyamoorthy, T. V. (1985). *India Since Independence: Studies in the Development of the Power of the State, Vol. 1, Centre State Relations: The Case of Kerala*. Delhi: Ajantha Publishers.

Schmitter, P. C. and Grote, J. R. (1997). *The Corporatist Sisyphus: Past, Present and Future*. Fiesole: European University Institute. Nota di Lavoro 55.

Seekings, J. (1997). 'SANCO: strategic dilemmas in a democratic South Africa'. *Transformation*, 34, 1–31.

Seekings, J. (2000). *The UDF: A History of the United Democratic Front in South Africa, 1983–1991*. Cape Town: David Philips.

Seema, T. N. and Mukherjee, V. (2000). 'Gender governance and citizenship in decentralised planning'. Paper Presented at the *International Conference on Democratic Decentralization*, Thiruvananthapuram, 23–27 May.

Sharma, R. (2003). 'Kerala's decenratlisation: idea in practice'. *Economic and Political Weekly*, XXXVIII(36).

Shefter, Martin (1994). *Political Parties and the State: The American Historical Experience*. Princeton: Princeton University Press.

Schiller, J. (1996). *Developing Jepara in New Order Indonesia*. Clayton: Monash Asia Institute.

Schmidt, J. P. (2003). *Cultura Política e Comportamento Eleitoral em Santa Cruz do Sul*. Santa Cruz do Sul: mimeo.

Schmidt, J. P. et al. (2002). *'O Vale do Rio Pardo – Caracterização Político-Institucional'*, *relatório de pesquisa*. Santa Cruz do Sul: mimeo.

Scholte, J. A. (2000). *Globalization: A Critical Introduction*. Basingstoke: Macmillan.

Schönleitner, G. (2004). *'Deliberative health councils and local democracy in Brazil: politics, civicness, and institutions'*. PhD thesis, University of London.

Schulte Nordholt, H. (1994). 'The making of traditional Bali: colonial ethnography and bureaucratic reproduction'. *History and Anthropology*, 8, 89–127.

Schulte Nordholt, H. (2002). 'A genealogy of violence'. In F. Colombijn and T. Lindblad (eds), *Roots of Violence in Indonesia*. Leiden: KITLV Press.

Schulte Nordholt, H. (2003a). 'Renegotiating boundaries. access, agency and identity in post-Soeharto Indonesia'. *Bijdragen tot de Taal-, Land- en Volkenkunde*, 159, 550–89

Schulte Nordholt, N. (2003b). 'Pelembagaan civil society dalam proses desentralisasi di Indonesia'. In H. Schulte Nordholt and Gusti Asnan (eds), *Indonesia in Transition. Work in Progress*. Yogyakarta: Pustaka Pelajar.

Selo Soemardjan and Kennon Breazeale (1993). *Cultural Change in Rural Indonesia: Impact of Village Development*. Surakarta: Sebelas Maret University Press.

Shiva, V. (1989). *Staying Alive: Women, Ecology and Development*. London: Zed Books.

Sidel, J. (1999). *Capital, Coercion, and Crime. Bossism in the Philippines*. Stanford: Stanford University Press.

Siegel, J. (1998). *A New Criminal Type in Jakarta: Counter-revolution Today*. Durham/ London: Duke University Press.

Sjögren, A. (2000). 'Organised interests, public spheres and democratisation in Uganda'. Project Proposal. Department of Political Science, Stockholm University.

Skocpol, T. (1992). *Protecting Soldiers and Mothers: The Political Origins of Social Policy in the United States*. Cambridge: Harvard University Press.

Smit, W. (2001). 'The changing role of community based organizations in South Africa in the 1990s: with emphasis on their role in development projects'. In A. Tostensen, I. Tvedten and M. Vaa (eds), *Associational Life in African Cities: Popular Responses to the Urban Crisis*. Uppsala, Sweden: Nordic Africa Institute.

Smith Alhadar (2000). 'The forgotten war in North Maluku'. *Inside Indonesia*, 63.

Smith Kipp, R. (1996). *Dissociated Identities: Ethnicity, Religion, and Class in an Indonesian Society*. Ann Arbor: The University of Michigan Press.

Smith, L. and Hanson, S. (2003). 'Access to water for the urban poor in Cape Town: where equity meets cost recovery'. *Urban Studies*, 40(8), 1517–48.

SPB (1996). '*People's campaign for 9th Plan: an approach paper*'. Thiruvananthapuram: Kerala State Planning Board.

SPB (1997). *Janakeeyasoothrana Prasthanam*, (Malayalam). Thiruvananthapuram: Kerala State Planning Board.

SPB (1998). *Report of the Working Group on Evolving Formula for Inter Redistribution of Plan Grants to Local Bodies*. Thiruvananthapuram: Kerala State Planning Board.

SPB (1999). *Ayalkootta Sanghamam '99*, Part I and II, (Malayalam). Thiruvananthapuram: Kerala State Planning Board.

SPB (n.d). *Power to the People, People's Plan – Ninth Plan, A Note Training Programme for Resource Persons*. Thiruvananthapuram: Kerala State Planning Board.

Stewart, A. (2001). *Theories of Power and Domination: The Politics of Empowerment in Late Modernity*. London: Sage.

Stirrat, R. L. (2003). 'The concept of Social Capitals in CEPA, IMCAP and SLAAS', *Poverty Issues in Sri Lanka, Towards New Empirical Evidence*. Orugoda watte.

Stokke, K. (2002). 'Habitus, capital and fields: conceptualising the capacity of actors in local politics'. Unpublished paper, Seminar on 'Local Politics and Democratisation in Developing Countries', University of Oslo, 12 March.

Sudarno Sumarto, Sulton Mawardi, Syaikhu Usman, Nina Toyamah, Jacqueline Pomeroy, and Roger Montgomery (1998). *Monitoring the Regional Implementation of Indonesia's Structural Reforms and Deregulation Program: West Java Site Visit Monthly Report No. 1*. Jakarta: Social Monitoring and Early Response Unit.

Sunstein, C. R. (2003). 'The law of group polarization'. In J. S. Fishkin and P. Laslett (eds), *Debating Deliberative Democracy*. Oxford: Blackwell.

Sutherland, H. (1979). *The Making of a Bureaucratic Elite: The Colonial Transformation of the Javanese Priyayi*. Singapore: Heinemann.

Syaikhu Usman, (2002). 'Regional autonomy in Indonesia: field experiences and emerging challenges'. Working paper. SMERU Research Institute.

Tamrin Amal Tomagola (2000). 'The Halmahera of North Moluccas'. In O. Törnquist (ed.), *Political Violence: Indonesia and India in Comparative Perspective*. Oslo: University of Oslo Centre for Development and the Environment.

Tarrow, S., (1994). *Power in Movement. Social Movements, Collective Action, and Politics*. Cambridge: Cambridge University Press.

Tharakan, P. K. M. (1982). 'The Kerala Land Reforms (Amendment) Bill, 1979: a note'. In Sheo Kumar Lall (ed.), *Sociological Perspective of Land Reforms*. New Belhi: Agricole Publishing Academy.

Tharakan, P. K. M. (1984). 'Socio-economic factors in educational development: case of nineteenth century Travancore'. *Economic and Political Weekly*, XIV(46–46), 1913–28, 1955–67.

Tharakan, P. K. M. (1990). *The Ernakulam Total Literacy Programme*. Thiruvananthapuram: Centre for Development Studies, mimeo.

Tharakan, P. K. M. (1992). 'Socio-religious reforms movement and demand for indications of development: Thiruvithamkoor, 1860–1930'. In Alok Bhalla and P. J. Bumks (eds), *Images of Rural India in the 20th Century*. New Delhi: Sterling.

Tharakan, P. K. M. (1996). 'Towards a humane community: local efforts and economic liberalization'. In K. A. Manikumar (ed.), *History and Society, Essay in Honor of Professor S. Kadhirvel Sixtieth Birth Anniversary Celebrations*. Madras.

Tharakan, P. K. M. (1997). *History as Development Experience Desegregated and Deconstructed Analysis of Kerala*. Unpublished PhD thesis, Mahatma Gandhi University, Kottayam.

Tharakan, P. K. M. (1998). 'Socio-religious reform movements: the process of democratization and human development: the case of Kerala, South-west India'. In L. Rudebeck *et al.* (eds), *Democratization in the Third World, Concrete Cases in Comparative and Theoretical Perspective*. London: Macmillan.

Tharakan, P. K. M. (2000). 'Kerala Rashtreeyam: Swathamthriyathinu Munpum Pinpum', *Samakalika Malayala Varika*, (Malayalam), Special Issues, 7 January, 98–102.

Tharakan, P. K. M. (2003). 'Community participation in school education, experiments in the state of Kerala'. In R. Govinda and Rashmi Diwan (eds), *Community Participation and Empowerment in Primary Education*. New Delhi: Sage Pub.

Tharakan, P. K. M. (2004). 'Ernakulam revisited: a study of literacy in the first totally literate district in India'. In Malavika Karlekar (ed.), *Paradigms of Learning: The Total Literacy Campaign in India*. New Delhi: Sage Pub.

Therborn, G. (2001). 'Into the 21st century: the new parameters of global politics', *New Left Review*, 10, 87–110.

Thomas, H. (ed.) (1995). *Globalization and Third World Trade Unions*. London Zed Books.

Törnquist, O. (1989 and 1991a). *What's Wrong with Marxism? Vol. 1: On Capitalists and State in India and Indonesia. Vol. 2: On Peasants and Workers in India and Indonesia*. New Delhi: Manohar.

Törnquist, O. (1990). 'Communists and democracy in the Philippines'. *Kasarinlan*, 6(1–2) (also in *Economic and Political Weekly*, 6–13 July, 20 July 1991).

Törnquist, O. (1991b). 'Communists and democracy: two Indian cases and one debate'. *Bulletin of Concerned Asian Scholars*, 23(3).

Törnquist, O. (1993). 'Democratic "empowerment" and democratisation of politics: radical popular movements and the May 1992 elections in the Philippines', *Third World Quarterly*, 14(3) (also in *Kasarinlan* 8(3) and 9(3), 1993.)

Törnquist, O. (1995). *The Next Left?: Democratisation and Attempt to Renew the Radical Political Development Project: The case of Kerala*, (with P. K. Michael Tharakan). Uppsala: Nordic Institute of Asian Studies, NIAS Report Series, No. 24.

Törnquist, O. (1997). 'Civil society and divisive politicisation: experiences from popular efforts at democratisation in Indonesia'. In E. Özdalga and S. Persson (ed.), *Civil Society, Democracy and the Muslim World*. Swedish Research Institute & Curzon Press, Istanbul.

Törnquist, O. (1998). 'Popular politics of democratisation: Philippine cases in comparative and theoretical perspective'. In M. Mohanty and P. N. Mukherji with O. Törnquist (eds), *People's Rights: Social Movements and the State in the Third World*, Delhi: Sage.

Törnquist. O. (1999). *Politics and Development: A Critical Introduction*. London: Sage.

Törnquist, O. (2000). 'Dynamics of Indonesian democratisation', *Third World Quarterly*, 21(3), 383–423.

Törnquist, O. (2001a). 'Comparative notes on democratic decentralization in Indonesia', *Renai: Jurnal Politik Local and Social-Humaniora*, 1(4), 31–62.

Törnquist, O. (2001b). 'Movement politics and development: the case of Kerala', *Social Scientist*, 29(11–12), 57–87.

Törnquist, O. (2002a). 'Conceptualising substantial democratisation', Paper to the 1st Annual Conference of the Network on Local Politics and Democratisation in Developing Countries: Local Politics: Actors and Approaches, Oslo, 17–19 October 2002.

Törnquist, O., (2002b). *Popular Development and Democracy: Case Studies with Rural Dimensions in the Philippines, Indonesia and Kerala*. Geneva and Oslo: UNRISD and SUM.

Törnquist, O. (2003a). 'Assessing problems and options of democratisation'. In Lars Rudebeck (ed.), *Democracy as Actual Practice: What Does Democracy Really Bring?*, Uppsala: Collegium for Development Studies at Uppsala University.

Törnquist, O. (2003b). 'Indonesia and the international discourse on democratisation: problems and prospects'. In Adi Prasetyo, Stanley, Priyono, A. E. and Törnquist, Olle *et al.* (eds), *Indonesia's Post-Soeharto Democracy Movement*. Jakarta: Demos.

Törnquist, O. (2004). *Towards and Alternative Assessment of Democratisation: The Case of Indonesia*. University of Oslo: mimeo.

UFRGS/IFCH (2001). *Desenvolvimento Regional, Cultura Política e Capital Social: Pesquisa empírica como subsídio à atividade parlamentar no Rio Grande do Sul, Relatório de análise dos resultados*. Laboratório de Observação Social, Porto Alegre.

UNDP (2002). *Human Development Report: Deepening Democracy in a Fragmented World*, New York and Oxford: Oxford University Press.

Vanguard, Newspaper, Lagos.

Vickers, A. (1991). 'Ritual written: the song of the ligya, or the killing of the rhinoceros'. In H. Geertz (ed.), *State and Society in Bali*. Leiden: KITLV Press.

Villarin, T. (2004). 'Finding meaning in local governance through popular participation at the *barangay-bayan*'. In Estrella, M. and Izatt, N. (eds), *Beyond Good Governance – Participatory Democracy in the Philippines*. Manila: Institute for Popular Democracy.

Wainwright, H. (2003). *Reclaiming the State: Experiments in Popular Democracy*. London: Verso.

Webster, E. and G.Adler (2000) 'Exodus without a map?: the labour movement in liberalizing South Africa'. In Beckman, B. and L. M.Sachikonye (eds).

Weekley, Kathleen (2000). '*What kind of populism is that?: the politics of the Estrada Presidency*'. Presented to the annual meetings of the Association for Asian Studies, 9–12 March, San Diego, California.

White, B. and Gutomo Bayu Aji (2000). 'The changing character of local politics: notes on a village in Yogyakarta from independence to reformasi'. Revised paper prepared for the Percik International Seminar 'Dinamika Politik Lokal di Indonesia', Yogyakarta.

Whitehead, Laurence (2002). *Democratization. Theory and Experience*, Oxford and New York: Oxford University Press.

Widlund, I. (2000). 'Paths to power and patterns of influence: the Dravidian parties in South Indian politics'. D. Phil. dissertation, Uppsala University.

Wihana Kirana Jaya and Dick, H. (2001). 'The latest crisis of regional autonomy in historical perspective'. In G. Lloyd and S. Smith (eds), *Indonesia Today: Challenges of history*. Singapore: Institute of Southeast Asian Studies.

Wood, R. L. (2001). 'Political culture reconsidered: insights on social capital from an ethnography of faith-based community organizing'. In B. Edwards, M. W. Foley and M. Diani (eds), *Beyond Tocqueville: Civil Society and the Social Capital Debate in Comparative Perspective*. Hanover and London: University Press of New England.

Wooldridge, D. (2002). 'Introducing metropolitan local government in South Africa'. In S. Parnell, E. Pieterse, M. Swilling and D. Wooldridge (eds), *Democratising Local Government. The South African Experiment*. Cape Town: UCT Press.

World Bank (1992). *Governance and Development*. Washington, DC: World Bank.

World Bank (1995). *World Development Report 1995. Workers in an Integrating World*. Oxford: Oxford University Press.

World Bank (1997). *World Development Report 1997: The State in a Changing World*. Oxford: Oxford University Press.

World Bank (1999). *Entering the 21st century: World Development Report, 1999–2000*. New York: Oxford University Press.

World Bank (2000). *World Development Report 2000/2001*. Washington, DC: World Bank.

World Bank (2003). *Decentralizing Indonesia: A Regional Public Expenditure Review*. Jakarta: World

Wright, E. O. and Fung, A. (1999). 'Experiments in empowered deliberative democracy: introduction'. University of Wisconsin, Department of Sociology, www.ssc.wisc.edu/~wright/deliberative.html (13 April 2001).

Xali, M. (2002). 'They are killing us alive': a case study of the impact of cost recovery on service provision in Makhaza Section, Khayelitsha'. In D. McDonald and J. Pape (eds), *Cost Recovery and the Crisis of Service Delivery in South Africa*. Cape Town: Human Sciences Research Council Publishers.

Zachariah, M. and Sooryamoorthy, R. (1994). *Science for Social Revolution?: Achievements and Dilemmas of a Development Movement*. New Delhi: Vistaar.

Zald, M. N. (1996). 'Culture, ideology, and strategic framing'. In D. McAdam, J. D. McCarthy and M. N. Zald (eds), *Comparative Perspectives on Social Movements: Political Opportunities, Mobilizing Structures, and Cultural Framings*. Cambridge: Cambridge University Press.

Index

Printed and bound in the United States of America